D1248858

French Canadians
in Massachusetts Politics,
1885–1915

French Canadians
in Massachusetts
Politics,
1885–1915

Ethnicity and Political Pragmatism

Ronald A. Petrin

Philadelphia
The Balch Institute Press
London and Toronto: Associated University Presses

© 1990 by Associated University Presses, Inc.

All rights reserved. Authorization to photocopy items for internal or personal use, or the internal or personal use of specific clients, is granted by the copyright owner, provided that a base fee of $10.00, plus eight cents per page, per copy is paid directly to the Copyright Clearance Center, 27 Congress Street, Salem, Massachusetts 01970. [0-944190-07-3/90 $10.00 + 8¢ pp, pc.]

Associated University Presses
440 Forsgate Drive
Cranbury, NJ 08512

Associated University Presses
25 Sicilian Avenue
London WC1A 2QH, England

Associated University Presses
P.O. Box 488, Port Credit
Mississuaga, Ontario
Canada L5G 4M2

The paper used in this publication meets the requirements
of the American National Standard for Permanence of Paper
for Printed Library Materials Z39.48-1984.

Library of Congress Cataloging-in-Publication Data

Petrin, Ronald Arthur, 1950–
French Canadians in Massachusetts politics, 1885–1915 : ethnicity
  and political pragmatism / Ronald A. Petrin.
  p. cm.
  Includes bibliographical references.
  ISBN 0-944190-07-3 (alk. paper)
  1. French Canadians—Massachusetts—Politics and government.
  2. Massachusetts—Politics and government—1865–1950. I. Title.
F75.F85P48 1990
974.4'004114—dc20   88-64126
                                         CIP

PRINTED IN THE UNITED STATES OF AMERICA

F
75
.F85
P48
1990

Contents

Tables

Acknowledgments

Many persons have helped me in the preparation of this book, which has been a long time in the making. Two mentors and friends have helped more than anyone else and deserve my heartfelt thanks. Ronald P. Formisano and George A. Billias (Clark University) have counseled and criticized the project through each stage of development and read each draft with care, to my profit. If the final result has any clarity of thought or expression, it is because of their patient and generous efforts to clarify my ideas, refine my research, and improve my prose. My intellectual debt to them is great; my gratitude for their friendship is still greater.

I wish to thank here others who, directly or indirectly, have contributed to this work. Jordan D. Fiore, Stephanie Husek, and William Cole (Bridgewater State College), and Joel Cohen and Maury Klein (University of Rhode Island) contributed much to my early training as a historian. Asgeir Asgeirson, Bill Baller, Gail Campbell, Bob Kolesar, Don Smith, and Bruce Zellers helped me to survive the vicissitudes of graduate student life and gave me their friendship and moral support, without which this project would never have been completed. To them, and to many others who cannot be named here, lest the list grow too long, I offer my thanks and gratitude. I hope that they will find some value in this book.

I owe many institutional debts, and wish to acknowledge the kind assistance of the staffs of the following: American Antiquarian Society; Anna Maria College Library; the Library, French Institute, and Community Studies Program of Assumption College; Boston Public Library; Goddard Library and Computer Center of Clark University; Fall River Public Library; L'Association Canado-Américaine Library; Massachusetts State Library; Southbridge Public Library; Spencer Public Library; University of Massachusetts at Boston Library; Worcester Historical Society; Worcester History Group; and Worcester Public Library. Assumption College, Bryant College, Clark University, Framingham State College, Pine Manor College, and the University of Massachusetts at Boston all provided part-time employment opportunities while my research and writing progressed.

I am especially grateful to Oklahoma State University. The Dean's

Incentive Grant program of the College of Arts and Sciences provided vital summer support for three critical years as I revised and completed the manuscript. Dawn Carr, Susan Oliver, Donna Portwood, and Toni Battles typed many drafts of the manuscript with patience, care, and cheer. OSU, which sits on the edge of the Great Plains, is indeed very far from the ocean and woodlands of New England, which I never expected to leave. But the Department of History has provided the intellectual environment and personal encouragement I needed to finish the manuscript, for which I am very grateful. In this regard I especially wish to thank W. Roger Biles, James Huston, H. James Henderson, Michael Smith, and Joseph Stout Jr. I would also like to thank the *Historical Journal of Massachusetts* and the French Institute of Assumption College for permission to use materials previously published by them.

Last but by no means least, I wish to thank my family. My parents long nourished and encouraged my intellectual curiosity and I feel deep grief that I did not complete this work in time for my father to share the pleasure of seeing the book. To my wife I owe my greatest debt, for she has sacrificed much for my sake, sustained me with her love, and given me two precious children. To Liz, and to Daniel and Michael, I dedicate this book.

French Canadians
in Massachusetts Politics,
1885–1915

1
Introduction

In the late nineteenth century, immigration, together with large-scale industrialization, profoundly and permanently altered American society and politics. The accelerated growth of the nation's cities, the spectacular ascendancy of its industrial corporations, and the diversification of its population in terms of national origin, religion, and culture all revolutionized the American landscape and have continued to shape the national experience throughout the twentieth century. Since the Civil War the American political system has struggled, with considerable success, to accommodate and contain the multitude of class, racial, and ethnoreligious conflicts that industrialists and immigrants sent into whirl during the last century.

Immigration produced deep and continuing political consequences that ultimately transformed American political culture. From the massive movement that brought millions of newcomers to the factories and farms of the United States sprang new political forms and styles, and novel attitudes towards government and politics that became vital elements of twentieth-century American democracy. Nativism—a deep-seated fear of and hostility toward immigrants—intensified in the late nineteenth and early twentieth century. Concurrently, ethnoreligious conflicts periodically spilled over into politics. Bitter battles fought over public policy relating to such cultural issues as control of education, the regulation of drinking, and sabbatarian legislation, stemmed ultimately from religious and ethnic diversity. Equally important, immigrants formed their strongest and closest relationship to the political system at lower levels of government through the operations of the local political machine. Machine politics appealed to immigrants mainly because it emphasized the values of reciprocity and mutual assistance and because it provided them a means by which to interject their communal values and group interests into politics. Urban political machines served the vital function of gradually integrating the mass of immigrants into American politics and of introducing them to the methods and mores of the American form of government.[1] Perhaps most significant, the urban machine embodied a new political style or

15

ethos based on a system of values alien to the rural Yankee-Protestant tradition that had inhibited the development of positive government. The legitimization of this alternative political style during the first decades of the twentieth century constituted the most enduring and profound political consequence of immigration and its primary contribution to the development of American political and social democracy. For without the conjunction of the pragmatic with the reformist approach to government the history of American political life since the Great Depression would have taken a far different course.[2]

Nowhere in the United States was the impact of industrial development and ethnoreligious diversification greater than in Massachusetts. Within four decades of the Civil War, industrialists and immigrants had transformed the economic and social composition of the Bay State and the outline of the modern state had become visible. By the turn of the century the government of Massachusetts had begun to devise methods by which to balance the public's interests with those of the great industrial corporations which, by virtue of their vested wealth and power, had assumed a commanding role in economic development. Likewise the scions of Beacon Hill had begun fulfilling, through measures of social legislation, the demands of laborers and reformers for social justice and security.[3]

Meanwhile, the process of politics itself was transformed as new men and new groups contested for a place in the political arena. By the 1920s, as J. Joseph Huthmacher pointed out, the political transformation of the Bay State reached a new level of maturity.[4] As this study shows, the two dominant features of the "new politics" described by Huthmacher—ethnic recognition politics and the alignment of the new immigrants with the Democratic party—emerged during the Progressive Era and may be glimpsed in the history of the political assimilation of French Canadians in Massachusetts. Although their influence in government remained disproportionately smaller than their share of the state's population, their political style and issues of concern had begun to influence the political parties and municipal government by the beginning of this century.

Political pragmatism best characterizes the style of politics fashioned by French Canadians during the early phase of their political assimilation. It describes their relationship to political parties as well as their approach to politics. The political assimilation of French Canadians was marked by their relatively slow absorption into the electorate, political organizations, and governmental institutions but also by a rapid acculturation to the methods and mores of American politics. Like other groups, French Canadians brought to politics their own particular style and concerns, shaped partly by their pre-immigration history and the conditions of life upon settlement but also by their political, social and economic interactions with other groups both in society at-large and within specific community contexts.[5] Subjective ethnic self-identification as *Canadiens* hindered social assimilation, but it stimulated the acculturation of the ways and norms of American political culture, and contributed to a pragmatic style of politics.[6] Preoccupied with protecting and advancing their group interests, French Canadians displayed a penchant for seeking and seizing political opportunities to enhance the status of their group and protect or enhance its material and cultural well-being. Political pragmatism often placed ethnic loyalty above party loyalty and subordinated group rivalries to the practical gains and psychic rewards derived from politics. Consequently, the relationship between French Canadians and political parties varied from place to place and over time within a given community, and can be comprehended neither as a uniform, reflexive response to Franco-Irish cultural and religious tensions nor in terms of loyalty to party, platform, or principle. French Canadian ethnicity remained un-Americanized insofar as it led them to identify strongly with neither the Democratic nor Republican party for long. Whatever their particular association at any time and place, most remained *Canadien* at heart, and consequently an unpredictable and, from the perspective of political parties and politicians, an unreliable force in politics.

Recognition politics became the focal point of the French Canadian political style, particulary after 1895. Recognition, above all, meant securing nominations for elective office, gaining positions of visibility within political party organizations, and holding elective and appointive public offices, all symbolic of public acceptance and respect for the group as a whole.[7] For French Canadians, the psychological rewards bestowed through recognition politics were vital. Their experience in Canada had predisposed them to assuming a defensive mentality toward all English-speaking peoples.[8] Their disposition in New England—juxtaposed between two formidable English-speaking groups, native Protestant Yankees and immigrant-stock Catholic Irish—burdened them with an acutely difficult dilemma as their identity and self-esteem as a group were doubly threatened. Yankee confidence in the historic mission of the so-called Anglo-Saxon race and its presumed cultural superiority, on the one hand, and the dominance of the Irish within the American Catholic Church and in politics, on the other hand, challenged the *Canadien* belief in the providential mission of French Catholicism in North America.[9]

Two solutions to this dilemma presented themselves: a retreat into ethnic enclaves or an adaptation to the realities of life in an alien land.

Retreat, an elusive quest, characterized the intial period of immigration and community-building. During this phase French Canadians clung to their inherited national mythology; they adhered to the ethos of *la survivance*. *La survivance* asserted the superiority and distinctiveness of *Canadien* Catholic culture and demanded its preservation in North America. The creation of the so-called Little Canadas of New England was inspired by this ethos, so eloquently expressed by the historians of the French Canadian epic in America.[10] On behalf of *la survivance*, French Canadians erected fortresses of *Canadien* culture, mentally and physically organized around the magnificent cathedrals that sprang up in the dismal proletarian districts of New England cities and towns. The invisible, encompassing walls of kin, culture, and faith would, it was the prayer, protect the *habitants* within Little Canadas from the assimilative forces assailing them from without.

The cultural isolation implied by the dream of *la survivance* ultimately proved impossible, as the history of French Canadians in New England after World War II demonstrates. Indifference to assimilation may have been possible for many common *Canadiens* who labored and lived within the confines of factory, family, and parish life deep within Little Canada. For the upwardly mobile middle class of businessmen and professionals, however, cultural isolation more quickly proved problematic. The mantle of leadership within the ethnic community pushed them to its periphery, where they were positioned to mediate between the culture of their origin and the culture of their host society. New England soon became their home, if not their homeland. As they tied personal fortune and fame to the institutions of their adopted land, adaptation became essential to their prosperity and their prominence.

The *Canadien* leadership initially had viewed the United States as an alien and malignant environment that threatened the survival of their culture and had advocated isolation within Little Canada as a strategy for ethnic survival. But by the 1880s some leaders began adopting a more benign view of American society as they accepted the reality that New England would become the permanent home of thousands of *Canadiens*. Their confidence in the preservation of their heritage grew, moreover, as Little Canadas flourished, testifying to the successful transplantation of Quebec's culture to New England. In the end, however, cultural isolation as a strategy for survival gave way to the need for greater participation in American life. Espousing a pluralist vision of American society, which allowed for cultural diversity through the maintenance of ethnic identities, leaders began arguing that political participation could help to protect and promote French Canadian culture.

The pragmatic style of French Canadian politics evolved from the need to devise a strategy of ethnic survival suitable to the group's position in Massachusetts. The culturally-charged political situation in the Bay State before 1895 led most newly mobilized French Canadian voters to align themselves with the Democratic party. After that time, many French Canadian voters remained inclined to vote for the Democratic party in presidential and gubernatorial contests, perceiving it as the guardian of their cultural and economic interests. After 1895, however, recognition politics became increasingly important as both parties competed for growing numbers of *Canadien* voters. The symbolic rewards of recognition politics attracted French Canadian voters and their leaders who sought the acceptance of the American community. Ethnic elites found recognition politics especially attractive. The prestige they accrued through political participation eased the burden of their ambivalent status and ameliorated to some extent the doubts they harbored about their self-worth as hyphenated Americans. Identification with the dominant culture might help propel their success in the larger community, they reasoned. Recognition politics enhanced their status within the French Canadian community as well for it cast them in the role of group spokesmen, solidifying the bond between them and other members of the group. Most important, the honors bestowed on particular individuals through the political process appeared to affirm publicly a respect for the group as a whole and an assurance of its acceptance by other Americans. Thus, for *Canadien* voters and political activists, recognition politics became more effective than cultural isolation as a means of mollifying feelings of inferiority that threatened their group identity and self-esteem.

Several generations of *Canadiens* tended countless looms and spinning frames in such cities as Fall River, Lowell, and Lawrence and in a host of smaller manufacturing towns in central Massachusetts. Long after the clatter of the machines had grown silent, the French language echoed in the homes and schools and along the sidewalks of many neighborhoods such as The Flint in Fall River. Long after the millyards had been deserted by the textile corporations, French Canadians persisted, though theirs was a "quiet presence."[11]

French Canadians formed a significant, but long-neglected, part of the people and history of New England for more than a century. Rising in number from thirty-seven thousand in 1860 to nearly six hundred thousand in 1900, they comprised more than 10 percent of the region's population by the turn of the century. They amounted to a still larger proportion of the inhabitants of New England's once-bustling textile communities. Given their sizeable numbers, their concentration in New England, and their central role over eight decades in the region's industrial life, it is surprising that French Canadians remained unnoticed by historians until quite recently.

This lack of scholarly interest may be explained in large degree by the self-imposed isolation that enabled the group to resist assimilation until after World War II. Unlike some immigrants, French Canadians arrived in the United States imbued with a fervent national identity. Their experience in Canada had instilled in them a distinct "we group" feeling and a minority mentality. Upon settling in New England they waged a determined and well-organized effort to preserve their group identity—a struggle they termed *la survivance*. Their efforts on behalf of *la survivance* proved remarkably successful: compared with other ethnic groups they resisted assimilation for a much longer time. As late as the 1960s, French-language parishes—complete with religious services in French and parochial schools in which French was the language of instruction—remained common.

The pattern of French Canadian settlement helps account for the success of *la survivance*. Settled mostly in New England, they remained physically as well as culturally close to their homeland. Their concentration in the workingclass neighborhoods of manufacturing centers provided, moreover, a critical population mass in which an ethnic culture could thrive. Finally, the hostilities they encountered because of *la survivance* enhanced their consciousness as outsiders and stimulated their resolve to dwell among, but live apart from, other New England inhabitants.[12]

The rediscovery of ethnicity in the 1960s stimulated and quickened the pace of study of many groups, including French Canadians.[13] Numerous studies explored the causes of their migration from Quebec, the process of adjustment to industrial life, and the creation of ethnic communities, or Little Canadas. Historians now have a better appreciation of the origins, development, and persistence of French Canadian culture.[14]

But the political assimilation of French Canadians merits further investigation because the contours of their political activity have remained obscure. When compared with the numerous studies dealing with the political life of other ethnic groups—the Germans, Irish, Italians, Jews, and Poles—the French Canadians might almost be said to represent a forgotten people.[15] This generalization holds true especially for their earlier period of assimilation: the era between the Civil War and World War I. Several studies, to be sure, have shed light on the political life of French Canadians before 1920, but they have offered limited interpretations and overlooked important aspects of the group's political experiences. In this book, I explore questions that have either been overlooked or incompletely studied. When did French Canadians become a significant political force? When did they begin seeking and holding public offices in significant numbers? With which political party were they associated? Did their political alignment change or remain constant before 1920? If did they prefer one party over another, why did they do so? Did their party preference vary from one community to another? What impact did the group's famous feuding with the Irish Catholic hierarchy have upon its relationship with the two political parties? Did the religious and cultural rivalry between the Irish and *Canadiens* drive French Canadians into the Republican party, as many analysts have claimed? Or did political pragmatism exercise a greater influence than ethnic animosity on French Canadian political preferences?

Massachusetts offers several distinct advantages for a case study of the political behavior of French Canadians. The Commonwealth contained more French Canadians than any other state after 1870. By 1900 about a quarter million *Canadiens* lived in the state, representing nearly half of the total in New England and nearly a third in the United States. Although they did not constitute as large a proportion of the total population as in other New England states, French Canadians ranked third among the Bay State's ethnic groups, after the Irish and English-speaking Canadians. By 1900 *Canadiens* formed about 9 percent of the population and their position within the state's ethnic mix changed little through 1920 despite the influx of many new immigrants.

The *Canadien* pattern of settlement within Massachusetts facilitates their study. Although a few French Canadian immigrants or their children could be found in most communities across Massachusetts, the majority were concentrated in a relatively small number of manufacturing towns and cities. Employment opportunities largely determined where they settled. French Canadians quickly found employment in three of the most rapidly expanding industries in the state—textiles, shoes, and construction. By 1885 no other ethnic group in the state was as dependent on these industries. Consequently, nearly two-thirds of all French Canadians lived in communities where either the textile or shoe industry was dominant in 1885; this pattern remained essentially unaltered for twenty years. By then, 80 percent of all *Canadiens* in Massachusetts lived in places where they numbered at least one thousand.

Although they shared certain features, these centers of settlement differed in many ways: in terms of size, time of arrival and rate of growth of the *Canadien* population, its position vis-à-vis other groups in the community, and its occupational distribution. Such differences in community context affected the political assimilation of French Canadians, as did their sharply defined ethnic identity and their determined efforts to maintain that identity in New England. Comparing the political experience of French Canadians in different communities within the same state makes it possible to point out how local social and political structures differentially affected their political assimilation.[16]

French Canadians are of interest also because they often have been mistakenly included among the New Immigrants who aligned themselves with the Republican party. French Canadians cannot exactly be considered New Immigrants, for this term usually refers to southern and eastern European immigrant groups who began arriving in the United States in large numbers between 1890 and 1915—Poles, Russian Jews, Lithuanians, and Greeks, for example. French Canadians, by contrast, began arriving in New England before the Civil War and their numbers swelled shortly after that conflict. Although their migration continued after 1890 and coincided with the New Immigration, French Canadians may be distinguished from the New Immigrants in several ways: their early arrival, their dominant position within the New England textile industry by 1900, the considerable size of the second, American-born generation, and the size of their middle class by 1900. Perhaps most significant, the *Canadiens*, unlike most other immigrant groups, arrived with a well-honed ethnic identity and had become a significant force in Massachusetts politics as early as 1900, a generation before the political arrival of the New Immigrants. Because of their unique position among immigrant groups in Massachusetts, French Canadians enable us to re-evaluate the connection between ethnicity and politics in the late nineteenth and early twentieth centuries.

The relationship of French Canadians to political parties assumes a special significance because many scholars have claimed that the group deviated from the pattern of political alignment ascribed by the "new political historians" to Catholic immigrant groups in the nineteenth century. Over the past two decades historians have retraced the evolution of American electoral politics by systematically analyzing the social group bases of mass voting behavior. In their studies Lee Benson, Ronald P. Formisano, Richard J. Jensen, Paul Kleppner, and others have emphasized the relationship between ethnic and religious identification and political affilation in the nineteenth century and have deemphasized the importance of economic distinctions in influencing American voters.[17] As they broadened the scope of study of American political history, these historians uncovered and sought to explain previously obscure voting patterns, contributing much to our understanding of the political behavior of many ethnic and religious groups in the past.

Extending and elaborating the insights of Gerhard Lenski and Samuel Lubell concerning the social and political implications of religion, the new political historians focused on religion as a particularly salient influence on nineteenth-century electoral behavior.[18] In their view, partisan identifications "mirrored irreconcilable conflicting values emanating from divergent ethnic and religious subcultures" more than they reflected economic class differences as earlier historians had believed.[19] Based on their analyses of the distinction between the "pietistic" and "ritualistic" religious orientations, these historians have argued that religious belief systems—which encapsulated and articulated the values and attitudes of different social groups—shaped the electorate's perception of political parties and affected voter preferences.[20] Pietistic groups, encompassing most native-stock and many foreign-stock Protestant voters, tended to support the Republican party while ritualistic groups, including most foreign-stock Catholics as well as certain Protestants—for example, German Lutherans—were more often attracted to the Democratic party.[21] Consequently, political parties became "coalitions of social groups sharing similar ethnocultural values."[22]

According to these historians, voters in the nineteenth century, as in the twentieth, responded to a multitude of conflicting pressures which at times could divert normally Democratic voters into Republican columns and vice versa.[23] Given the wide range of factors affecting political behavior, however, the strength and consistency of the relationship between foreign-born Catholic groups and the Democratic party, particularly before the mid-1890s, is striking. Non-English-speaking Catholic immigrants, who usually viewed religion and ethnicity as inseparably intertwined, often resented and resisted the domination of the Catholic Church in America by the Irish hierarchy. Such ethnoreligious tensions created cross-pressures for these groups and conceivably could have led to anti-Democratic voting, as the Irish were so strongly identified with the Democratic party. It is important to emphasize, however, that most often this did not happen. As Kleppner's survey of the voting habits of Catholic subgroups points out, most Catholic ethnic voters, even when they lived in close proximity to the Irish, remained strongly Democratic despite their religious and cultural differences with the Irish.[24]

Viewed from this perspective, the French Canadians in the Northeastern states represent an intriguing case because scholars have often viewed them as the exception to this rule. In the Midwest, French Canadians usually voted with other Catholic groups. In New York and New England, however, the cultural collision between the Irish and French Canadians reportedly divided the French-speaking electorate and "even gave the Republicans marginal majorities in some contexts."[25] In Massachusetts, for example, Franco-Irish conflict "often led the French Canadians to vote against the Irish party, the Democrats."[26] This interpretation of French Canadian political behavior represents the traditional view, which postulates that the French Canadians of New England tended to align themselves with the Republican party from 1892 until the 1920s primarily because of their antipathy toward the Irish.[27]

I would suggest, however, that French Canadians were less exceptional than previously realized. An analysis of French Canadian voting in presidential and gubernatorial elections from the 1880s to 1920 indicates that the group tended to favor Democratic candidates. Contrary to traditional views of French Canadian voting, religious and cultural rivalry between French Canadians and the Irish was not the central determinate of their behavior, although it did pointedly affect *Canadien* politics on occasion. Instead, it is important to analyze the impact of ethnicity and religion on politics within particular community contexts. Emphasizing the changing role that ethnicity and religion played in politics over time and place does extend the essential insights of the so-called ethnocultural analysis but also modifies it by stressing the increasing potency of recognition politics during the Progressive Era. Whereas in the nineteenth century ethnic and religious variables encouraged the formation and maintenance of strong party identifications, recognition politics tended to weaken party loyalty after 1895, particularly on the local level, where French Canadians assumed a more pragmatic attitude toward political parties.

In chapter 2 I trace the development of rural society in Quebec and of French Canadian ethnic consciousness. I examine the causes of the migration and the course of settlement and adjustment to industrial life in Massachusetts, highlighting *Canadien* efforts on behalf of *la survivance* and the differences among the communities where they lived.

Chapter 3 is an analysis of the attitudes of Americans and French Canadian leaders towards naturalization, the activity—or inactivity—of the mass of *Canadiens* in seeking American citizenship, and discusses general electoral and officeholding patterns.

Chapter 4 is an examination of Massachusetts politics during the early 1890s and confirms the conventional view that most French Canadians gravitated toward the Democratic party during this period. Voting patterns indicate, however, that French Canadians remained marginally Democratic, not Republican, in state and national elections from 1895 to 1920, contrary to the traditional interpretation.

In chapters 5 and 6, I suggest how the relationship between French Canadians and the political parties became more complicated after 1895, as recognition politics became more important. After 1895

French Canadians became more aggressive in seeking recognition from the political parties, especially on the local level, and both political parties competed to accommodate their demands. The results varied among communities and within communities over time. These chapters make use of case studies to explore and contrast the relationship of French Canadians to political parties in such large cities as Fall River and Worcester and such smaller towns as Southbridge and Spencer. These case studies show that the relationship between French Canadians and the political parties may best be described as one of mutual exploitation. Neither party loyalty nor anti-Irish feeling played as large a part in determining *Canadien* political preferences as their desire for recognition. The antagonism between French Canadians and the Irish was by no means a constant, always affecting politics in the same way. Within the multi-ethnic world of these communities—replete with ethnic rivalries, intragroup feuding, and unlikely alliances—the political choices of French Canadians were rarely a simple, automatic, almost reflexive reaction against the Irish, but rather the product of a complex calculus of political conflict and accommodation.

2

La Survivance and the Little Canadas of Massachusetts

The histories of the people of New France and New England have been intertwined since their beginnings. Different in origin, culture, and faith, French Canadians and New Englanders lived as enemies within competing colonial empires in North America from the early seventeenth century until the British finally conquered Canada. Wolfe's victory on the Plains of Abraham in 1759 altered the course of empire forever, and affected, albeit in different ways, the evolution of both peoples. In a sense the Little Canadas of Massachusetts, the offspring of French Canadian emigration and of New England industrialism in the late nineteenth century, were conceived in Montcalm's defeat.

La Survivance and the Evolution of Rural Society in Quebec

For the people of New England the outcome of the Great War for Empire held a much different meaning than for people of French Canada. Before a generation had passed New England Yankees had thrown off the yoke of empire. Protestant in faith, English in culture, and free of colonialism, New Englanders spread their influence across the seas and across the continent with great zeal. After liberation New England society itself was transformed. Through the nineteenth century its agriculture declined and its rural poplulation migrated westward and cityward. Stimulated by the prosperity of its commerce and its industries, the cities of the region grew rapidly. By 1865 parts of New England, particularly Massachusetts, had become an urban industrial society that contrasted sharply with the rural society of Quebec. By then, however, the economic evolutions of the two regions began to pull their distinct cultures into closer contact.

For the *Canadiens* the conquest of Canada meant that they would remain a subjugated people for at least a century. Within Quebec they created an insulated, rural, and militantly French Catholic culture. Proud of their French heritage and resentful of their English rulers, generation after generation resisted assimilation. Self-conscious and inward-looking, the people of French Canada focused on *la survivance*—the collective effort to survive as a French-speaking Catholic people in North America that they believed was their mission.

New France underwent a profound transformation in the century after 1760. While New England entrusted its future to the sea, the power loom, and the factory, French Canada found refuge in the soil, the ploughshare, and the family farm. As in New England, the process of change in Quebec was a gradual mutation. With the conquest, commercial life passed into British hands, but the life of the rural *habitants* remained largely undisturbed. The *Canadiens* were guaranteed the exercise of their religion and language as well as the continuation of their civil law and seigneurial land system.[1] Such toleration had long-lasting consequences. The seigneurial land system stimulated the settlement of French Canadians within a relatively compact area inside the immense province. Unlike the Acadians, the *Canadiens* retained a homeland that grounded their struggle for cultural survival that focused on the preservation of their religion and language.[2] Within this homeland "the social organization of French Canada was simplified and proceeded along a single line of social development—rural development."[3] By the end of the eighteenth century an overwhelmingly rural society had evolved in French Canada.

The so-called peasant society that developed within French Canada encouraged the insularity of French Canadians, inhibited their assimilation, and nurtured the growth of their ethnic group consciousness. The nearly self-sufficient family farm served as the primary unit of the new rural society, and landowning families, grouped together in rural neighborhoods or *rangs*, formed the nucleus of the parish. The village, inhabited by retired farmers and the local bourgeoisie—merchants, professionals, and clerics—completed the structure of the local community within which most French Canadians passed their lives.[4] The routine of work and family life organized everyday life, and loyalty to the family superseded all other. Religion had an important place in rural society, but the church's influence was limited before 1840 and, according to one historian, the "faithful were not exceptionally religious or virtuous."[5] By virtue of its control over education, and thus any access to higher social status, the church gained a considerable influence in shaping the outlook of French Canada's rural elite. It "assured the spread of its ideology, its vocabularies of motives, and its languages" within the worlds of business and politics, especially after midcentury.[6]

Comparatively prosperous and prolific, the French Canadians looked with hope toward the future at the beginning of the nineteenth century, for their survival seemed assured. Their language, faith, and mores seemed safeguarded by the physical and cultural isolation fostered by rural development. Living almost wholly within the sheltered confines of their peasant society, the French Canadians multiplied rapidly, so that sheer numbers alone might have insured their survival.[7] The bonds of kinship, common language, religion, and culture contributed to their subjective self-identification as a people distinct from other Canadians. Such bonds provided a cluster of shared values and beliefs that found expression through the communal institutions of rural society. To the extent that French Canadian ethnic identity had its origins in rural society, it may be viewed as a kind of "tribal ethnicity."[8]

Although dominant within their Quebec homeland where they constituted a majority of the population, the French Canadians had a minority status within Canada. Continual rivalry and periodically virulent conflict between themselves and English-speaking Canadians accentuated the feeling among *Canadiens* that they were a conquered people whose autonomy and cultural survival remained threatened. From this sense of insecurity concerning their eventual fate within Canada stemmed a psychology of persecution and inferiority which fueled the *Canadiens'* obsession with national survival, *la survivance.*[9]

"The French-Canadian ideology," as Marcel Rioux explained, "has always rested on three characteristics of the French Canadian culture— the fact that it is a minority culture, that it is Catholic, and that it is French."[10] Acutely aware of their minority status within their own nation, the elite of French Canada superimposed a nationalist ideology upon the tribal ethnicity of the *habitants* during the middle of the nineteenth century. The Rebellions of 1837–39, the Union of Upper and Lower Canada (1841) and Confederation (1867), all of which threatened the survival of French Canada, stimulated the ethnic consciousness of the French Canadians. The Catholic church consolidated its position in French Canada in the aftermath of these events and played a crucial role in formulating and spreading this nationalism. Under its direction, French Canadian nationalism assumed its distinctive form—fusing inseparably the French language and Catholicism and making both essential components of the *Canadien* national identity.[11] As one historian put it:

> In few countries other than French Canada was loyalty to Catholicism . . . so closely associated with an attachment to a language, and ultimately to a form of culture embodied in a given ethnic group.[12]

The close identification between language and religion led the French Canadians to believe that language was the guardian of one's faith, and that loss of language would lead to loss of faith, and ultimately to the loss of one's ethnic identity. For French Canadians, consequently, *la survivance* became identified with the preservation and transmission of their *foi, langue* and *moeurs*.[13]

Ironically, French Canadian nationalism waxed as the rural society at its heart waned. French Canadian leaders romanticized the *habitants'* rural way of life and sanctified home and family as vital repositories of the French Canadian cultural heritage. Large families, the core of French Canada's peasant society, had a central role in the ideology of *survivance*, for "the revenge of the cradle" was part of the strategy in the battle with *les Anglais*. The equilibrium of rural society rested, however, upon a precarious relationship between the family and the land. Large families were essential to the continuation of traditional French Canadian society but were simultaneously the source of its instability.[14] This "demographic contradiction" Everett Hughes described in this way:

> The rural society turns, then, about a relation of family to land. The farm must be fertile enough and large enough to feed and clothe the family— ideally, enough so to provide money for education or a start elsewhere for the children who do not inherit land. The family, in turn, must be large enough, and possessed of enough skill and solidarity to run the farm and keep it free of burdensome debt. But such a family, by its very size, endangers the farm in every generation. It becomes a function of the family to scatter its members, leaving but one son behind to inherit and to sire the next generation of farmers.[15]

French Canada's rural society began to falter primarily because population growth outpaced the productivity and the availability of arable land. Low productivity, the result of continuing use of traditional agricultural practices and technology, became a chronic defect of Quebec's agricultural system. Extensive planting compensated in part for declining soil fertility, but the *habitants'* resistance to change kept their farms inefficient. Meanwhile, in the half-century between 1794 and 1844, the population of the province increased 400 percent. The rural system expanded its boundaries to accommodate this increase; French Canadian settlement crept northward up the valley of the St. Lawrence, across the river to the narrow band of fertile soil along the southern fringe of the Canadian shield, and up the Ottawa River. Yet, in those fifty years, the area occupied by French Canadians increased only 275 percent. As a result, land grew increasingly scarce and expensive after 1820. With little cash to buy the land that imperial policy made available elsewhere, the *habitants* subdivided existing farms in the seigneurial counties of Quebec. Within the traditional homeland of the French Canadians, farms declined in size and fertility but families did not. While harvests grew lean, the rural population bulged, becoming more dense and less prosperous. With each passing year the conflicting currents of low soil productivity, high human fertility, and land scarcity further undermined the foundations—and the future—of Quebec's rural society.[16]

To these problems others were added, so that by the 1830s crisis seized rural Quebec. Wheat, the primary food crop, was also the major cash crop. An over-reliance on wheat drained the soil of nutrients, aggravating the problem of low productivity. As the output of wheat declined, alternative grain crops, potatoes, and peas gained in popularity. But less wheat meant a lower standard of living, for less wheat not only meant less bread but less cash as well. Recurring crop failures between 1830 and 1850, first in wheat, and then in potatoes, compounded the misery. Without adequate development in commerce or industry to relieve the burdens of agricultural decline, disillusion and despair gripped the habitants.[17] The agricultural crisis deepened the feelings of insecurity French Canadians harbored about their survivance, as did political events during that period.

While preparing the ground for the adoption of a nationalist ideology, the agricultural crisis also created the conditions from which emigration would spring. As early as the 1840s the farms and factories to the south of Quebec beckoned the dissatisfied and the adventuresome. The fertile prairie of the American West and the bustling manufacturing towns of New England promised economic opportunity. True, the dispersal of the French Canadians away from their blighted rural life appeared to threaten la survivance. But for thousands of Canadiens there existed no alternative: physical survival demanded emigration.

Immigration and Adjustment to Industrial Society

Confronted after midcentury by bleak economic prospects at home, thousands of Canadiens took flight. Trekking southward and westward to the United States, they sought economic opportunities the overworked and crowded farms of Quebec could no longer furnish. A mere trickle before the Civil War, the stream of immigrants grew to surprising proportions after 1860.[18]

By 1920 three-quarters of all French Canadians in the United States lived in New England.[19] The lumber industry and the farmlands of the Midwest attracted some French Canadians, but the need for unskilled labor created by the expansion of industry in New England drew most of the emigrants. Between 1840 and 1900 the net migration from French Canada to New England came to about 350,000 persons. Besides these permanent settlers, an equal number probably crossed the border only to return to Canada after a temporary stay.[20] During the first two decades of the twentieth century the influx of *Canadiens* into New England slackened as the pace of industrialization in Quebec quickened and absorbed the surplus rural population. But the French Canadian stock continued to grow, augmented by natural increase. From 1900 to 1920, about 108,000 persons of French Canadian descent were added to the region's population.[21] Comparing their concentration in New England to that of Mexicans along the southern U.S. border, one observer in the 1920s speculated that a plebescite might result in the loss of parts of New England to Canadian annexation.[22]

The ebb and flow of French Canadian immigration into the United States, like that of other immigrants, followed the American business cycle. The volume of immigrants swelled in times of prosperity—as during the rapid expansion of the textile industry just after the Civil War—and then shrank during depressions. Unlike other immigrants, however, French Canadians in New England could easily return home when hard times hit, and many did so.[23]

The migration of French Canadians to New England followed changes in that region's economy as well, resulting in an uneven distribution of *Canadiens*. In large measure the pattern of their settlement reflected the economic opportunities available in the various states. Before 1850 they settled mostly in northern New England. Thereafter, most French Canadian immigrants settled in southern New England, where industrial expansion was more vigorous.[24]

Massachusetts, the most populous and prosperous of the New England states, attracted the largest number of emigrants from Quebec. After 1870 it contained more French Canadians than any other state in the Union. In 1900, between 150,000 and 275,000 persons of French Canadian origin inhabited the Bay State, representing nearly half of all French Canadians in New England and nearly a third of those in the United States. By 1920, Massachusetts contained three times as many as either Maine, New Hampshire, or Rhode Island.[25]

The French Canadians in Massachusetts, however, did not constitute as large a proportion of its total population as in New Hampshire, Rhode Island, or Vermont. They were, nonetheless, an important part of the Bay State's population.[26] They ranked third among the state's ethnic groups, after the Irish and English-speaking Canadians, and first among non-English-speaking immigrants. The Irish were the predominant ethnic group in Massachusetts; more than a fourth of its population was first or second generation Irish in 1885. The French Canadians, by contrast, represented only a twentieth of the state's population in 1885, roughly the same proportion as the English or English Canadians. Other groups each made up less than 3 percent of the total. Nearly half of the state's immigrants hailed from Ireland, while only one in eight had formerly lived in Quebec. By 1895 French Canadians formed about 7.5 percent of the total population and about 14 percent of the foreign-born. Thereafter, until 1920, despite the influx of many southern and eastern European immigrants, the position of the French Canadians within the state's ethnic mix changed relatively little.[27]

French Canadian immigrants, unlike the Irish of Boston when they first arrived, found employment quite quickly in the rapidly expanding industries in Massachusetts.[28] By 1885, thirty-seven thousand French Canadian-born workers formed nearly 5 percent of the state's total workforce and they constituted even larger proportions of all workers in manufacturing (7.1 percent) and of those in the textile industry (16.6 percent). Three-quarters of all *Canadien* immigrants were employed in manufacturing and two of every five worked in textile mills.[29]

Although French Canadians could be found in other industries, they were unusually concentrated in the textile industry, especially in the manufacture of cotton goods. By 1885 they represented the single largest group in cotton textiles, although other groups—notably the Irish and English—followed close behind them in order of importance. More than 70 percent of *Canadien* females in manufacturing worked as cotton mill operatives, a high proportion compared with other immigrant groups. Another 20 percent of *Canadien* women were employed by the woolen, paper, shoe, and clothing industries. Together these five industries contained more than 90 percent of all French Canadian female immigrants in manufacturing. French Canadian male immigrants were less concentrated in the cotton textile industry than females. Only 31 percent of *Canadien* males in manufacturing were cotton mill operatives. This occupation was by far the single largest source of employment, but significant proportions of *Canadien* males found other jobs. The building and shoe industries together, for example, employed nearly 30 percent of the *Canadiens*. Among other immigrant groups none were as concentrated in three industries—cotton textiles, building, and shoes—as the French Canadians.[30]

The occupational distribution of French Canadians remained essentially unchanged throughout the rest of the century. First and second generation *Canadiens* alike were concentrated in manufacturing to an unusual degree. Compared with other immigrant groups, relatively few French Canadians were employed in domestic and personal service, or in trade and transportation. By 1895, about 30 percent of all cotton mill operatives in Massachusetts were French Canadians; their numerical superiority in that industry was challenged only by the Irish. In industries outside of textiles French Canadians rarely made up more than 10 percent of the labor force and were greatly overshadowed by the Irish.

In 1895, as ten years earlier, the concentration among French Canadian workers in just three industries was exceptional. In terms of specific occupations for males, cotton mill operative was still the single largest occupation among French Canadians (19.5 percent), followed by laborers (9 percent), boot and shoe makers (7.2 percent), and carpenters and joiners (5.9 percent). These four occupations headed the list of the twenty occupations in which there were at least 750 French Canadian males. No other occupation contained more than 5 percent of the French Canadian male workforce in 1900.[31]

The opportunities for unskilled labor drew French Canadians to Massachusetts "not in quest of a higher standard of living but to avoid a lower."[32] The expansion of the textile industry created such jobs; the number of wage-earners in the cotton textiles increased from 38,500 to more than 92,000 between 1860 and 1900. The spread of new technology within the industry permitted immigrants with little or no prior experience in industry to work in the mills by reducing the level of skills required of workers. The boom and bust pattern of growth in the industry, coupled with very low wages, diminished its appeal among native-born Americans and the Irish. As these groups exited the cotton mills in search of better wages and working conditions, French Canadians replaced them. By the end of the nineteenth century, *Canadiens* had moved up into semiskilled and skilled jobs within the industry.[33]

Despite low wages and long hours, certain conditions within the textile industry made it attractive to recently arrived immigrants. Textile corporations often provided housing and credit for employees. While such practices sometimes led to exploitation, they made entry into American urban industrial society less difficult. The textile industry also offered employment possibilities for women and children. Again, this could and did lead to abuses. But for immigrants coming to Massachusetts from rural backgrounds in which children shared in the work, it seemed natural to expect children to help support the family. More often than not it was not a matter of choice; the income derived from working children was a necessary supplement to the income of the head of the household whose annual earnings could not sustain a large family. Among textile workers, French Canadians were hardly exceptional in this regard.[34]

French Canadian Centers of Settlement

Employment opportunities largely determined where French Canadians settled in Massachusetts. Nearly two-thirds lived in places where the boot and shoe or textile industries were dominant in 1885; this residential pattern had changed little by 1905. The concentration of

Canadiens in the state's textile centers was especially notable. In 1895, for example, nearly three-quarters inhabited the cities and towns where there was at least one cotton textile establishment, and a third lived in the handful of major textile centers. More urban than the total state population, the French Canadians were unusually concentrated in large cities (except for Boston) and in larger towns, but these places varied greatly in terms of the proportion of their inhabitants who were Canadien.[35]

An examination of forty-two French Canadian centers of settlement indicates much diversity among them, making it difficult to say that any one locality was typical.[36] French Canadian centers were usually manufacturing cities and towns in which a substantial portion of the workforce was employed in the production of textile or leather goods. But the centers differed significantly in terms of the size and rate of growth of the French Canadian population, its position vis-à-vis other groups in the community's ethnic mix, and the occupational distribution of French Canadians.

Three types of French Canadian centers of settlement may be distinguished on the basis of such differences—primary cities, secondary cities, and secondary towns.[37] The six primary cities (Fall River, Lowell, Holyoke, Worcester, New Bedford, and Lawrence) having an average Canadien population over ten thousand, contained more than 40 percent of all French Canadians in Massachusetts in 1895. In these cities—the chief foci of immigration after the Civil War—nearly one in five inhabitants was Canadien, while two-thirds of them had been born in Quebec.[38]

Such secondary cities as Fitchburg and Marlboro differed from the primary centers mainly in terms of the size of their French Canadian populations. The twelve secondary cities had, on the average, only a third as many Canadiens as the larger cities, and the Canadiens made up a smaller percentage of their residents (13 versus 18 percent). As in the primary cities the Irish often ranked first in size among ethnic groups despite the relatively rapid growth rate of the French Canadian populations.[39]

Several features of the secondary towns set them apart from the cities. French Canadians had settled in many of these communities—for example, Southbridge and Spencer—before the Civil War. Located mostly in central Massachusetts, in or near Worcester County, some of these communities had attracted Canadien immigrants as early as the 1840s.[40] These localities, usually small, single-industry towns dominated by one or two cotton or woolen mills, did not undergo the rapid industrial expansion characteristic of the larger cities after the Civil War.[41] Consequently, fewer French Canadians settled in these communities in the 1880s and 1890s when immigration peaked. The early settlement and slower growth rate of the *Canadien* population in the secondary towns diminished the difference in size between the first and second generation French Canadians. By 1895 about half of the *Canadiens* who inhabited these towns were the children of immigrants.

The occupational distribution of the French Canadians and their place within the ethnic mix of the secondary towns also differed from that of the cities. The smaller towns did not offer the diversity of economic opportunities common in larger cities. As a result, far fewer French Canadians found jobs as white-collar workers or in the trades, and a greater proportion worked in the textile mills or shoe factories. Finally, the French Canadians, rather than the Irish, almost always ranked first among the ethnic groups in the secondary towns, and the gap between them and the second-ranking group was often far greater than in the cities.

Grouping French Canadian centers of settlement into these three catagories serves a useful purpose, for it reveals some of the differences among these communities. Unfortunately, it also blurs important distinctions among centers within the groups. It is important to emphasize that the adjustment of French Canadians to industrial Massachusetts differed in many ways from place to place.[42] The context of a particular community affected the ways *Canadiens* interacted with other groups and the way they behaved in politics.

Differences among the primary cities may be highlighted by contrasting Fall River with Worcester. French Canadians were practically unknown in Fall River until after the Civil War, but by 1895, twenty-five thousand strong, they represented the largest single concentration of *Canadiens* in Massachusetts. The rapid development of the cotton textile industry attracted throngs of rustic *Canadiens* to Fall River during the 1870s. Until that decade the city's textile workers were mostly British and Irish immigrants with a proclivity for trade unionism. The influx of thousands of impoverished French Canadians, desperate for any kind of work, however low the wages and long the hours, and who, at least upon arrival, displayed an indifference towards unions and a willingness to be used as strike-breakers, transformed the city. It became a cauldron of seething economic and cultural rivalries that pitted English and Irish unionists against the French Canadians. In the aftermath of a bitter strike in 1879, relations between the Catholic Irish and French Canadians, which had been generally cordial through the 1870s, flared up during an acrimonious religious controversy over the appointment of a *Canadien* curate to the parish of Notre-Dame de Lourdes. The so-called Flint Affair embittered relations between the two groups. As the arrival of new immigrants over the next twenty years pushed the French Canadians up the occupational ladder, they came to view the unions more favorably and their relationship between their Irish co-religionists became less strident.[43] One would expect that the fierce class warfare and intense ethnic antagonisms in Fall River might have influenced the political behavior of the French Canadians. To be sure, Franco-Irish hostility was an important influence on *Canadien* politics but political alignments were not always predicated on this conflict alone.[44]

When contrasted with the virulence that characterized group relations in Fall River, labor and ethnic conflicts in Worcester appear muted. French Canadians had settled in Worcester in substantial numbers by 1860 but their number did not increase as rapidly as in other primary cities because Worcester was not a major center of textile manufacturing. By 1895 their population reached nearly ten thousand, however, and comprised the fourth largest concentration in the state. Despite the size of the colony, *Canadiens* remained a minority in Worcester. The Irish, who formed nearly a quarter of the city's people, greatly overshadowed them, while Swedes outnumbered them by a small margin. Economic rivalries were probably not as bitter as in Fall River because the *Canadiens,* like other groups, were not so dependent upon a single industry. Within Worcester's diversified and largely un-unionized industries immigrants could be found in a wider range of occupations. And, unlike Fall River, no great religious controversy severely strained relations between the city's two major Catholic groups before 1900.[45]

Occupational differences between the French Canadians in the two cities, as well as their early arrival in Worcester, affected the number of French Canadian males who became voters. In Worcester more *Canadiens* found work in shoe factories and in the building trades than in Fall River, where most worked as cotton mill operatives. Having been in the United States longer and having worked their way into more stable and better paying occupations, 20 percent of Worcester's *Canadien* males were naturalized in 1885, as opposed to only 13 percent in Fall River.

Despite the greater rate of naturalization, French Canadians in Worcester gained few local offices. In part, their diminished role in municipal affairs stemmed from their minority status within the city. Comprising less than 10 percent of the total population, they were not in a position to make effective their demands for recognition. Settled primarily in the predominantly Irish wards of the city, moreover, they often vied for office against the Irish and lost. By way of contrast, the *Canadiens* in Fall River formed the largest single ethnic group, had a majority status in Ward Six, and used their numerical superiority to acquire a substantial number of local political offices and at least some influence in local affairs.[46]

Southbridge provides yet another example illustrating the differences among French Canadian centers of settlement and how community context affected politics. As in Worcester, French Canadians settled in Southbridge before the Civil War. But, in contrast with both Worcester and Fall River, they constituted about half of the town's population as early as 1875, and far outnumbered the Irish, who, though they were the second largest ethnic group, made up about 10 percent of the townspeople. One fourth of Southbridge's *Canadien* males worked in its textile mills and a fifth found employment in the town's prospering spectacle industry. The town's sizeable *Canadien* population supported a good number of *Canadien* businessmen and tradesmen. Nearly 20 percent of French Canadian males were naturalized in 1885. Within this context, French Canadians aligned themselves with the Irish in the Democratic party and early acquired a voice in town government. A similar pattern prevailed in Spencer, a shoe town a few miles north of Southbridge. There the French Canadians had settled early and made up nearly 40 percent of the population by 1895.[47] In subsequent chapters, I will explore in greater detail the relationship between different community contexts and the political activity of French Canadians.

Cultural Adaptation and Conflict

Between 1860 and 1900, thousands of French Canadians departed Quebec in search of brighter prospects in New England. For many, leaving Canada meant not only abandoning their homes but also raised the fearful possibility of losing their language and their religion. Such was surely the case for those who left before the Civil War or who dispersed themselves throughout the Midwest.[48] Resettlement in New England did not imply the loss of culture, however, once more *Canadiens* began to arrive. Neither easily nor quickly did most French Canadians adopt the culture of their new home.[49] Instead they preserved and adapted the culture of rural French Canada to conditions of life in New England.

When transplanted to an urban and industrial setting, the traditional rural way of life of the *habitants* was bound to undergo a transformation. Gone were the familiar fields and farms; in New England most French Canadian immigrants congregated in urban villages, living near the mills in which they labored. Surrounded by English-speaking Protestants as well as Irish and other Catholics whom they previously regarded as *les étrangers*, the French Canadians themselves became the aliens.

Lofty spires reached above the factory towers that beckoned Quebec's *habitants*. Church bells and factory bells symbolized the two poles around which the lives of many *Canadiens* were organized in New

England. Six days a week urban *habitants* heeded the call to work in hope of future prosperity and property. On Sunday their churches summoned them to worship and to the remembrance of their collective past.

Linking past to present and present to future, Little Canada imparted continuity to the lives of displaced rural *habitants*, drawing like-minded immigrants together while isolating them from other urban dwellers. Outside the brick and granite walls of the great factories, the laborers built for themselves an invisible world of institutions that wove new color and rich texture into the Commonwealth's old and thick cultural fabric. The Little Canadas of New England were surely places, defined in space by the commanding spires of the magnificent churches that arose amid the clusters of tenements in the proletarian districts of centers of French Canadian settlement. But they were more than mere places. Their institutions—family, parish, and associations—ordered those aspects of life not governed by the factory bells or the foreman's bark. Within the web of relationships with their folk, the *Canadiens* worshiped, bought and sold, loved and died, rejoiced and mourned. Within them the customs, the mores, and the habits of speech of Quebec survived and flourished in New England. The community of Little Canada sheltered their national culture and nurtured their nascent ethnic identity.

Impelled by economic necessity, many French Canadians exchanged the farmyard for the millyard, and the plowhorse for the spinning-frame or loom.[50] Far fewer proved as willing to forfeit their faith, language, or customs. Transplanted from its indigenous rural setting, the culture of the *habitants* did not wither, as many of their leaders had feared. Instead it flourished. The concentrated pattern of their distribution, the proximity of the settlements to Quebec, their deeply-rooted ethnic consciousness, and their predominantly workingclass status all contributed to the creation of Little Canada wherever two or three hundred families gathered. The institutions of Little Canada—the national parish with its church, school, religious societies, fraternal associations, and French language newspapers—and the cultural conflicts arising from their resistance to assimilation further stimulated an ethnic "we-group" feeling and led French Canadians to cling tenaciously to the ideal of *la survivance*.

The pattern of French Canadian settlement was one of concentration, not dispersal. Relatively few manufacturing centers contained most of the *Canadiens*, and it was in these centers of settlement that their culture flourished. Poor, often unskilled and unfamiliar with the routine and rigors of industrial life, *Canadiens* first sought jobs, shelter, and companionship upon arrival. Sharing a common culture and language as well as the impoverishment and low social status of the workingclass, the immigrants found some of their needs satisfied by institutions of their own making. Isolated from the other inhabitants by virtue of cultural and economic differences, the uprooted *habitants* actually had little choice but to rely on their own resources.

But they were not entirely alone, for the French Canadian immigration was one of families more than of individuals, and in this respect, they differed from some other immigrant groups.[51] Family and kinship ties proved invaluable in finding employment and housing and provided emergency economic and moral support during personal crises or when hard times hit. The symbiotic relationship that developed between family and the textile industry, moreover, encouraged the preservation of strong family bonds on practical grounds, reinforcing the cement of sentiment. The traditionally large and close-knit French Canadian family aided the immigrants in their adjustment to industrial life, providing a sense of continuity and stability in the midst of the disorienting and potentially debilitating process of immigration.[52] Beyond the family, parish life offered the solace of religion and whatever comforts the hearing of a familiar tune or tale or sharing of memories could provide.

The propinquity of Quebec gave the French Canadians an advantage in transplanting and maintaining their culture in New England. For the *Canadiens*, migration did not necessarily cause so sudden and complete a rupture with the past as for such other immigrants as Russian Jews or Poles.[53] Return trips to Quebec were comparatively easy and common. *Habitants* crossed the border time and again on temporary visits to friends and relatives.[54] As "commuting immigrants" they could more easily maintain close ties with their families and friends than could trans-Atlantic immigrants.[55] Although the leaders of French Canada condemned and discouraged emigration at first, they quickly accepted what they could not change. After 1880 they came to view the enclaves of *Candien* culture in New England more favorably and assisted their development. Quebec provided much of the leadership, both religious and lay, crucial to the early success of *la survivance* in New England. Later, second-generation elites were often educated in the classical colleges and universities of the homeland.[56]

The national parish, with its school and societies, was the heart of Little Canada.[57] Like many other immigrants, French Canadians associated the loss of language with the loss of faith. The establishment of national parishes under the direction of French Canadian priests, they believed, was essential to their ethnic survival. For French Canadians, attending an English-speaking church, *les églises irlandaises* (the Irish churches), jeopardized not only one's soul but one's ethnic identity as well. Confessing one's sins and following a Sunday sermon in English often proved difficult if not impossible. French Canadians also missed the traditional pomp and pageantry associated with the rituals of religious life in Quebec. These familiar displays the immigrants found much diminished in an Irish parish; the Irish religious tradition leaned towards austerity—a tendency that had been reinforced by the attempts to soothe and accommodate Yankee prejudice against "popish pageantry." The parish system of the well-endowed, virtually established church in Quebec had provided inexpensive religion and offered an unusual degree of participation for laymen in parish governance. Many *Canadiens* viewed the costs of maintaining one's faith in New England prohibitive and their role in parish affairs circumscribed. In response many French Canadian parishes were formed. At great expense and effort, grand churches were erected, imparting an air of permanence to *Canadien* colonies.[58]

The parish school sought to preserve both language and faith not so much among the immigrants themselves but among their children. *La survivance* implied that immigrants should retain their customs, faith, and language and transmit them to following generations. This goal, of course, threatened to perpetuate linguistic and cultural differences among Catholics in America, and was clearly aimed at resisting assimilation. If successful, the parish school would extend the divisive effects of the immigration far into the future, bypassing the assimilative efforts of the Irish-American hierarchy and the public school system.[59]

Mutual aid societies and fraternal associations also played a central role in promoting *la survivance*. Founded to provide for the economic and social needs of the immigrants, they buttressed traditional values as well. While helping French Canadians to face the uncertainties of life, they promoted the ideal of a collective culture as well as that of collective security. Within these societies were often found the nucleus of parish organization. From their membership usually arose the leadership needed to create parishes and to maintain a French Canadian community separate from the larger society.[60] The same leadership also forged important connections with the larger society, for in articulating the aspirations of their group they drew recognition from outside their group.[61]

The creation of French Canadian institutions in Massachusetts began in Worcester County in the 1840s under the missionary priests Zephryrin Levesque and Napoleon Mignault. These early efforts achieved only limited success as the immigrants were few and their resources meager. Not until 1868 was the first French Canadian parish in Massachusetts founded in Pittsfield. The following year parishes were established in Worcester, Southbridge, Lowell, and Holyoke. Institutional development progressed more rapidly in the early 1870s as the boom in the textile industry swelled the stream of immigrants from Quebec. By 1873 about a dozen parishes and mutual aid societies had been formed in the state.[62]

The industrial depression of the mid-1870s diminished the flow of immigrants and slowed the pace of institutional development. In the face of economic adversity many French Canadians fled industrial life, returning to the temporary shelter of rural Canada. But among those who remained, additional fraternal societies were formed; their number doubled between 1873 and 1881. The resurgence of the immigration in the mid-1880s stimulated a decade of rapid institutional growth. More than a dozen parishes and twice as many mutual aid associations were founded during the 1880s in Massachusetts, indicating that French Canadians were becoming a fixture of urban life in New England. By 1891 thirty-five *Canadien* parishes, ranging in size from two hundred to two thousand families and enrolling more than eleven thousand children in twenty-five schools, existed in Massachusetts.[63]

The "institutional completeness" of French Canadian colonies differed from community to community.[64] Larger *Canadien* populations in the cities supported a greater number and wider range of institutions than those in most smaller towns. Cultural-recreational organizations and political clubs were common in the cities, particularly in the primary centers such as Fall River and Worcester, but were absent in many secondary towns. Many towns lacked even a separate French Canadian parish.[65] Ethnic institutions expressed and stimulated *Canadien* group consciousness and probably slowed the rate of assimilation, as indeed they were intended to do. Simultaneously the social networks created by their institutions provided the French Canadians with group-minded leadership and served as the organizational basis for political action. Ethnic politics and demands for recognition on the local level could be expected to be more intense wherever institutional development was more advanced.

The creation of Little Canadas explicitly was aimed at resisting assimilation and preserving the *Canadien* ethnic identity in America. These efforts on behalf of *la survivance* drew the French Canadians into conflict with both Irish Catholics and English-speaking Protestants. Both groups looked askance at the development of a separate and distinct *Canadien* subcommunity within their midst. For their part, the French Canadians viewed any opposition to their efforts as part of a plan for "pan-Saxonization" and as a continuation of the struggle for ethnic survival that they had known in Canada. Arriving in the United States with a well-honed sense of French Canadian nationalism, they were already prone to taking a defensive stance in the face of hostility.

Mutual suspicion and fear occasionally erupted into open conflict and contributed to the vehemence with which *Canadiens* pursued *la survivance*.[66]

Franco-Irish conflict centered about the creation of separate French Canadian parishes. In the minds of the most zealous and militant proponents of *la survivance*, the need for national parishes lay in the incompatibility between the Irish and French Canadian characters. No doubt differences in temperament, expressed in different customs of worship, did contribute to conflict.[67] The fundamental source of disagreement, however, had more to do with the French Canadian belief that their language and their religion were inseparable. As Hamon expressed it, *"La religion et la langue sont les deux gardiennes naturelles de la nationalité d'un peuple."* Among *Canadiens* the belief that *"Qui perd sa langue, perd sa foi,"* was common.[68] Such ideas ran contrary to the prevailing policy of the American Catholic Church in the late nineteenth century, which proposed rapid assimilation of the immigrants.[69] Group differences over the administration of parish finances and personal struggles for status and power within the church were the immediate issues behind the occasionally virulent instances of Franco-Irish religious controversy.[70]

Difficult as it is to gauge the depth of the hostility that existed between the Irish and the French Canadians, it is still easy to exaggerate the implications of dramatic conflicts. Individual conflicts were the product of particular situations and personalities, but they provided occasions for fulminations by the French Canadian press and remain well-remembered highlights of the Franco-American epic. On the other hand, the founding of many *Canadien* parishes went smoothly, had the encouragement of the hierarchy, and provoked no open animosities.[71]

The response of French Canadians to various crises differed, moreover. The controversy over the establishment of a French Canadian parish in North Brookfield, for example, provoked a storm of protest among some French Canadians of Worcester. It received much publicity because it resulted in the mass excommunication of several hundred *Canadiens* who defied the ecclesiastical authority of Bishop Beaven of Springfield.[72] Rev. Jean Berger, one of the principals in this episode, militantly proclaimed that the "whole issue may be summed up in the following phrase: 'The Irish church for the Irish, the French church for the French Canadians.' "[73] Some of Worcester's *Canadien* leaders concurred and called for a national congress in order to "defend our rights and particularly, to obtain justly our due from the clerical authorities in this country." Pleaded Felix D. Fontaine, who chaired a mass meeting in Worcester on this controversy,

We have been oppressed and brow-beaten by the bishops of other nationalities until it is impossible to bear with it longer. Justice for the French-speaking Catholics is an unheard-of-thing.[74]

Not all Worcester French Canadians viewed the issues in such clear-cut and oversimplified terms. J. Arthur Favreau, editor of *L'Opinion Publique*, the city's French-language daily, for example, declined to act as secretary at the meeting, "as he was not in favor of the movement, as he understood it."[75] Felix A. Belisle warned that "in his opinion the meeting was a trap for the unwary."[76] *L'Opinion Publique*, like other French Canadian newspapers, was critical of Berger and counseled the rebellious *Canadiens* to obey the bishop's dicta and "remain faithful to the faith of [their] fathers." The pastors of two of the three French Canadian parishes in Worcester warned their flocks against involvement in the rebellion and severely criticized its leaders.[77]

Finally, not all the French Canadians of North Brookfield supported Berger's demand for a separate parish. Berger had nearly four hundred followers when the controversy broke out in September 1900. After the excommunication, this number steadily dwindled. By October the original lay leaders of the rebel religious association came to view Berger as the primary obstacle to the formation of a national parish and sought a peaceable compromise with the bishop. By November Berger's following had been halved and the controversy petered out.[78]

In contrast with the high visibility the issue had in Worcester, the French Canadians of Spencer, the town located between North Brookfield and Worcester, remained unagitated. Although reportedly in sympathy with their fellow *Canadiens*, few attended the mass meeting held in Spencer organized by Dr. Marc Fontaine. Indeed, most of the speakers and those in attendance at the Spencer meeting had come from Worcester and North Brookfield for the occasion.[79]

French Canadian efforts on behalf of *la survivance* brought them into cultural conflict with English-speaking Protestants as well. In large measure such conflict lay rooted in anti-immigrant and anti-Catholic feeling common during this period, which occasionally erupted in hysteria. The Haverhill school controversy of 1887–89 (see Chap. 4) and the growth of the American Protective Association in the early 1890s in Massachusetts exemplify such incidents of hysteria and gave vent to anti-*Canadien* as well as anti-Irish prejudice. Underlying both incidents were the growth of Irish political influence and the robust development of Catholic institutions in the Bay State's cities during the 1880s. Particularly disturbing to the nativists was the growth of the Catholic parochial school system, and especially the founding of

French Canadian schools that aimed explicitly at preventing assimilation by making French the language of instruction. According to Albert Bartlett, one of the principals in the Haverhill school controversy, which revolved around the issue of language,

> The danger in the establishment of these large schools lies in the separation of the people, not only by religious, but also by social and racial lines; in the mutual jealousy and suspicion engendered; in the teaching and practice that the German or French or any other foreign language has equal claim here with English; in short, in separating us into strongly-divided classes by the impressionable years of youth, and thereby destroying the conformities and sympathies which grow up in minds made alike by a common development' and which form the strength of a republican state.[80]

Coupled with periodic trouble encountered over the founding of *Canadien* parishes, incidents of Yankee hostility reinforced the feeling of separateness that French Canadians brought from Quebec.

The rural society that evolved in Quebec after the conquest of Canada by Great Britain isolated the French Canadians within Canada and provided the foundation for *la survivance*. Stimulated by cultural and political conflict with the English-speaking Canadians, French Canadian nationalism grew stronger in the mid-nineteenth century as the rural society upon which it was based began to falter. The deepening agricultural crisis in Quebec forced thousands of French Canadians to emigrate after the American Civil War. Drawn to the manufacturing centers of New England in search of economic well-being, the *Canadiens* came with a well-defined ethnic identity that they sought to preserve. This identity flourished when transplanted to New England's urban environment.

Concentrated in comparatively few centers of settlement close to their Quebec homeland, the French Canadians successfully erected the institutional framework necessary to maintain their culture. Little Canadas isolated the mass of French Canadians from assimilative influences, and cultural conflicts arising from *Canadien* efforts on behalf of *la survivance* fortified the sense of alienation. Consequently, the French Canadians assumed an essentially defensive posture in their relations with other groups.

3
Naturalization, Officeholding, and Voting

Initially opposed to mass naturalization, French Canadian spokesmen eventually became its proponents. Most *Canadien* immigrants, however, remained indifferent to exhortations to become citizens. Legal barriers and certain socioeconomic factors account in part for the low rate of naturalization but the circumstances of their immigration and their way of life in New England were probably more salient influences. Despite the group's low naturalization rate, the number of French Canadian voters increased as their political influence grew. French Canadians tended to vote Democratic in presidential and gubernatorial elections between 1888 and 1920. But officeseeking and officeholding patterns show that the relationship between French Canadians and the political parties was complex and varied from one community to another.

Naturalization represented an important step for an immigrant in the process of his adjustment to American life. Whatever else it may have meant to an immigrant, naturalization reflected a commitment to remain in the United States as a permanent resident and to pursue his fortune within the American framework. It was a decision made by an individual willing to sever at least a legal connection with his past. Although an immigrant might retain fond memories of and harbor deep sentiments for his former way of life, naturalization made him legally an American and opened the door to fuller participation in the American community. A stranger still in many ways—his labor exploited, his habits and speech the objects of ridicule—the immigrant gained through naturalization legal equality with other citizens; upon naturalization a newcomer could vote and hold public office. Naturalization provides an appropriate starting point for a discussion of the political assimilation of an immigrant group.

Born Again: The Loyal American

Naturalization held different meanings for different people. Native-born Americans viewed naturalization from one perspective, and even

45

among immigrants themselves perspectives differed. Americans often saw naturalization as conferring political liberty—specifically the franchise—upon those less fortunate than themselves. They expected all immigrants to seek the blessings of American liberty and republican government. Such blessings should be extended to foreign-born Americans, they agreed, but only gradually and only selectively—to those newcomers perceived as worthy of liberty, who were willing and capable of the change of heart needed to relinquish their previous national loyalty and identity and became Americans in spirit.

Several measures were used to evaluate the worthiness of immigrants for citizenship. Some states, like Massachusetts, erected, beyond the federal residence requirements, formidable constitutional obstacles to the right to vote. The Bay State permitted only an adult male immigrant who could "read the Constitution in English and write his name" to qualify for suffrage. Literacy in the English language was the legal measure of an immigrant's worthiness for citizenship in Massachusetts.[1] Beyond literacy there existed other informal standards by which immigrant groups could be evaluated. The rate at which members of a particular group became citizens was one such standard. The extent to which enfranchised immigrants made political choices in the public interest rather than in terms of self-interest of their group was another.

These criteria revealed, in the eyes of Americans, the willingness of immigrants to become true citizens of the republic, in spirit as well as in residence. The fundamental issue of language underlay the first two measures. Since the ability to read English was a prerequisite for enfranchisement, the number of immigrants who qualified for voting represented the degree to which a particular group was willing to learn English. What was for many an alien language was taken as a yardstick of their commitment to America's institutions and its way of life. From this perspective, continued use of his native tongue symbolized an immigrant's resistance to Americanization.

Another aspect of an individual's national identity was at issue in the third criterion. The political choices of naturalized immigrants, Americans hoped, would reflect an identification with the American people without regard to national origin. Americans viewed the introduction of ethnic identity or group interest into the political arena as both unwise and un-American. Truly patriotic voters would vote for the best man regardless of the candidate's national origin, these Americans believed. The editor of a small-town newspaper in Massachusetts summarized these sentiments in a sentence: "This is America and as citizens we are all free and equal, and we must sink all racial feelings in the desire to benefit our common good."[2] In short, Americans viewed naturalization as symbolic of a change of heart in which an immigrant renounced not only loyalty to another government but also shed his national identity in order to assume another and thus be born-again—an American.

An apparent lack of interest in American citizenship among French Canadians provoked periodic criticism of the group by Americans, especially before 1900. Such criticisms reveal the fears and worries underlying the American perspective on naturalization. Initially critical of the impermanent character of the emigration from Quebec, Americans later worried about what impact the development of the Little Canadas would have on American society and politics.

In 1880 the Massachusetts Bureau of Labor Statistics summarized the attitudes towards French Canadians, as expressed by persons interviewed in preparing a report on the obstacles to labor reform in the Bay State:

> They are a horde of industrial invaders, not a stream of stable settlers. Voting, with all that it implies, they care nothing about. Rarely does one of them become naturalized. . . . All they ask is to be set to work, and they care little who rules them or how they are ruled.[3]

Until 1880 the transience of *Canadien* immigrants worried some Americans who feared that they would not settle down and "become part of the American people."[4] During the 1870s and 1880s, however, French Canadians established many parishes, schools, and associations; many former *habitants* were in fact becoming permanent New England inhabitants. Old fears gave way to new.

The growing number of *Canadiens* and the militant assertion of their culture with the explicit aim of preserving it within New England aroused new apprehensions. Some critics feared that French Canadians would remain an undigested lump within American society. Others imagined that the network of parishes spreading throughout New England would ultimately be linked with Quebec, thereby threatening to unite New England with Quebec under a papal banner. While some Americans welcomed the possibility of annexing Canada to the United States, others pointed to the perplexities that such a step would bring to American political life. They warned against annexation and the growth of the French Canadian presence in New England.[5]

Francophobes emphasized the threat French Canadians and their institutions seemed to pose to cherished and traditional New England institutions—particularly the common public school and the town meeting. Some nativists viewed the French Canadians as unfit for citizenship and incapable of assuming the responsibilities of self-government because of their Catholic and French heritage. From the nativist perspective—one frequently charged with powerful racial and anti-Catholic impulses—the Roman Catholic clergy, and especially the Jesuits, dominated the French-speaking population of Canada.[6] As a result, they believed, French Canadians lacked "training in self-government and sympathy with the institutions amid which they were transplanted."[7]

Francophobes pointed out, with some accuracy, that French Canadian religious and cultural institutions constituted a deliberate attempt on the part of *Canadien* leaders to circumvent the assimilation of immigrants to American life. Carroll Wright, head of the Massachusetts Bureau of Labor Statistics, for example, noted this tendency among the French Canadians early in the 1880s. Wright had warned the *Canadiens* that their insistence upon a distinct and separate cultural existence within the republic was, and would remain, the primary source of prejudice against them.[8] Although he himself later grew more tolerant and more accepting of French Canadians, Wright's original assessment remained valid for some time.[9] About a decade after Wright's warning, an alarmist explained the dangers associated with the French Canadian presence in these terms:

> We have thus rapidly developing among us an organized community opposed to Americanization, secluded by all possible efforts on the part of its leaders, from the assimilating influences which affect other immigrants, and having on its banners the inscription: *Notre Religion, Notre Langue, et Nos Moeurs.* It is an organization ruled by a principle diametrically opposed to that which our forefathers brought to these shores, and which has made New England what it is. The one depresses to the lowest point possible what the other exalted to the highest, the principle of personal responsibility with the freedom which this involves.[10]

Nativists argued also that the institutions and character of the French Canadian immigrants would lead to an erosion of the sense of common trust and good will necessary for the survival of the American republican form of government. With the alleged subversion of public schools by parochial schools and the substitution of the ward caucus for the town meeting, they feared, politics would be reduced to "mutual jealousy and suspicion" among groups divided against each other on the basis of class and race. Instead of being a "people whose strength is unity, we may become a heterogeneous collection of different nationalities with diverse allegiances."[11] Nativists feared the loss of social homogeneity, upon which many Americans believed their republic was founded, and the creation and persistence of ethnic divisions in politics. Unless French Canadian immigrants became reborn Americans by way of naturalization, the nativists predicted that the American republic, its social life, and its political life would be forever altered.

Most native-born Americans in the late nineteenth century, and even much later, could not envision the United States as a nation of peoples culturally and linguistically diverse. They deeply trusted the capacity of American society to assimilate the strangers arriving at its borders. But they always expected that newcomers would, and should, aspire to become Americans. In the end, they hoped, all immigrants would become Americans at heart as well as in residence.[12] Carroll Wright expressed succinctly this point of view to the French Canadians assembled before him at a public hearing in 1881:

> I wish you to remember one thing, however, and that is that while this land is open to all, and a welcoming hand is extended all without regard to nationality, the people of the United States will always look with disapprobation upon any attempt on the part of settlers to be other than American citizens . . . *you cannot be loyal Americans and loyal French Canadians at the same time* [emphasis added].[13]

Naturalization: A Change of Heart?

French Canadians in New England, especially the more affluent and influential professional and middle classes who sought acceptance by the Americans, grew sensitive to such criticisms and reacted strongly. They defended their group against the charges that *Canadiens* were somehow inferior to other groups. Denying certain charges, they excused others. They remained fundamentally at odds with their critics because each had a much different vision of American society.

Although the French Canadian view of naturalization, of American society, and of the purpose of their immigration changed over time, most *Canadien* leaders never accepted the point of view of the Americanizers. In 1881 they did not attempt to refute Wright's contention that American citizenship was an either/or proposition. Their silence on this point indicated not that they agreed with Wright but rather that they were primarily concerned with combating the "calumny," "prejudice," and "malice" that they contended inspired the comments publicized by the bureau. One suspects, however, that the French Canadian leaders who met with Wright knew, perhaps better than he, that their national churches, schools, and associations betrayed their intention to resist assimilation. They tried to demonstrate that the specific charges in the bureau report were not applicable to all *Canadiens* in New England. They presented detailed evidence relating to the number of French Canadian voters, property-holders, merchants, and professionals as proof that *habitants* were not merely sojourners. At the same time and for the same reason, they listed the number of *Canadien* parishes, schools, and associations.[14] Therein lay the rub. Wright was reluctant to press the point, and thus further to antagonize or discourage the French Canadians. He pointed out in his summary of the meeting, nevertheless, that

> . . . it would have been very easy to have combatted the evidence given at the hearing, and to have introduced much testimony to support the statements contained in the report of last year.[15]

Indeed, he included in the same volume of bureau *Reports,* which contained an account of his meeting with the French Canadians, a report on the ethnic composition of the state's voting population in 1875 that showed how few *Canadiens* had become voters.[16]

Unless national pride had clouded their vision, the French Canadian leaders meeting with Wright must have realized that the bureau's report, though erroneous in some details, presented a largely accurate picture of the migration in its early stages. Part of their dilemma in refuting the description was that many French Canadian leaders up to that time had viewed as odious the permanent settlement of French Canadians in the United States and had encouraged repatriation to the Canadian soil. Certainly they had rejected, and many abhorred still in 1880, the idea that French Canadians should become citizens in Wright's meaning of the term. After 1880, however, these leaders altered their views of American society and of the *Canadien* immigration. As they adopted a pluralistic vision of American society, they entertained the notion that *Canadiens* could become legal citizens of the United States while remaining French Canadians at heart—in faith and in language.

The differences between the advocates of Americanization and the French Canadian leaders may best be seen in the meaning each attributed to naturalization. For the Americanizers, naturalization signified a change of heart within the immigrant—an outward manifestation of an internal spiritual transformation that a newcomer had experienced. In this sense the Americanizers viewed naturalization as akin to a religious conversion by which an immigrant became a born-again American.[17]

Before the 1880s many French Canadian leaders viewed naturalization similarly, as representing a change of heart implying the loss of one's national identity. In their eyes, however, such a change was an ignoble apostasy and betrayal of one's heritage. Consequently, they discouraged the mass of French Canadians from taking an oath of allegiance to the government of their new domicile. They viewed American society as being overly materialistic and spiritually indifferent, and as such a flawed and wicked place unfit as a permanent abode for the French people in North America. Naturalization was prescribed only for those few who planned to remain in the states and who, carefully shielded within French Canadian institutions, could avoid the contagions of the American way of life. Most French Canadians, they hoped, would be repatriated, not naturalized. Those who did become citizens endangered their French Canadian identities; but properly protected they could serve as the trustees of the rights and interests of their alienated compatriots.[18]

"*Devenez légalement Américain, mais soyez toujours cordialment Canadiens,*" summarizes the attitude toward naturalization before 1880.[19] Those few *Canadiens* who planned to remain in the United States should become citizens. Rather than being integrated themselves into American society, however, naturalized French Canadians were to become the stewards of *Canadien* interests within the republic. "*Restons français, avant tout soyons Canadiens;*" such was the admonition to naturalized *Canadiens*.[20]

As the stream of immigrants swelled in the 1880s the dream of repatriation evaporated. The successful transplantation and rapid growth of French Canadian institutions allayed fears among French Canadian leaders, in Quebec as well as in the United States, that the emigres would become apostates. By the late 1880s, once the institutional framework of the thriving Little Canadas seemed to safeguard their cultural heritage, *Canadien* leaders gained greater confidence that their culture would survive. Although living in New England, French Canadians, it now seemed possible, could remain *Quebecois* at heart and in spirit.

With this development, the attitude of French Canadian leaders toward American society changed. Instead of being a hostile and alien place, American society came to be viewed as one providing liberty and opportunity—liberty for the individual to pursue his own beliefs, and opportunity for each different group to educate its young and to develop its distinctive qualities. This new, positive image conceived of America as a pluralistic society. Amalgamation, assimilation, and the loss of one's French Canadian identity need not necessarily be the destiny of the *Canadiens* in New England. Accordingly, French Canadian leaders argued that unity among Americans did not preclude diversity among them. As one *Canadien* explained, "*La variété des branches ne détruit pas l'unité de l'arbre; la diversité des races ne nuit pas davantage a l'unité de la nation.*"[21]

Although Americanizers certainly did not share this vision, French Canadian leaders often expressed such sentiments. *Canadien* spokesmen were now more apt to say: "*Ma foi, à l'Amérique! Et mon coeur, à la chère Province de Québec!*"[22] With their acceptance of permanent residence as compatible with the retention of French Canadian culture, mores, and faith, the attitude toward naturalization shifted. Rather than remaining an anathema to be avoided at practically any cost, naturalization became for the French Canadian leadership a means by which the group's interests and culture could be safeguarded and promoted. Properly led, a mass of voters could become the guardian of their culture within American society. Naturalization, after all, some *Canadien* leaders reasoned, was merely a legal contract between an individual and a government in which loyalty to the state was exchanged for its protection under the law.[23]

While serving as a device by which *Canadien* rights and interests could be protected, greater naturalization might also gain the recognition French Canadian leaders believed their group deserved, they now reasoned. Naturalization might also fend off detractors who frequently pointed to the low naturalization rate as an indication of the undesirability of French Canadian immigrants. Insofar as Americans measured the relative merits of a particular immigrant group in terms of its naturalization rate, the image of the French Canadians might be improved.[24] Thus by 1900, French Canadian leaders viewed naturalization as a strategy by which members of the group could become voters for the benefit of the group, and yet not necessarily become Americanized. Naturalization need not signify, as they feared earlier, a change of heart.[25] It might also mean the opportunity to remain "*Canadiens de coeurs et de pensée*" and "*perpétuer sous le drapeau américain les traditions et les virtues de sang français.*"[26]

Canadien Political Indifference

How the mass of ordinary French Canadian immigrants felt about naturalization may best be judged inferentially, by the extent to which they became citizens. Compared with most other immigrant groups, few French Canadians became American citizens, at least until 1920. In 1885 fewer than 20 percent of adult French Canadian males in Massachusetts were naturalized—the lowest rate of naturalization among foreign-born groups in the state.[27] Fifteen years later, despite a change in attitude on the part of their leaders, at least 58 percent, and possibly as many as 75 percent, of eligible *Canadiens* remained legal aliens. By 1910 only 35 percent of adult French Canadian males in the Bay State were legal voters; fewer than 3 percent had declared their intention of becoming citizens. While constituting 5 percent of the state's adult male population, French Canadians formed less than 3 percent of its legal voters. Greater progress was evident by 1920 when 42 percent of *Canadien* males had become naturalized citizens and another 17 percent had declared their intention of doing so (see table 3.1). Nevertheless, com-

Table 3.1

Percentage of eligible French Canadian
males who were naturalized, had
first papers, were aliens, or
whose status was unknown,
Massachusetts, 1885-1930

	Naturalized	First papers	Aliens	Not reported
1885	18.2	n/a	81.8	n/a
1900	n/a	n/a	57.8	n/a
1910	35.1	2.6	57.4	4.9
1920	42.3	16.8	39.8	2.1
1930	51.3	13.3	32.0	3.4

SOURCE: Massachusetts Bureau of Statistics of Labor, Report 19 (1888), p. 188; U.S. Bureau of the Census, Twelfth Census of the United States: 1900, 1:914-29; Thirteenth Census of the United States: 1920, 2:826-41; Leon E. Truesdell, The Canadian Born in the United States (New Haven: Yale University Press, 1943), p. 108. Foreign-born males could take out their first papers, i.e., declare their intention to become citizens, once they reached eighteen years of age. They then could be naturalized after a two-year waiting period, if they satisfied the requirement of five years continuous residence in the United States.

pared with other ethnic groups, they lagged behind. Viewed in terms of their rate of naturalization, the mass of French Canadians appear to have thought little about becoming American citizens. Politics remained for most a concern secondary to their social and economic preoccupations.

Statutory language and residency restrictions and the hostility of French Canadian leaders toward naturalization help account for the low rate of the 1880s. The persistence of the low rate in the early twentieth century for French Canadians in New England may be explained in part by certain socioeconomic variables, but the circumstances of their immigration and conditions of life in New England were probably the most salient determinants affecting their naturalization rate.

French Canadian leaders gave a number of reasons for the low naturalization rate in 1881, but emphasized the stringent legal requirements for citizenship in Massachusetts, especially regarding literacy in English. Many French Canadians, they explained, arrived at an older age and found it difficult to learn English or to understand the customs of American life. Because few older immigrants acquired property—a difficult task in light of the low wages of the textile industry in which most found employment—few became citizens. Younger immigrants, however, were said to find the language barrier less formidable and were naturalized as soon as they otherwise qualified.[28]

Other factors prevented French Canadians from applying for citizenship, according to their leaders. The recency of their arrival precluded satisfying the legal residence requirements for many. Their love of Canada and hope of returning to their homeland, moreover, made many immigrants reluctant to become American citizens. Finally, the nearness of Quebec to New England made the trip home easy, raised the expectation of repatriation, and encouraged frequent visits to Quebec that made it more difficult to meet residence requirements.[29]

These explanations seemed plausible in 1880. Carroll Wright admitted that "considering the obstacle of language" the *Canadiens* were "doing well," but he pointed out that the attitude of the leaders toward naturalization up to that time had not made things easier.[30] The relative importance of language and length of residence in the United States as barriers to citizenship may be evaluated, and they lend some credibility to the explanations given by *Canadien* leaders. In 1885 the naturalization rate among French Canadian immigrants literate in English was higher than among *Canadiens* at large. The Irish had the highest naturalization rate among immigrants because of their early arrival and longer residence in Massachusetts. English and Scottish immigrants, many of whom arrived about the same time as the French Canadians, had a naturalization rate closer to 50 percent. For English and French Canadians, considered separately, the rate was closer to 40 percent in each case.[31] The difference between the rates among English, Scottish, and Canadian immigrants suggests that Canada's proximity to New England had a negative effect on naturalization and was a more important influence than language on all Canadians.

A comparison of French Canadian naturalization rates in different centers of settlement suggests that length of residence was, as *Canadien* leaders argued, an important factor in the 1880s. A larger proportion of French Canadians were legal voters in 1885 in those communities where they had settled in sizeable numbers before 1860. In Pittsfield, for example, where the first French Canadian parish in Massachusetts had been founded in 1869, 37 percent of adult *Canadien* males were naturalized—twice the average for the state. Naturalization rates tended to be higher in other centers of early settlement—Marlboro, Southbridge, Spencer, and Sutton to name a few. In Worcester, where the *Canadiens* had arrived early, 22 percent of the adult males were voters in 1885, while in Fall River, in which the French Canadians arrived later, only 13 percent were voters.[32]

From 1885 to 1910 French Canadians in New England generally, and in Massachusetts particularly, became naturalized citizens more slowly than their countrymen in other parts of the United States and more slowly than most other immigrants. By 1910, on the national level as well as in Massachusetts, French Canadians had a naturalization rate somewhat higher than more recently arrived immigrants, such as Greeks, and somewhat lower than other immigrants, such as the British, who arrived before or about the same time as the *Canadiens*. For old immigrant groups in Massachusetts in 1910 about 53 percent were naturalized; about 18 percent of new immigrants had become voters. The naturalization rate among French Canadians was 35 percent, and for English Canadians, 47 percent. By 1920 the percent of naturalized French Canadians had climbed to 41 percent, an increase of six percentage points, a smaller gain than for most other immigrant groups.[33]

If naturalization did not always represent a change of heart on the part of an immigrant, it did reflect a commitment to permanent residence in the United States. As an immigrant became more familiar with America and as the memories of his homeland grew dim, he was more likely to become a citizen.[34] It is not surprising, therefore, to find that length of residence in the United States correlates highly with naturalization rates among immigrant groups. The longer an immigrant remained in the United States the more likely he was to learn English and to satisfy the legal requirements of residence. He was, moreover, more likely to get a better job and perhaps acquire some property. Thus, by 1920 immigrant groups that had been in the United States longer usually had a higher naturalization rate (see table 3.2).[35]

The proximity of Canada to the United States somewhat modified this generalization's applicability to both English- and French-speaking Canadians. If naturalization is best understood as a commitment to reside in the United States, why Canadians were generally slower to become citizens or even to declare their intention to do so becomes comprehensible. A comparison of motives for coming to and staying in the United States helps to make this clear. As much as the golden door attracted them, anti-Semitism drove Russian Jews away from their homes. Given the long distances involved and the quality of life they could expect in Imperial Russia, few would have been inclined to return. Russian Jews had a comparatively high rate of naturalization. Italians and Greeks, who arrived about the same time as Eastern Jews, had a lower rate of naturalization. While economic conditions may have driven the Italians and Greeks to America, conditions at home did not prevent them from returning once their fortunes had been made. Many did return despite

Table 3.2

Rank ordering of twenty-three immigrant groups by percentage of
foreign-born males, twenty-one years of age and over,
who are naturalized and by length of residence
in the United States, United States, 1910

	Percent naturalized	Index of length of residence	Rank percent naturalized	Rank index of length of residence
Germany	69.5	69.8	1	2
Wales	69.2	66.9	2	3
Ireland	67.8	70.0	3	1
Sweden	62.8	51.2	4	13
Switzerland	61.8	58.6	5	10
Denmark	61.6	54.6	6	12
England	59.4	62.3	7	4
Norway	57.1	58.8	8	8
Netherlands	56.8	59.1	9	7
Scotland	56.5	60.4	10	5
Canada-Other	53.9	55.5	11	11
France	49.6	59.9	12	6
Canada-French	44.7	58.7	13	9
Belgium & Luxemburg	43.0	44.7	14	15
Finland	30.6	38.6	15	17
Rumania	28.8	24.9	16	22
Russia	26.1	36.9	17	18
Portugal	24.9	48.1	18	14
Austria	24.6	41.3	19	16
Italy	17.7	36.0	20	19
Spain	16.4	33.7	21	20
Hungary	14.3	29.2	22	21
Greece	6.6	7.7	23	23

SOURCE: U.S. Bureau of the Census, Thirteenth Census
of the United States; 1910, 1:877, 1068.   See note 35.

the distances. But the return trip was much easier still for Canadians, and encouraged their expectations of returning to their homeland.[36]

The language barrier explains, in part, why fewer French-speaking Canadians became citizens than their English-speaking countrymen. Many non-English-speaking immigrants showed a livelier interest in naturalization than the French Canadians and were quicker to learn English. A study of textile mill workers, for example, showed that French Canadians were more likely to speak English on their arrival than other immigrants, but that other groups learned English more quickly once in the states. Among immigrants who had been in the

United States for less than five years, for example, 41 percent of *Canadiens* but only 16 percent of Greeks spoke English. Among immigrants in the states for more than ten years, 75 percent of Greeks spoke English but the proportion of French Canadians who spoke English was only 84 percent.[37]

A comparison of naturalization rates among French Canadians in different parts of the United States emphasizes the importance of language as a primary barrier to citizenship in New England. By 1910 twenty-four states accounted for 95 percent of the *Canadiens* in the United States. Of the twenty-four states, French Canadians in Massachusetts had the lowest rate of naturalization except for Maine. In 1910 about 45 percent of *Canadiens* had become citizens nationally. In Massachusetts the proportion was only 35 percent, as contrasted with 67 percent in North Dakota and 62 percent in Wisconsin (see table 3.3). French Canadians outside New England generally acquired citizenship at about the same rate as other immigrants having a comparable length of residence.[38] Of about 160 cities in the United States having twenty-five thousand persons in 1900, nearly fifty had at least one hundred adult French Canadian males. A comparison of these cities showed that the proportion of French Canadians who were aliens was much higher in the cities of New England. In Fall River, Holyoke, and Worcester, for example, aliens constituted between 45 and 60 percent of the adult *Canadien* male population. In cities outside New England, generally fewer than one in five French Canadian adult males remained aliens.[39]

Why language appears to have been less a barrier to naturalization beyond the boundaries of New England may in part be due to differences among state laws regarding naturalization, but other forces were also important.[40] A study of French Canadians in selected urban (mostly New England) and rural areas (primarily North Dakota and Wisconsin) in 1920 showed that *Canadien* immigrants in the middle and central states had a longer period of residence than those in New England. Nearly 80 percent of male French Canadian immigrants in rural areas had arrived in the United States before 1901, as compared with only 62 percent in urban areas.[41] French Canadians outside New England were also more likely to be farmers and to own property—conditions that contributed to a higher rate of naturalization. In North Dakota, for example, in 1900, 70 percent of the state's thirteen hundred families of French Canadian descent were farm families, and more than 75 percent owned their homes. In Wisconsin, only a third of French Canadian families lived on farms but more than 60 percent owned their homes. In Massachusetts, however, only seven hundred of forty-four thousand French Canadian families lived on farms and less than 20 percent owned their homes (see table 3.4).[42]

Table 3.3

Political condition of French Canadian-born males
twenty-one years of age and over,
in twenty-four selected states,
1910-1920

| | Percent naturalized | | Percent having first papers | | Percent either naturalized or having first papers |
	1920	1910	1920	1910	1920	1910
United States	47.0	44.7	15.5	3.9	62.5	48.6
Illinois	76.0	68.6	5.5	2.2	81.5	70.8
North Dakota	74.5	67.3	6.4	4.3	80.9	71.6
Colorado	72.2	58.1	8.3	8.5	88.5	66.6
Montana	71.5	69.3	11.3	6.8	82.8	76.1
Minnesota	71.4	65.0	13.0	6.5	84.4	71.5
Iowa	70.6	55.7	7.8	1.8	78.4	57.5
South Dakota	69.6	66.7	3.7	7.8	73.3	74.5
Michigan	64.3	62.1	15.9	10.8	80.2	72.9
Ohio	64.0	62.5	10.7	2.3	74.7	64.8
Washington	59.8	58.8	15.6	6.0	75.4	64.8
California	59.1	62.7	9.5	6.5	68.6	69.2
Kansas	58.7	59.5	10.5	1.7	69.2	61.2
Nebraska	56.8	62.0	16.2	3.3	73.0	65.3
Wisconsin	56.6	62.4	18.2	15.0	74.8	77.4
New York	54.9	53.7	11.0	3.3	65.9	57.0
New Jersey	54.4	45.6	13.1	4.9	67.5	50.5
Pennsylvania	53.7	55.5	12.0	3.5	65.7	59.0
Rhode Island	52.2	44.1	22.8	2.9	75.0	47.0
Missouri	50.0	52.9	6.2	3.0	56.2	55.9
Vermont	43.3	48.9	11.1	1.9	54.4	50.8
New Hampshire	41.7	37.8	14.6	1.9	56.3	39.7
Massachusetts	41.3	35.1	16.8	2.6	58.1	37.7
Connecticut	40.2	35.7	13.8	2.1	54.0	37.8
Maine	35.5	29.8	15.3	2.1	50.8	31.9

Calculated from: U.S. Bureau of the Census,
Thirteenth Census of the United States; 1910, 1:1069,
1073, 1085; Fourteenth Census of the United States;
1920, 2:826-41.

Table 3.4

Percentage of naturalized French Canadians
and percentage of French Canadian families
living in nonfarm and hired homes, for
twenty-four selected states, 1900-1910

| | Percent of French Canadian-born males, 21 years of age who are naturalized 1910 | | Percent of families of French Canadian parentage who: (1900) | | | |
| | | | Live in non-farm homes | | Live in homes they do not own | |
	%	Rank	%	Rank	%	Rank
Montana	69.3	24	71.9	15	37.0	21
Illinois	68.6	23	82.6	9	57.7	10
North Dakota	67.3	22	29.7	24	17.5	24
South Dakota	66.7	21	38.2	23	32.9	23
Minnesota	65.0	20	60.7	20	40.9	20
California	62.7	19	79.4	12	46.5	14
Ohio	62.5	18	87.4	6	57.9	9
Wisconsin	62.4	17	66.4	18	35.7	22
Michigan	62.1	16	75.9	13	43.0	19
Nebraska	62.0	15	52.2	21	44.6	17
Kansas	59.5	14	42.3	22	44.0	18
Washington	58.8	13	71.5	16	46.3	15
Colorado	58.1	12	82.1	10	51.0	13
Iowa	55.7	11	63.0	19	45.7	16
Pennsylvania	55.5	10	87.0	7	62.6	7
New York	53.7	9	82.0	11	58.1	8
Missouri	52.9	8	70.0	17	57.4	11
Vermont	48.9	7	74.3	14	52.9	12
New Jersey	45.6	6	96.8	3	73.7	5
Rhode Island	44.1	5	98.6	1	85.1	1
New Hampshire	37.8	4	93.4	5	75.6	4
Connecticut	35.7	3	95.5	4	83.2	2
Massachusetts	35.1	2	97.7	2	81.1	3
Maine	29.8	1	85.4	8	63.3	6

Calculated from: U.S. Bureau of the Census, Twelfth Census of the United States; 1900, 1:742-50; Thirteenth Census of the United States; 1910, 1:1069, 1073, 1085.

A study of about eighteen hundred French Canadian adult male immigrants in Fall River, Southbridge, Spencer, and Worcester, based on the manuscript schedules of the 1900 U.S. Census, provides additional evidence confirming the relationship between literacy, length of residence, age of arrival, occupation, property ownership, spousal nativity, and naturalization (see table 3.5). From this analysis, the impact of the legal language barrier is especially apparent. Among immigrants who could speak English or read and write, between 41 and 47 percent were naturalized; among those who could neither speak English nor read and write, only 5 to 6 percent were naturalized. The evidence shows that immigrants with longer residences in the United States or who had arrived in the United States while under twenty years old were also more likely to become citizens, as were those with white-collar occupations, those who owned their homes, or those who married non-French Canadian wives. Nevertheless, only 34 percent of the *Canadiens* were citizens in 1900, probably for the same reasons their leaders had given twenty years earlier. True, between 70 and 80 percent could read and write or speak English, but nearly 30 percent had been residents for fewer than 10 years and nearly 50 percent had immigrated when they were at least twenty years old. More significantly, most French Canadian immigrants were blue-collar workers or unskilled laborers and more than 80 percent did not own their homes or had married within their ethnic group.

The Seamless Fabric of Life and Labor: *Habitants* of Little Canada

The lack of interest in citizenship among most French Canadians may best be understood by considering the circumstances attending their way of life in New England: the differing attitudes of *Canadiens* towards naturalization, the pattern of life within Little Canadas, and the geographic proximity of Quebec to New England.

While French Canadian leaders urged their countrymen to become citizens after 1880, they exhorted them to remain French Canadian at heart. But few ordinary French Canadians living in New England seemed willing to burden themselves with the schizophrenic existence implied by the logic of their leaders. The leaders expected too much of the *habitant* mill workers who saw easily enough the paradox of becoming an American in order to remain a French Canadian.

Habitants had come to the manufacturing centers of New England to escape the poverty of rural Quebec, not consciously to fulfill the mission of *la survivance*. Within the community structure of Little Canada, French Canadian immigrants found familiar habits of speech and social

Table 3.5

Socioeconomic variables and naturalization among
French Canadian adult male immigrants, 1900

| | PERCENT | | |
	Naturalized	Alien	Total
Can Read and Write (1282)	49.9	53.1	100
Cannot Read and Write (570)	5.6	94.4	100
Can Speak English (1478)	41.5	58.5	100
Cannot Speak English (374)	5.1	94.9	100
Length of Residence			
1-9 years (538)	13.2	86.8	100
10-19 years (536)	36.8	63.2	100
20-29 years (387)	47.0	53.0	100
30 or more years (391)	46.8	53.2	100
Age at Arrival			
1-9 years (313)	47.9	52.1	100
10-19 years (615)	46.2	53.8	100
20-29 years (442)	28.5	71.5	100
30 or over (482)	15.1	84.9	100
Occupation			
White Collar (296)	61.8	38.2	100
Blue Collar (1121)	33.5	66.5	100
Laborers (304)	17.8	82.2	100
Others (131)	15.3	84.7	100
Own Home (247)	53.4	46.6	100
Rent Home (1155)	32.1	67.9	100
Spouse French Canadian (1215)	33.0	67.0	100
Spouse Other (203)	48.3	51.7	100
TOTAL (1852)	34.2	65.8	100

Source: Manuscript schedules of the 1900 U.S. population census
for Fall River, Enumeration District Nos. 106, 115, 143; Southbridge,
Enumeration District No. 1678; Spencer, Enumeration District No.
1684; and Worcester, Enumeration District Nos. 1732 and 1734. The
analysis includes all French Canadian-born males twenty years of age
or older in each district. Those immigrants who had taken their
first papers are included among the naturalized.

intercourse. By their standards their culture seemed safe and life comfortable enough. Consequently, the urgent need to become naturalized in order to protect and preserve their cultural heritage, which resounded in the speeches of the French Canadian middle class more assimilated to American life, escaped ordinary Canadiens.[43]

The pattern of life within Little Canada, existing synchronistically within a larger pattern of migration, employment, and culture that linked industrial New England to rural Quebec, discouraged naturalization. Most French Canadians in Massachusetts lived in tight-knit urban villages within manufacturing cities and towns. Inside these enclaves they found it easy to maintain their cultural heritage. Ethnic parishes, schools and associations isolated them from the wider world of the host society, reinforced their ethnic identity, and inculcated in their children a sense of being different—of being French Canadian. French-speaking business and professional men, who serviced their needs, promoted the insularity of their group but also diminished the need for immigrants to learn English or otherwise become involved with the larger community.

The fabric of life in Little Canada combined cycles of family, social, and religious life with routines of factory work. While tending to isolate the French Canadians from other groups within a given community, life and labor within Little Canada bound Canadiens to social and economic patterns of greater breadth. The railroad cars that carried thousands of Quebecois south to the manufacturing centers of New England cheaply also could return many north to home as well. Sojourners who had saved enough to finance a farm in Quebec could re-emigrate with little difficulty. Others who had immigrated with some intention of remaining in the United States could easily flee industrial life and find temporary refuge from its uncertainties in rural Quebec. Finally, the networks of kin, work, and rail within New England facilitated the movement of Canadien textile workers from one manufacturing center to another when a strike or quarrel disrupted the routine of factory life.

The nearness of New England to Quebec stimulated a steady flow of people back and forth across municipal, state, and national boundaries, making French Canadians among the most mobile immigrants. Coincidentally, it encouraged the insularity of the Canadiens within New England industrial centers. As the "birds of passage," the disheartened, or those simply lonely for relatives and old friends boarded northbound trains, new faces, fresh and eager, disembarked to take their places in the church pews and to harness themselves to the spinning frames and stitching machines abandoned by the departing Canadiens. Newcomers brought with them old and familiar habits of speech, and news and gossip from home, reinforcing linguistic as well as sentimental ties with the homeland. French-speaking clergy from Canada maintained the discipline and distinctiveness of the immigrants' faith and ritual. Teachers from Quebec instructed the children of immigrants in parish schools. Older American-born students completed their education in the secondary schools and colleges of Quebec. Railroad ties thus maintained the bonds of kinship and culture, sustained the symbiotic relationship between the people of New France and the economy of New England, and strengthened the ethnic identity of the French Canadians living there.

Enmeshed in a way of life that transcended recognized boundaries but linked them closely to each other through far-reaching networks of kin, culture, and jobs, most ordinary *habitants* found no pressing need to become American citizens. They remained *Canadiens*, secure in their faith, living and working amid their kind, and always close at heart as well as in distance to their homeland. Politics remained for most of them a concern secondary to their social and economic concerns. For some, the acquisition of property or the perception of political or economic opportunities, which lay beyond the confines of Little Canada, sparked greater interest in naturalization. For the majority of French Canadians in New England, however, acquiring American citizenship appears to have neither symbolized a change of heart nor a means of safeguarding their culture; rather, it was merely a legal technicality that added precious little filling to the warp of their lives.

Officeholding and Voting Patterns

Although the great mass of French Canadians remained indifferent to their leaders' behests to become American citizens, the number of *Canadien* voters in Massachusetts steadily increased from 1875 to 1910, as did the number of officeholders and candidates for public office. In 1880 there were probably fewer than two thousand French Canadian voters in the Commonwealth.[44] Within five years, the number of *Canadien* voters doubled. By 1885 French Canadian immigrants formed 4 percent of adult males in the state; fewer than 1 percent of the state's 440,000 qualified voters, however, were French Canadian.[45] Except in Southbridge and Spencer there were few *Canadien* officeseekers or officeholders before 1888. French Canadian political mobilization began in earnest after 1887. By 1890 there were at least ten thousand French Canadian voters in the Commonwealth, concentrated in such a way as to make them crucial to Democratic victories in gubernatorial contests during the early 1890s, and they were increasingly active in politics. From 1887 to 1895 French Canadian candidates for town offices in Southbridge and Spencer totaled 130, while nearly sixty town offices were filled by *Canadiens*. Together, Fall River and Worcester produced more than thirty French Canadian candidates for city council and school committee in the same period. Among the primary cities, more than forty city council seats were occupied by *Canadiens* between 1891 and 1895.

The political influence of French Canadians in Massachusetts, measured in terms of voters and political activists (candidates for office and officeholders) expanded significantly after 1895. During the 1890s the number of *Canadien* voters in the state doubled, to twenty thousand by 1900, and probably doubled again over the next ten years. By 1910 first and second-generation French Canadian voters comprised about 5 percent of the electorate in Massachusetts.[46] Between 1895 and 1915 two hundred French Canadian candidates vied for positions in the Massachusetts General Court, of whom fifty-six sat in the House of Representatives. French Canadian officeholding in twenty-two towns surveyed expanded dramatically during this period, particularly in Southbridge and Spencer. In 1895 only nine French Canadians held local town offices, about 2 percent of the total offices considered. By 1910 *Canadiens* held about seventy offices, approximately 13 percent of the total offices in these towns. French Canadian officeholding in urban centers also increased during this period, from less than 3 percent of the total offices surveyed in seventeen cities in 1895 to nearly 6 percent in 1910. In the primary cities alone, some 260 city council seats were held by French Canadians from 1896 to 1915. Because French Canadians had gained a secure foothold in local politics by 1900, the Democratic party commonly included a *Canadien* name on its slate of candidates for statewide elective office after 1900.

As French Canadians became more politically aware, the question becomes whether the group exhibited party preferences in Massachusetts. Did the group tend to vote Republican as David Walker argued in his study of French Canadian voting? Walker based his conclusions on an analysis of elections in thirty New England communities with substantial French Canadian populations, including nine in Massachusetts. His analysis relied upon a comparison of changes in the Democratic percentage of the two-party vote over time. Because the average Democratic vote in his selected communities was usually less than 50 percent of the total between 1896 and 1924, he concluded that French Canadians exhibited a Republican tendency during this period.[47] As he pointed out, the earlier belief that the group had always preferred the GOP was not entirely accurate; in three elections (1908, 1912, and 1916) a majority of French Canadians probably supported Democrats William Jennings Bryan and Woodrow Wilson. Nevertheless, he concluded,

Table 3.6

Average percent Democratic of the
two-party vote for president in selected
French Canadian Communities and in
Massachusetts, 1884-1924

YEAR	French Canadian[a]	State	State,[b] Adjusted
1884	43.3	45.5	41.6
1888	46.2	45.2	42.6
1892	48.7	46.6	44.1
1896	28.7	27.4	24.6
1900	39.8	39.7	35.6
1904	39.3	39.1	34.8
1908	39.6	36.9	33.7
1912	50.8	52.6	49.3
1916	51.2	48.0	45.2
1920	33.3	28.9	26.7
1924	33.1	28.5	25.2
Mean	41.2	39.8	36.6

[a]This sample includes the nine Bay State communities used by
David B. Walker, Politics and Ethnocentrism: The Case of the Franco-
Americans (Brunswick, ME: Bowdoin College, Bureau for Research in
Municipal Government, 1961). These are: Chicopee, Fall River,
Fitchburg, Gardner, Holyoke, Leominster, Lowell, North Adams, and
Southbridge. These calculations as well as others relating to
presidential and gubernatorial elections are based on election
statistics found in Massachusetts, Public Document No. 43: "Number
of...Registered Voters and Persons Who Voted...Together With the
Number of Votes Received by each Candidate," 1890-1924, and
Massachusetts, Manual for the Use of the General Court, 1880-1920.

[b]Excluding Suffolk County; see note 49.

. . . if the eight presidential elections from 1896 to 1924 are taken as a unit
the [earlier] interpretation is basically accurate for a majority of these voters
in a majority of the contests.[48]

An analysis of the voting patterns in Walker's nine French Canadian
Bay State communities, using different methods, points to a different
conclusion. Distinctly French Canadian voting patterns may be better
viewed by comparing party preferences to those of a larger population.
A comparison of the average Democratic vote in Walker's communities
shows these averages were higher than the percentage of the two-party
vote received by Democratic candidates statewide in presidential elections (see table 3.6).[49] This Democratic tendency may be confirmed by a

Table 3.7

Pearsonian correlation coefficients (R)
showing the association between the
percent Democratic for the two-party vote
for president and percent French Canadian
of the population in nine
French Canadian communities,
1884-1916[a]

YEAR	R	YEAR	R
1884	.57	1904	.53
1888	.48	1908	.28
1892	.55	1912	.18
1896	.35	1916	.73*
1900	.44		

[a]See footnote a for table 3.6.

*Indicates significance at the .05
level of confidence.

correlational analysis that permits the historian to test the relationship between the proportion of the total population that was French Canadian and the Democratic vote. The analysis shows that the correlation between the two was quite high until 1892 and again in 1916 but dropped during Bryan's first two bids for the presidency, as might be expected from Walker's description. But contrary to Walker's view, it should be emphasized, the association between the French Canadians and the Democratic vote was positive, indicating that most *Canadiens* probably did not vote Republican (see table 3.7).

Was the Democratic voting tendency observed among Walker's selected cities and towns representative of other French Canadian communities? An analysis of voting trends in presidential and gubernatorial elections between 1888 and 1916 shows that conclusions based on Walker's communities alone probably overestimate the Democratic tendency. Nonetheless, the analysis, which included about seventy communities encompassing all of Worcester County and all those places in Massachusetts where French Canadians formed 20 percent or more of the population in 1895, reveals a positive, although relatively weak, association between the French Canadians and the Democratic vote. The relative weakness of this association becomes apparent when it is compared with the correlation between the Irish and the Democratic vote. In nine presidential elections, for example, the average

Table 3.8

Coefficients of determination (Multiple R^2) showing the percent of the variation in the Democratic vote in presidential and gubernatorial elections explained by percent Irish and percent French Canadian together and by French Canadian alone, 1888-1916

	Presidential		Gubernatorial	
	Irish and French Canadian	French Canadian alone	Irish and French Canadian	French Canadian alone
1888	.55	.19	.53	.16
1889			.43	.17
1890			.48	.16
1891			.51	.18
1892	.61	.23	.59	.23
1893			.57	.17
1894			.59	.17
1895			.52	.19
1896	.53	.11	.57	.16
1897			.56	.19
1898			.63	.34
1899			.59	.28
1900	.66	.20	.68	.22
1901			.63	.20
1902			.53	.18
1903			.55	.15
1904	.66	.22	.60	.23
1905			.67	.24
1906			.63	.29
1907			.39	.16
1908	.68	.14	.62	.16
1909			.65	.20
1910			.67	.31
1911			.65	.26
1912	.48	.12	.68	.25
1913			.59	.18
1914			.66	.18
1915			.64	.15
1916	.63	.23		

Table 3.9

Partial correlation coefficients
(Pearson's R) showing the association
between the percent Democratic vote
in presidential elections and percent
French Canadian and percent Irish of
the population, in sixty-seven communities,
1884-1916

Variable 1	Percent Democratic		
Variable 2	Percent French Canadian		
Variable 3	Percent Irish		

	Zero-order partials		Partial coefficients	
YEAR	R_{12}	R_{13}	$R_{12.3}$	$R_{13.2}$
1884	.29	.42	.30	.43
1888	.45	.60	.54	.65
1892	.50	.61	.61	.69
1896	.36	.65	.44	.68
1900	.47	.68	.61	.75
1904	.49	.67	.63	.75
1908	.41	.73	.55	.78
1912	.36	.60	.42	.63
1916	.51	.63	.63	.71

All the above coefficients are significant at least
at the .01 level of confidence.

Pearsonian correlation coefficient for the French Canadians was only
.43, while for the Irish it was .62.[50] Assuming that both groups independently contributed to the Democratic vote,[51] the Irish and French Canadians together explained upwards to 68 percent of the variation in all
but three state elections. As might be expected, the Irish contribution
was considerably more significant than that of the French Canadians
(see tables 3.8, 3.9, and 3.10).

The relative weakness of association between French Canadians and
Democratic voting suggests diversity in *Canadien* voting. This diversity
may be illustrated best by contrasting the patterns found in the towns of
central Massachusetts to those in the primary cities.[52] The group of
central towns included all those towns in or near Worcester County in
which the French Canadians formed at least 25 percent of the population in 1895. For these communities the correlation between the Democratic vote and French Canadians, while low until 1896, was
consistently higher afterwards, reaching a peak of .81 in 1916, for
presidential elections. When the two deviating cases of Palmer and

Table 3.10

Partial correlation coefficients
(Pearson's R) showing the
association between the percent
Democratic vote for governor and
percent French Canadian, and
percent Irish of the population,
in sixty-seven communities, 1888-1915

YEAR	Zero-order partials		Partial coefficients
	R_{12}	R_{13}	$R_{12.3}$
1888	.41	.61	.50
1889	.41	.51	.48
1890	.41	.57	.49
1891	.44	.57	.52
1892	.49	.59	.60
1893	.42	.64	.53
1894	.43	.65	.55
1895	.44	.58	.53
1896	.41	.64	.52
1897	.44	.61	.55
1898	.59	.54	.69
1899	.53	.56	.63
1900	.48	.68	.64
1901	.46	.65	.59
1902	.44	.59	.53
1903	.39	.63	.50
1904	.49	.61	.61
1905	.50	.65	.65
1906	.55	.59	.66
1907	.41	.48	.46
1908	.41	.68	.54
1909	.46	.67	.60
1910	.57	.60	.70
1911	.53	.62	.66
1912	.51	.66	.66
1913	.43	.64	.55
1914	.44	.70	.59
1915	.40	.70	.54

All the above coefficients are significant at least at the .01 level of confidence.

Table 3.11

Pearsonian correlation coefficients (R)
showing the association between the
percent Democratic of the total
vote for president and percent
French Canadian, 1884-1916

Year	Central towns (n=10)	Central towns[a] (n=8)	Primary cities (n=6)
1884	.20	.54	.65
1888	.32	.50	.55
1892	.24	.54	.59
1896	.61*	.70*	.35
1900	.48	.84*	.42
1904	.59*	.75*	.67
1908	.47	.63*	.64
1912	.42	.72*	.66
1916	.81*	.89*	.39

[a]Excluding Palmer and Sutton.

*Indicates significance of .05 level of confidence.

Sutton are excluded from this group, the correlation coefficients for presidential elections were always .60 or higher, indicating a strong association. In contrast to these towns, the relationship between the French Canadians and the Democratic vote in six primary cities, although usually positive, appears weaker and more erratic.[53] The overall trend suggests, nonetheless, that the French Canadian tendency was marginally Democratic (see tables 3.11, 3.12, and 3.13).[54]

An examination of French Canadian candidates for the Massachusetts General Court sustains the hypothesis that the *Canadiens* in larger cities tended to be less Democratic than their counterparts in smaller towns. Urban Republican *Canadien* candidates for the lower house, for example, outnumbered Democrats by two to one; in towns the opposite was true. Among those candidates who won election urban Republicans outnumbered Democrats twenty-eight to four while among representatives elected from the towns Democrats outdistanced Republicans sixteen to eight. Overall, since the cities elected more French Canadians and had a greater number of candidates, Republicans were more numerous. Nearly half of all *Canadien* candidates were Republicans; only one-third were Democrats. Within the lower house of the general court between 1896 and 1915 two-thirds of French Canadian representatives were Republicans (see tables 3.14 through 3.17).[55]

Considered separately, voting and officeholding patterns suggest dif-

Table 3.12

Pearsonian correlation coefficients (R)
showing the association between the
percent Democratic of the total
vote for governor and percent
French Canadian, 1888-1915

	Central towns (n=10)	Central towns[a] (n=8)	Primary cities (n=6)	Walker's sample (n=9)
1888	.32	.50	.63	.32
1889	.36	.64*	.71*	.54
1890	.32	.59	.85*	.53
1891	.41	.60	.72*	.49
1892	.29	.49	.66	.57
1893	.35	.65*	.63	.59
1894	.21	.45	.61	.49
1895	.21	.53	.61	.70*
1896	.65*	.83*	.40	.54
1897	.41	.74*	.32	.42
1898	.44	.76*	.27	.54
1899	.50	.64*	.26	.67*
1900	.62*	.89*	.29	.66*
1901	.72*	.79*	.35	.74*
1902	.59*	.58	.37	.79*
1903	.62*	.77*	.32	.70*
1904	.54	.70*	.57	.51
1905	.46	.69*	.40	.61*
1906	.63*	.81*	.38	.79*
1907	.73*	.60	.65	.46
1908	.48	.70*	.11	.54
1909	.44	.78*	.39	.44
1910	.62*	.77*	.36	.56
1911	.17	.55	-.28	.75*
1912	.49	.74*	.41	.70*
1913	.20	.68*	.34	.69*
1914	.30	.67*	.28	.82*
1915	.24	.64*	.24	.61*

[a]Excluding Palmer and Sutton.

*Indicates significance at .05 level of significance.

Table 3.13

Characteristics of communities in different
groupings of French Canadian centers

	Percent of the state's total French Canadian population (1905)	Percent of the total population in the community which was:	
		French Canadian	Irish
Walker's centers			
Southbridge	2.4	51.3	8.9
Fall River	12.1	26.8	17.5
Holyoke	5.4	25.4	27.3
Gardner	1.2	22.7	9.8
Lowell	8.4	20.6	28.6
Chicopee	1.9	22.5	19.7
North Adams	1.9	20.2	16.5
Fitchburg	2.8	20.0	17.8
Leominster	1.1	18.8	14.5
Central towns			
Southbridge	2.4	51.3	8.9
Sutton	.6	48.2	3.4
Spencer	1.1	36.8	12.0
Ware	1.2	33.8	16.4
Dudley	.4	25.4	12.5
Ludlow	.4	24.4	7.7
Sturbridge	.2	27.7	12.5
Millbury	.5	26.8	17.3
Grafton	.5	22.7	16.5
Palmer	.6	17.6	16.0
Primary cities			
Fall Rive	12.1	26.8	17.5
Holyoke	5.4	25.4	27.3
Lowell	8.4	20.6	28.6
New Bedford	6.3	20.0	10.2
Lawrence	4.8	16.0	24.6
Worcester	5.1	9.3	23.8

Table 3.14

French Canadian candidates
for state representative,
Massachusetts, 1896-1915

	Total #	Total %	Republicans #	Republicans %	Democrats #	Democrats %	Other #	Other %
Cities	150	100	80	53.3	42	28.0	28	18.7
Towns	44	100	14	31.8	27	61.4	3	6.8
Total	195	100	94	48.4	69	35.6	31	16.0

Source: Tables 3.14 through 3.17 are based on an
examination of the names of all candidates running for
either state representative or the state senate between
1896 and 1915 in the following counties: Berkshire, Essex,
Bristol, Hampden, Hampshire, Middleses, and Worcester.
These counties contained the bulk of the French Canadian
population.   French Canadian candidates were identified by
surname from Massachusetts, Public Document No. 43, 1896-
1915.

ferent conclusions about the French Canadians in Massachusetts. Voting patterns point to a Democratic tendency among French Canadians between 1890 and 1915; officeholding patterns suggest divergent tendencies. A closer look at the cities and towns that generated many of the candidates shows that French Canadians were very pragmatic in their approach to politics. While leaning towards the Republican party after

Table 3.15

Successful French Canadian
candidates for state representative,
Massachusetts, 1896-1915

	Total #	Total %	Republicans #	Republicans %	Democrats #	Democrats %	Other #	Other %
Cities	32	100	28	87.5	4	12.5	0	0
Towns	24	100	8	33.3	16	66.7	0	0
Total	56	100	36	64.3	20	35.7	0	0

Table 3.16

French Canadian candidates
for state senator and state
representative, Massachusetts,
1896-1915

	Total		Republicans		Democrats		Other	
	#	%	#	%	#	%	#	%
Cities	160	100	82	51.3	45	28.1	33	20.6
Towns	52	100	14	26.9	34	65.4	4	7.7
Total	212	100	96	45.3	79	37.3	37	17.4

1895, *Canadiens* in the cities turned to the Democratic party when it suited their interests. The reverse is true about the French Canadians in the towns. As case studies of two cities—Fall River and Worcester—and of two towns—Southbridge and Spencer—indicate, the relationship between the French Canadians and the political parties may best be described as one of mutual exploitation. Neither party loyalty nor anti-Irish feeling played as large a part in determining *Canadien* political preferences as their desire for recognition. Thus, an appraisal of French Canadian political behavior suggests that ethnic and cultural determinants of political choices should be considered within the context of particular communities lest the logic of cultural conflict distort by oversimplification the variations of a group's political tendencies.

Table 3.17

Percent of French Canadian
candidates for state
representative in
Massachusetts who won election,
1896-1915

	Total	Republicans	Democrats	Other
Cities	21.3	35.0	9.5	0
Towns	54.5	57.1	59.3	0
Total	28.7	38.3	29.0	0

4

French Canadians and Massachusetts Politics, 1885–1895

French Canadian political preferences, like those of other groups, lay rooted largely in pragmatic considerations of group self-interest. Arriving with a well-developed ethnic identity, *Canadiens* established an institutional framework aimed at preserving that identity and resisting the loss of their traditional values through assimilation. Their highly visible and determined efforts on behalf of *la survivance* created tensions between themselves, Yankee-Protestants, and the Irish in Massachusetts. Outbursts of cultural conflict enhanced the *Canadiens'* awareness of themselves as an embattled minority group and shaped their party preferences. The relationship between culture and politics was complex, however, and did not always yield similar results. Party preferences among the French Canadians varied, depending on their perception of which party was more accommodating or more threatening to their interests at any given time.

Between 1888 and 1895 most French Canadian voters leaned toward the Democratic party. Frightened by a flood of anti-immigrant and anti-Catholic feeling sweeping Massachusetts, some of which was aimed directly at them, French Canadians, who previously had shown little interest in politics, mobilized to protect their rights. The Republican party, which catered to the nativist and anti-liquor movements, gained little from this mobilization. The Democratic party, which offered French Canadians the political recognition they sought, defended Catholic rights, and focused on tariff reform as an electoral campaign issue, attracted more of the new voters.

Initial Political Activity

Few French Canadian immigrants had become voters in Massachusetts by 1880. Most remained preoccupied with the difficulties of their social and economic adjustment and their leaders were largely hostile to naturalization. Even so, the group had begun to have an impact, albeit limited, on the political life in some French Canadian centers. A few *Canadiens* were appointed or elected to local offices before 1880 in such places as Lowell, Fall River, Holyoke, Southbridge, and Spencer.[1] By 1880 about thirty French Canadians held some form of public office in eleven communities despite the small number of French voters.[2]

French Canadians exhibited greater interest in politics during the 1880s. As French Canadian leaders changed their attitude toward American citizenship, they promoted interest in naturalization and politics by establishing political clubs.[3] Such clubs provided vital assistance by teaching immigrants to read and write English—a requirement for citizenship in Massachusetts—and by defraying the legal expenses of naturalization. Social gatherings, picnics, and bazaars, aimed at raising funds for these clubs, also fostered a sense of community among French Canadians.[4] Naturalization clubs linked individuals to an ethnic group and to American society as a whole by making the rite of passage to citizenship a collective effort. Lectures and discussions sponsored by the clubs stimulated interest in political issues while encouraging greater awareness of the group's minority position within American society. Perhaps most important, the clubs generated a nucleus of politically conscious activists, some of whom used the clubs as springboards to local office.[5] Consequently the number of French Canadian voters increased quite rapidly during the 1880s, rising from less than two thousand in 1880 to about four thousand in 1885, and to about ten thousand by the end of the decade.[6]

The political preferences of French Canadians before 1888 are difficult to determine since few were voters or held political office. One knowledgeable French Canadian, C. Herbert De Fosse, speaking of the French Canadians in New England, claimed in 1899 that about 75 percent were Democrats in 1885.[7] The accuracy of De Fosse's observation is uncertain, but a comparison of Fall River and Spencer suggests that local situations played an important role in affecting party preferences.

In Fall River, French Canadians aligned themselves with the Democratic party during the 1870s, cooperating with their Irish co-religionists. E. J. L'Herault, for example, served as Democratic committee treasurer in Ward One, where Irish Democrats predominated, in 1877, and Reverend P. J. B. Bedard won the Democratic nomination for school committee the following year. French Canadians reportedly voted Democratic during this period although political leaders such as L'Herault and Pierre F. Peloquin, Regular Democrats, opposed Benjamin Butler's bid for governor on the Democratic ticket in 1878.[8] By 1880, however, French Canadians in Fall River began shifting to the Republican party.

Labor and religious disputes with the Irish, especially a bitter struggle over the appointment of a *Canadien* pastor for the Notre Dame de Lourdes parish in Ward Six, contributed to this shift. The Republican party, which accommodated French Canadian demands for some influence in local affairs, eased the transition. *Canadien* voters cast their ballots against Butler in 1883, and against President Grover Cleveland in 1884, while French Canadian office seekers in the city won on Republican ballots.[9]

French Canadians in Spencer, unlike those in Fall River, probably voted for Butler in his contests for the governorship in 1882 and 1883. Butler, the Democratic candidate who faced fierce competition in both races, appealed directly for the support of *Canadien* voters who, numbering about 150, formed about 10 percent of the town's electorate. Speaking in Spencer late in his campaign in 1883, he attacked restrictions on the franchise, especially the requirement that voters be able to read and write English, in an obvious attempt to win French Canadian voters, who were still smarting from the criticisms of the group made in a recent report of the state's Bureau of Labor Statistics. George D. Robinson, the Republican candidate who visited Spencer the following day, accused Butler of "angling" for French Canadian voters with "pretended love for the poor Canadian," and warned them against being duped by the wily Democratic governor.

Robinson's admonition probably went unheeded. In 1878 when Butler first ran for governor, losing Spencer 244 to 523, there had been fewer than fifty French Canadian voters. As the number of French voters increased, so also did Butler's vote. By 1883, the number of *Canadien* voters had grown and Butler received twice as many votes as he had received five years earlier. The Republican vote meanwhile rose only to 577, suggesting that newly naturalized French Canadian voters favored Butler. This conclusion is reinforced by the emergence of a Franco-Irish Democratic alliance in local politics in 1882, which aimed at securing greater representation for both groups in town government. The election of a French Canadian Democrat to the board of selectmen in the spring of 1884 testified to the effectiveness of this alliance.[10]

The drive among French Canadians for greater political involvement in the 1880s had the protection of the group's interests or rights as its primary objective. Political recognition was a critical part of this strategy, and French Canadian party preferences often hinged on this factor. In local politics, they manifested what some contemporary journalists called clannishness. One sympathetic observer noted of the French Canadians in Southbridge in the 1880s that they were becoming Americanized rapidly and made good citizens. But, she added,

. . . they at the same time preserve a certain peculiar pride in their nationality. . . . Instead of entering into politics as directly and unreservedly as the Irish-Americans, they think more of a class representation in bestowing official honors and not infrequently hold caucuses of their own to select candidates for various town offices to be represented to the general party caucuses as the representative of their race.[11]

William MacDonald, in a similarly sympathetic account of the French Canadians in New England, commented in 1897:

It does not appear that the French Canadians are inclined to attach themselves en masse to any one political party . . . In local elections it is frequent testimony that they are not to be counted on to support either party or any general policy, but are liable to put their votes up for sale, not for money, but for political or social concessions.[12]

MacDonald disliked such political practices, and he frowned upon the "zealous and systematic measures used by the French Canadians to keep themselves apart."[13] "Whatever the reality may be," he wrote of la survivance, "the appearance is un-American."[14] MacDonald, like others, was confident that French Canadian efforts to resist assimilation could only retard and not prevent "the inevitable absorption of their race in the cosmopolitan American people."[15] Henry Loomis Nelson, editor of Harper's Weekly, like MacDonald, was critical of the French Canadians' "rudimentary" understanding of politics, but did not believe that the growth of their political influence posed any serious threat to American democracy in the long run.[16] Although Nelson's conclusion proved correct, neither he nor MacDonald completely understood how profoundly the character of political life would be transformed. The coming of political age for the French Canadians helped to change the nature of politics in Massachusetts in ways that surely would have distressed both.

The Democratic Coalition, 1888–1892

By 1890 the French Canadians in Massachusetts had begun to play a significant role in state as well as local politics. Canadien voters, about ten thousand strong, represented only 2.5 percent of the state's voting strength but they gained influence beyond their number because they were concentrated in relatively few cities and towns. The six primary cities contained nearly 40 percent of the state's Canadien voters, and thirteen towns in central Massachusetts held nearly 25 percent. Together, these nineteen communities accounted for almost two-thirds of French-speaking voters.[17] A strong French Canadian vote in these pockets could swing the outcome of local elections.[18] It played a crucial role in giving the Democratic party several of its few victories in the late nineteenth century. As Nelson pointed out in 1893:

> In every one of the six New England states, except Vermont, votes equal in number to the solid French-Canadian vote would suffice to reverse the political supremacy if they should be transferred from the prevailing party to the minority. In the presidential election just held this vote played an important part, especially in Massachusetts. It is said that most of the French-Canadians voted for the Democratic candidate because of the injuries inflicted on farmers of Quebec by the McKinley Tariff. However that may be, it is the fact that the French-Canadian vote was a matter of much solicitude to the politicians of both parties, and it is its growing importance in American politics that makes the immigration of interest in this country.[19]

The Republican party retained firm control of Massachusetts during the decades between the Civil War and World War I. Only six times before 1900 and six times afterwards did the opposition win the governor's chair.[20] The Democrats, under the leadership of William "Billy" Russell, the popular "gentle reformer" and master politician of Cambridge, scored three successive victories early in the 1890s before falling victim to the twin forces of depression and nativism in 1893.

The success of the Democratic coalition reflected certain changes in the party and dissatisfaction within the reform wing of the Republican party. The Democratic party in Massachusetts consisted primarily of Yankee leadership and Irish rank and file voters. While Irish and Yankee politicians vied for control of the party, factional strife weakened the Irish-dominated urban wards. Divided against itself, the party had trouble coordinating its efforts to win state-level executive offices.[21] Poorly organized and lacking funds, the party remained vulnerable to freelance political adventurers who could rally the rank and file around a cause. Such was the case when Benjamin F. Butler drove a wedge between the leadership and the voters in 1882–83, winning control of the party and the governor's chair. Anti-Butler Yankee Democrats and young Republican reformers filled the gap left by Butler's defeat.[22] The incessant criticism of federal patronage policies voiced by the reformers during Cleveland's first term, however, conflicted with Irish demands for patronage.[23] As long as civil service reform remained the central issue, the fragile coalition remained severely strained. Reconciliation of these differences came towards the end of Cleveland's term, when William Russell made tariff reform the party's primary focus. On this issue both conservative reformers in search of an issue and Irish politicians in search of political power could agree. Realizing that Democratic victories would come only with Irish-Yankee cooperation, Russell nursed the political ambitions of the Irish while mollifying

Yankee qualms about them, forging an effective working relationship between them.[24]

Having lost the gubernatorial race in the two previous elections, Russell won three successive contests beginning in 1890, and the party recaptured the Boston mayoralty and took several congressional seats as well.[25] Russell's personal popularity, his strenuous efforts to extend the party's base of support beyond Boston, and his exceptional skills as an orator on the tariff issue were critical to these victories.

The first of Russell's victories stunned many Republicans who had grown accustomed to substantial majorities on election day. Russell outpolled his opponent by more than nine thousand votes in 1890, benefiting from higher turnout. Having won slightly more than 49 percent of the total vote in 1890, Russell repeated this performance in the next two elections. As turnout increased, however, his pluralities diminished. Winning by 6,400 votes in 1891, he led his foe the next year by a scant 2,500 votes—a mere 1.5 percent of the total vote.[26]

Many French Canadian voters contributed to these narrow victories. Governor Russell's demands for a lower tariff and reciprocity with Canada found a sympathetic ear among *Canadiens*, many of whom believed that the McKinley tariff was "impoverishing their people at home by the taxes which it imposed on barley, hay, eggs, and horses."[27] Democratic proposals for state reforms such as abolishing the poll tax as a prerequisite for voting and the enactment of progressive labor laws attracted French-speaking voters as well. Alert and humane Democratic politicians who led the party realized that their political success depended largely on meeting the interests of urban immigrants and establishing theirs as the labor party in Massachusetts. Josiah Quincy, elected to the general court in 1886, led a successful effort to pass legislation aimed at improving the working conditions of the state's laboring population and, at the same time, aimed at bolstering support for his party among the working class.[28]

The Democrats coupled their emphasis on issues attractive to French Canadians as members of the laboring class with an organizational campaign to bring the group under its wing. Under the direction of Josiah Quincy, the state's key campaign manager, the party provided subsidies for its press and recognition for its aspiring politicians. At the request of Democratic friends in Lowell, Benjamin Lenthier moved his newspaper, *Le National*, from upstate New York to that city in 1890. From that base, with funds funneled to him through Quincy, Lenthier expanded the scope of his influence. In 1891 *Le National* became the only French-language daily in New England, and the most popular French Canadian newssheet in the nation. By the summer of 1892 Lenthier owned sixteen newspapers in New England, including those in nearly every French Canadian center in Massachusetts. Lenthier's newspapers, dependent on Democratic funds, served as party propaganda organs assailing Republicans while praising Democrats and their policies.[29] Meanwhile, Joseph E. Marier, working for the state central committee, organized as many as forty-five French Canadian political clubs supporting Russell's campaigns.[30]

The upsurge of anti-Catholic feeling late in the 1880s, lasting until the mid-1890s, also contributed much to bringing French Canadian voters to the Democratic banner. During this period, French Canadians, like other immigrant groups in Massachusetts and elsewhere, came under attack.[31] The rise of Irish political power in the state's cities and growth of the parochial school system in the 1880s stimulated anti-Catholic prejudice. Controversy over Catholic schools arose in 1887 and was exacerbated in 1888 by the highly publicized Haverhill school controversy, which involved the refusal of a local school superintendent to approve a French Canadian school because it used French rather than English as the language of instruction.

The Gracy School Inspection Bill, an undisguised attempt to undermine the Catholic school system by requiring English as the language for all instruction, provoked fear among French Canadians that *la survivance* was in danger. Even though the bill never became law, it stimulated the political mobilization of the *Canadiens* in the late 1880s.[32] The Irish clergy, embroiled occasionally in internecine religious disputes with the French Canadians, generally opposed the French policy of bilingualism. In the face of general attack on Catholic schools, however, they closed ranks in defense of Catholic religious minority rights. The Democratic party, which championed their cause, benefited by the reconciliation of these two rival Catholic workingclass groups while the Republicans, inclined to exploit nativist fears for political gain, diminished their chances of garnering *Canadien* voters, who could have kept the governor's office in its grip.[33]

Republican campaign strategy in 1890–91 centered on challenging the Democratic tariff position and Russell's program of state reforms. As a counterpoint to the Democratic demand for the abolition of the poll tax as a requirement for voting, the Republicans cast doubt on the sincerity of Democratic intentions. One Republican speaker went so far as to claim that Democratic state policy was formulated by former slaveholders and supported the disenfranchisement of Southern blacks.[34] Republican stump speakers emphasized the tariff issue in their tour of industrial towns in southern Worcester county, arguing that protectionism was essential to the prosperity of all American working people, foreign-born included. Congressman Joseph H. Walker, for example, appealed to French Canadian voters in Southbridge, telling them that their economic interest lay with the GOP. "You, who came here from other countries for higher wages, should vote for the party that will keep them where they are," he said.[35] In Webster, a Democratic stronghold, a few days later Walker again pleaded with French Canadian voters, whom he identified as Democrats, to support the protective tariff.

> I ask you, Frenchmen, why don't you meet somewhere and tell your Democratic leaders that they must change their free trade ideas? If you want to be Democrats, be so, but don't, for heaven's sake, rob your wives and your children of your present wages in Webster.[36]

French Canadian voters in Southbridge, Webster, and other manufacturing towns in the region remained unimpressed by Walker's appeal, and instead gave John E. Russell solid backing. Russell, a Democrat popular in those towns, hammered away at the tariff issue with greater effectiveness. Russell argued that raw materials imported from elsewhere should be allowed to enter the United States freely, a very useful argument among the many woolen textile workers of Worcester County whose jobs depended on imported wool. He argued also that the McKinley tariff placed high duties on food products such as potatoes, beans, and onions, hindering their importation from Canada and causing scarcity and higher prices for working people in New England.[37] In addition, Republican charges that Democratic state senate candidate Charles Haggerty of Southbridge was "a Jesuit in disguise" seeking to appropriate public monies for Catholic schools, that public schools were threatened by the foreign influence in some localities, and that the Democrats sought the "rule of the minority and free rum" did not help Republican candidates in these towns.[38] The Democratic vote for governor in Southbridge, for example, jumped from 473 in 1889 to 533 in 1890 while only 17 votes were added to the Republican total. In Webster, Russell polled a hundred more votes than he had the previous year; the vote for his opponent increased by less than forty. As in 1889, Russell won more than 50 percent of the vote in these two towns. In nearby Spencer, where French Canadians remained divided in local elections during the 1880s, a "solid French vote" gave Russell a small majority in 1889.[39] The following year he won additional votes, apparently having won over some Republicans, and took Spencer with 53 percent of the vote. Russell's candidacy got a boost in Spencer by the nomination of a French Canadian Democrat, L. E. P. Moreau, for state representative in the Sixth Worcester County District, which included Spencer.[40]

Republican Congressman Joseph Walker of Worcester county interpreted GOP defeat in 1890 as a rejection of the McKinley tariff by the voters who, he believed, had been misled by Russell and the Irish Democrats. "People have been periodically deceived as to their interests since the formation of the government," Walker commented after election. "When they get at the facts, this decision will be reversed." Walker attributed his party's loss to self-seeking Democratic demagogues, offering this assessment of the Democratic coalition:

Extremes always meet socially, politically, and economically. Harvard College and the slums were the defenders and supporters of slavery when it existed. Harvard College and the slums today are against the masses of people in teaching free trade.[41]

Not all Republican observers agreed with Walker's evaluation of the campaign of 1890. Some believed overconfidence among Republicans was also to blame; too many Republicans had simply failed to vote. According to the *Worcester Daily Spy*, a Republican newspaper, some seven thousand voters "which Republican managers confidently believed would come to the polls yesterday did not come."[42] Turnout remained a preoccupation among some Republicans during the next gubernatorial contest. "Last year we lost the head of our ticket through Republican stay-at-homism," proclaimed one Republican campaigner in October of 1891.[43] Republicans grew more confident as the election approached because of the great increase in the number of registered voters throughout the state.[44]

The Republican Dilemma

These two views of the election of 1890 reveal the dilemma that Russell's coalition posed for the GOP in Massachusetts. Under his leadership and under the banner of tariff reform, the Democratic party was making significant gains among the state's non-Irish immigrant voters, especially among French Canadians. Renegade reformers and the unreformed urban working class, while essentially conservative in their social philosophies, threatened to overturn established Republican political principles and subvert Yankee-Protestant cultural dominance in the Bay State.[45] To preserve Republicanism, the GOP had to attract traditionally Republican voters to the polls; to insure its ascendancy, it also had to attract immigrant voters who, if unified, might soon predominate. Republican voters could be turned out by focusing on such cultural issues as prohibition, immigration restriction, and schools, but that strategy risked further alienating Catholic immigrant voters.

The high voter registration that the *Worcester Daily Spy* had noted in 1891 reflected the Republican choice of campaign strategy. In his speech as president of the Republican convention Henry Cabot Lodge outlined the four main issues of the campaign—protecting the ballot for southern blacks, a protective tariff, the defense of the public school system, and a return of the GOP to the standard of prohibition.[46] Lodge's speech signaled the party's willingness to court anti-Catholic and anti-liquor voters in its effort to defeat the nascent Democratic-Catholic majority.[47]

Republican campaign rhetoric during the next two elections echoed Lodge's themes. Editorials in the Spy, for example, blamed "unions—the product of the immigration of foreign labor to this country" for the eruption of industrial strife and the increase in crime. Both unions and foreign labor "made war on the apprentice system by which American boys learned a trade and rose to success." The decline of the apprentice system was said to lead to idleness, and idleness to crime. The editors of the Spy criticized naturalization laws as too lenient, opposed providing federal money to Catholic missions educating western Indians, urged immigration restriction, and warned of the dangers to the Republic inherent in Catholic efforts to create national churches and bilingual schools.[48]

In an editorial aimed at soliciting native-born voters in the "country towns," the Spy criticized Governor Russell's proposal to populate the abandoned farms of the state with families of Canadian or European descent. Praising the native rural American stock for its "individuality, its moral, intellectual, and manly qualities," the Spy warned that

... a change, and that for the worse, is making itself apparent in many country towns, where an entirely different class of people are taking the place of the typical New Englanders.

It continued:

The unfortunate thing about this incoming foreign population is not so much the fact that it is a foreign element, but that those who come are by no means the best examples of citizenship in other nations. The people who cannot make a success of life nearer home are certainly not the most likely to be desirable additions to society here. Some of the most unpleasant cities and towns, and the most undesirable to live in, are those manufacturing places that have attracted large numbers of the 'floating population' of Canada as operatives in mills and factories. It is the same influence, on a smaller scale, which is likely to prove unfortunate in country towns, as worn-out farms are taken up by the same kind of people.[49]

The following year the Spy expressed its relief that only twenty-five of the three hundred deserted farms catalogued by the state had been sold, not to "foreigners or even to French Canadians" but to "native American citizens."[50]

Such anti-Catholic, anti-foreign, and anti-labor rhetoric hardly could have been calculated to draw *Canadien* voters to the Republican banner. The GOP did make some effort, nonetheless, to solicit them. Republican speechmakers continued to explain the benefits of a protective tariff to immigrant workers in the manufacturing towns of Worcester County.[51] At Republican campaign rallies Irishmen, alleged to have converted to Republicanism, explained the reasons for their transformation.[52] As in earlier campaigns prominent French Canadian Republicans from New England attended party rallies and addressed their kinsmen in French on behalf of the GOP.[53]

Despite these efforts, French Canadian voters in the towns of central Massachusetts continued to favored the Democratic party. In his five contests from 1888 to 1892, Russell's vote in ten *Canadien* towns averaged nearly eleven percentage points above that he received in Worcester County communities where French Canadians formed less than 19 percent of the population (see table 4.1). The governor's forthright rejection of the school question as a legitimate issue, his denunciation of the Republican effort to inject religious and ethnic prejudice into the campaign, and his continued emphasis on the tariff question continued to attract *Canadiens*. As a result, the Democratic vote in French Canadian towns rose. Russell's support in Southbridge, for example, increased from 533 to 645 votes, giving him a majority of 57 percent in 1892, an increase of three percentage points over 1891. Russell took more than 50 percent of the vote in other *Canadien* towns—Webster, Dudley, Palmer, North Brookfield, Douglas, and Ware—as compared to only 38 percent in communities where *Canadiens* were not an important element of the population.

The candidacy of Joseph D. Blanchard, the first French Canadian from Southbridge to be nominated by either party for state representative, helped to keep the French vote in the Democratic camp in many of these towns until 1893.[54] In Spencer Democrats failed to renominate L.E.P. Moreau for state representative in 1891, giving the GOP an opportunity to draw French Canadian voters away from Russell by running a *Canadien* Republican for that position. Although French Canadian support for the Democratic representative candidate evaporated, Russell still took Spencer, in part because the local Republicans angered the *Canadiens* in a clumsy and controversial attempt to scratch French Canadian Democrats from the voting list.[55]

The Democrats attracted French Canadians not only with the tariff issue and by defending Catholic religious rights but also by opening for

Table 4.1

Percent Democratic of the
total vote for governor in
French Canadian and non-French Canadian
towns in central Massachusetts,
1886-1895

	Non-French Canadian[a]	French Canadian[b]
No. of cases	41	10
1886	35.3	44.9
1887	32.9	42.2
1888	32.4	42.7
1889	34.8	45.3
1890	36.6	47.7
1891	38.2	48.6
1892	38.3	50.3
1893	32.9	44.0
1894	25.5	35.6
1895	27.8	39.2

Source: Massachusetts, Manual of the General Court, 1886-1895.

[a]Includes those towns in Worcester County where French Canadians formed less than 19 percent of the population in 1895.

[b]Includes those towns in central Massachusetts where French Canadians formed 24 percent or more of the population in 1895: Southbridge, Sutton, Spencer, Ware, Dudley, Ludlow, Sturbridge, Millbury, Grafton, Palmer.

them the door to political position and influence. French Canadian state representative candidates from Southbridge and Spencer were very visible recognition and advertised Democratic goodwill towards the group throughout southern Worcester County. Democratic French Canadians were elected, moreover, to the selectmen's board in both towns in the early 1890s. Between 1888 and 1892 twice as many *Canadiens* ran for public office in Southbridge than during the previous four years, mostly as Democrats. Of the sixteen positions in town government held by *Canadiens* all but three were occupied by Democrats. After 1892 the French Canadians remained an important, and later, a dominant force within the Democratic party in Southbridge as well as in Spencer.[56]

Republican Victory, 1893–1895

The "old-time Republican majority" for which GOP leaders had been waiting since 1890 finally turned out in 1893, and the party recaptured the governor's office, which remained in its hands until 1904. The onset of hard times took its toll among Democratic voters. Republican campaign speakers had no trouble blaming the Democratic party for the nation's economic woes; in their view the tariff reductions effected under Cleveland caused the depression. In the small woolen textile towns of Worcester County, they stressed economic issues, pointing out repeatedly that 460 sets of woolen machinery lay idle, 10,000 operatives were out of work, and $460,000 in wages had been lost. At the Knowles loom works in Worcester alone, a thousand workers remained unemployed. French Canadian Republicans traveled the campaign circuit, to such towns as Spencer and Webster, to explain the tariff issue and its relation to the depression.[57] As wages fell, mills closed, and families suffered, Republican appeals to support a protective tariff assumed a new meaning among French Canadian voters.[58]

While economic conditions contributed to Democratic defections, the GOP benefited from the intensification of nativist hysteria. Nativist sentiment ran deep among certain segments of the state's electorate, and Republican leaders did not ignore this source of potential voters. Neither did they risk, however, an open alliance with the American Protective Association (APA) which emerged in Massachusetts in 1893; for blatant support of APA would further alienate Catholic voters, possibly keeping them in Democratic columns the depression notwithstanding. Republican leaders resolved the problem by entering into what one Republican leader privately called an *entente cordiale* with the APA. In 1894 and 1895 the Republican platform and state ticket were shaped so as to attract nativist voters, but Republican regulars focused on traditional national issues and avoided references to so-called state issues. APA speakers, meanwhile, stressed the school issue, demanded immigration restriction, and urged their supporters to vote for the GOP.[59]

With Governor Russell's retirement in 1893, the Democrats could no longer rely on his popularity to draw voters. Democratic campaigners responded only lamely to Republican charges concerning the economy, arguing that the downturn had been caused by thirty years of Republican policies—an argument unpersuasive among the unemployed.[60] Party leaders denounced the APA as an "oath-bound secret organization" and condemned its quiet but obvious liaison with the Republican party, but were ultimately unable to make the APA the central campaign issue.[61] As free-silver Democrats, led by George Fred

Williams, gained the upper hand within the party in 1895, the Democracy became hopelessly divided. Neither Irish Democrats nor Yankee reformers, who had joined together in supporting William Russell, could bring themselves to embrace the cause of free silver. Williams' bid for governor in 1895 produced the worst electoral defeat of the decade, barring only the debacle of the next year.[62]

Although the depression dampened the spirit of Democratic voters in the French Canadian towns of central Massachusetts, the GOP's affiliation with the American Protective Association probably kept most *Canadiens* out of Republican columns in 1894 and 1895, as the case of Spencer suggests. In 1894, when the APA made its bid for control of the Republican party, French Canadians in Spencer reportedly became unhappy with the GOP and threatened not to vote at all or to support other candidates. Dr. Charles Barton, after voting Republican for twenty-eight years, announced that he had decided to vote the straight Democratic ticket and believed that the "French citizens would vote *en masse* with the Democratic party on account of the APA."[63] Election results indicate that many *Canadiens* in Spencer may have indeed abstained or voted for the People's Party. Disaffection between the French and Republican party was evident in the town's spring 1894–95 elections as well. In Spencer, as in other French Canadian towns, Democratic fortunes slumped after 1892.[64]

Nativism, the Republican *entente cordiale* with the American Protective Association, and astute Democratic politics, which emphasized issues of interest to the *Canadiens* and catered to their desire for recognition, enabled Democratic politicians to attract French Canadians in certain cities and in central Massachusetts towns (see table 4.2). In Marlboro the election of Charles Favreau, a Democrat, to local offices starting in 1884 and to the general court in 1893, helped the Democratic majorities which that city regularly returned until 1893.[65] French Canadians from both parties held local office in Holyoke in the 1880s and early 1890s. *Canadien* voters, especially those of heavily French Precinct Two-A, voted Democratic during this period, and contributed to that city's strong Democratic vote in gubernatorial contests between 1886 and 1893.[66] That most French Canadians holding seats on the city council from 1894 to 1896 were Democrats also indicates a Democratic tilt during the early 1890s.[67] In Lowell, where French Canadians had formed an alliance with Yankee Republicans in the 1880s, the GOP's ties with the APA initially pushed them towards the Democratic party in the early 1890s. During those years three-time Democratic mayor William F. Courtney helped to keep them in the fold through patronage and by his marriage into a prominent French Canadian family.[68]

Table 4.2

Pearsonian correlation coefficients (R)
showing the association between
the percent Democratic of the total vote
for governor and percent French Canadian
of the population, 1888-1895

	Central towns[a] (n=10)	Central towns[b] (n=8)	Primary cities[a] (n=6)
1888	.32	.50	.63
1889	.36	.64*	.71*
1890	.32	.59	.85*
1891	.41	.60	.72*
1892	.29	.49	.66
1893	.35	.65*	.63
1894	.21	.45	.61
1895	.21	.53	.61

[a]See table 3.13 for the communities in each category.

[b]excluding Palmer and Sutton

*Indicates significance at .05 level of confidence.

Most French Canadian voters in Fall River and Worcester tended to favor Democrats as well. As in Lowell, *Canadiens* in Fall River had gravitated towards the GOP after 1880 in the wake of a bitter strike and the Flint affair.[69] By 1890 the tie between the two was shaken, as the French Canadians gave strong electoral suport to Democratic mayoral and gubernatorial candidates between 1889 and 1893. Paralleling the case in Lowell, the marriage of the young Irish mayoral candidate into a French Canadian family probably helped this transition.[70] Important also was the Democratic nomination of *Canadiens* for school committee and for ward alderman in Ward Six. Between 1889 and 1893 French Canadian Democratic nominees for local office outnumbered Republicans eight to four. Such recognition helped to heal the rift between the *Canadiens* and the local Irish Democracy (see table 4.3).[71] In Ward Six, the French stronghold and scene of the Flint affair, the vote for Democratic mayor John W. Coughlin rose from 35 percent in 1888 to 56 percent in 1891, while Governor Russell's increased from 40 percent to 58 percent (see table 4.4). During the same period Robert Howard, an outstanding labor reformer and ally of Josiah Quincy in the General Court, received even stronger backing in that ward.[72] Democratic candidates also gained strength in other wards where French voters were

Table 4.3

French Canadian candidates for local
public office in Fall River and Worcester,
1888-1895

	Fall River			Worcester		
	Total	Rep.	Dem.[a]	Total	Rep.	Dem.[a]
1888	3	2	1	1	1	0
1889	3	2	1	2	1	1
1890	4	1	3	1	0	1
1891	2	0	2	1	0	1
1892	1	0	1	0	0	0
1893	2	1	1	2	0	2
1894	3	3	0	2	1	1
1895	3	2	1	3	0	3

Sources: Fall River Daily Herald (1888); Fall River Daily Globe
(1889-95); Worcester Evening Gazette (1888-95).

[a]Candidates running as Independent Democrats were classified as
Democrats in this table.

important (see table 4.5).[73] Starting in 1893, however, the Democratic
vote in Ward Six began a precipitious decline. While the majority of the
city's Canadiens voted for Mayor Coughlin in 1893, a year in which the
GOP mayoral candidate was accused of having ties to the APA, Republican recognition was probably an important factor in regaining for
the GOP the bulk of the French vote afterwards.[74]

Although French Canadian voters in Worcester remained divided, the
Democratic party also made important gains among them in that city.
With the formation of several naturalization clubs in the 1880s, the
number of Canadien voters increased more quickly in Worcester than in
Fall River, and both parties competed for their votes.[75] The founding of
a French Republican Club and a French Democratic Club stimulated
"more visible consideration towards us on the part of other nationalities," as the editor of Le Worcester Canadien put it.[76] The Democratic party proved more successful in the competition for French
Canadian voters probably because it offered Canadiens better opportunities for public officeholding. Alexandre Belisle Jr., a Democrat
closely tied to the Ward Five Naturalization Club, was elected to the
first of his two terms as city councillor in 1888, the first Canadien to
serve on the council.[77] In 1890 and 1891 Democrats nominated Andre
G. Lajoie, early president of the Ward Six Naturalization Club, for a
councillor's spot.[78] Although Lajoie lost both races, John F. Jandron, a

Democratic lawyer, was appointed deputy sheriff for Worcester County early in 1890, a post he held until the Democrats lost the governor's chair.[79]

French Canadian voting patterns in Worcester prove difficult to discern; but electoral data, coupled with the recognition *Canadiens* received from the Democratic party, suggest that many were associated with that party (see tables 4.3 and 4.6).[80] In Wards Five and Six, which held 45 percent of the *Canadien* voters, they tended to vote Democratic. French Canadians also were active in the party's organization of those wards, serving as ward committeemen and convention delegates. French Canadian politicians from these wards appeared with party leaders on campaign platforms at rallies, urging their fellow French Canadians to support the party because French officeholders owed their positions to the Democracy.[81] In Ward Five, a Democratic stronghold, Precinct Two, the seat of Belisle's influence, consistently returned Democratic majorities of 80 percent or more. Because the other precincts in that ward having far fewer *Canadien* voters also voted Democratic but turned out majorities ranging between just 50 and 60 percent, the extraordinarily high Democratic vote in Precinct Two probably reflects

Table 4.4

Percent Democratic of the two-party vote
for president, governor, mayor, and alderman,
in Ward 6, Fall River, 1888-1896

	President	Governor	Mayor	Alderman
1888	37.9	39.7	34.8	28.4
1889		48.4	41.9	35.7[a]
1890		49.6	58.9	33.7[a,b]
1891		57.8	56.1	45.7[a]
1892	38.5	57.8	47.9	43.1[a]
1893		40.3	49.4	47.1
1894		34.5	34.6	25.8
1895		33.6	25.9	- [c]
1896	15.4	16.8	18.5	44.9

Sources: Massachusetts, Public Document No. 43, 1888-1896, and reports on local elections in the Fall River Daily Globe, 1888-1896.

[a]French Canadian Democratic candidate.

[b]Three-man race.

[c]No Democratic candidate.

Table 4.5

Percent Democratic of the two-party vote
for governor in selected wards, Fall River,
1888-1896

	Ward 6	5	9	1	3[a]	8[b]	R$_s$ [c]
1888	39.7	68.0	33.1	42.6	80.4	11.2	.067
1889	48.4	70.7	39.0	49.7	83.4	15.4	.321
1890	49.6	72.0	43.5	48.8	86.7	18.1	.250
1891	57.8	75.3	47.5	53.5	89.3	18.0	.454
1892	56.9	73.2	46.1	50.2	83.7	14.8	.400
1893	40.3	69.7	37.2	42.1	82.3	14.4	.067
1894	35.5	62.6	33.8	41.3	77.3	12.7	.050
1895	33.6	64.2	33.4	37.8	77.2	14.7	.067
1896	16.8	54.5	24.9	25.5	65.2	17.6	.083
% FC[d]	24.0	13.7	7.0	6.5	4.9	.3	

Sources: Philip A. Silvia, Jr., "The Spindle City: Labor, Politics, and Religion in Fall River, Massachusetts, 1870-1905 (Ph.D. diss., Fordham University, 1973), 863.

[a]Democratic banner ward.

[b]Republican banner ward.

[c]Spearman's correlation coefficient showing the relationship between percent Democratic vote and percent of the voters estimated to be French Canadian for all nine of the city's wards.

[d]The estimated percent of the voters who were French Canadian was derived by taking the number of French Canadian voters known to be in the ward in 1887 and dividing by the number of registered voters in the ward in 1890.   Only 587 French Canadian voters were registered in the city in 1887.   Because the number rose to only 629 by 1891, the distribution probably did not change significantly.

the combined strength of the Irish and French Canadian vote. In Ward Six, normally Republican, Lavoie's Precinct Two, where 80 percent of the *Canadien* voters in that ward lived, Democratic percentages were twice as high as in Precinct One, suggesting the same conclusion. In Ward Three, however, the Democratic vote was less strong in Precinct Two, where French Canadians were most numerous. Given that the officers of the Ward Three Naturalization Club were often Republican party activists and that French nominations for office usually came from the Republican party in that ward, it seems likely that most

Canadiens there favored the GOP. Although many French Canadians remained associated with the Democratic party in Worcester in 1895, things thereafter changed, both here and elsewhere.

With William Jennings Bryan's ascendancy on the national scale, the Democratic party turned its attention from free trade to free silver. Like many other Democratic voters, many French Canadians favored William McKinley over Bryan in 1896, partly because the free silver issue stirred them little but also because they found Bryan's evangelical style alien and discomforting. On the state level the nativist hysteria that had helped push *Canadiens* into the Democratic coalition between 1888 and 1895 abruptly subsided, creating an opportunity for the GOP to make gains among French Canadian voters. Having regained control of the state and local government, the Republican party replaced Democrats as the potential source of political recognition. The Democratic party, once again severely weakened by internal strife, out of power with dim prospects for electoral victory, could offer neither the leadership nor political recognition necessary to retain French-speaking voters in the primary French Canadian centers. In those cities a Franco-Republican alliance was forged by the GOP, which used political recognition to create a visible and practical bond between itself and the French Canadians. In the French Canadian towns of central Massachu-

Table 4.6

Precent Democratic of the two-party vote
for governor in three Worcester wards, 1886-1895

WARD PRECINCT	3 1	3 2	5 1	5 2	5 3	6 1	6 2
YEAR							
1886	77.3	77.2	54.8	87.4	68.5	19.5	47.7
1887	74.8	73.8	53.4	89.7	61.5	20.7	51.8
1888	65.2	66.9	46.0	82.9	59.0	20.3	43.8
1889	69.9	66.3	52.3	85.3	60.2	16.8	44.3
1890	73.9	69.0	50.3	86.3	58.1	20.2	46.8
1891	73.5	69.9	54.2	87.5	60.2	26.4	49.7
1892	73.8	69.7	56.3	87.7	51.7	25.9	51.4
1893	70.5	60.7	45.5	81.7	49.2	17.4	42.6
1894	68.0	60.1	40.1	80.5	46.1	12.1	37.8
1895	64.2	59.5	47.0	78.6	48.5	12.4	39.8

Calculations are based on electoral data derived from the
Worcester Evening Gazette, 1886-1895.

setts, however, the Franco-Democratic alliance of the Russell years, though weakened temporarily by the defection of *Canadien* voters in 1896, later persisted and grew stronger. The following two chapters examine the divergent paths that French Canadians followed after 1895 and highlight the increasing importance of recognition politics for French Canadians during the Progressive Era.

5

The Fragility of Urban Franco-Republican Alliances, 1896–1915

After the collapse of the Democratic coalition in the mid-1890s, many French Canadians in Massachusetts cities gravitated towards the Republican party. While Bryanites, led by George Fred Williams, retained control of the party apparatus, many Democratic voters—Irish as well as French Canadian—remained alienated and the Bay State Democratic party was deeply divided. Given this opportunity, the GOP recruited many *Canadien* voters recently mobilized by the political whirlwinds that intensified their interest in public affairs. By accommodating the ambitions of rising French Canadian politicians, the party broadened its electoral base, enabling it to re-establish its control of urban governments. Often holding in their hands the balance of power in municipal politics, French Canadians could sometimes extract from the GOP the recognition they desired. By associating themselves with the party in power, moreover, they could sometimes gain leverage in shaping public policy to conform with their interests, an opportunity the moribund Democratic party could not provide. The emergent Franco-Republican alliance rested more upon a foundation of mutual political pragmatism than upon a congruence of political principle.

The motley Republican coalition, encompassing Yankees, immigrant Protestants and assorted reformers as well as French Canadians, remained fragile and unstable, frequently unable to satisfy the divergent interests of its constituent groups. The failure of the GOP to accommodate continuing French Canadian demands for recognition and influence or the injection of class or cultural issues into politics easily could disrupt its delicate constitution, and drive French-speaking voters into Democratic columns. Such possibilities became more probable after 1900, once the Democratic party freed itself from the stranglehold that the Bryanites had held over the party since 1895. Only by carefully cultivating their political sensibilities could the Republican party keep firm its grasp on French Canadian voters. This proved difficult. Most French Canadians, who remained suspicious of both political parties despite their increasing involvement in political life, identified strongly with neither party. Their relationship to the parties was instead governed by political pragmatism.

Urban Officeholding and Voting Patterns

The influence of French Canadians in municipal affairs, measured in terms of officeholding, expanded significantly after 1895. In 1895 they held only thirty-four positions in seventeen cities.[1] By 1900 the number of officeholders increased to sixty, and ten years later to seventy-seven. Occupying less than 3 percent of all positions in these cities in 1895, French Canadians formed nearly 6 percent of all officeholders fifteen years later. Although few French Canadians served on school committees or in administrative offices, they proved relatively more successful in acquiring elective positions on city councils and appointments to governing boards (see table 5.1). As might be expected, Canadiens were more successful in securing city council seats in those cities where they formed a larger proportion of the population, and the leverage gained by council membership often opened the way to other offices. Three-quarters of all French Canadian officeholders were found in the eight cities in which the group made up 20 percent or more of the population (see table 5.2).[2] Holyoke, Chicopee, and Marlboro—the three cities where the Canadiens were most successful in becoming city councillors—alone accounted for nearly 50 percent of all other positions.[3] Elsewhere their success varied widely, but by 1910 fourteen of the seventeen cities had at least three Canadien officeholders, reflecting the progress the group had made since 1895.[4]

Changes in the party affiliation of French Canadian city councillors in these seventeen cities illustrate the shift of Canadiens to the Republican party after 1895. In 1895 ten of the sixteen (62 percent) city councillors whose party affiliation could be determined were Democrats. By 1898 the number holding council seats nearly doubled and Republicans outnumbered Democrats sixteen to ten. Two years later Republicans had gained six additional seats while Democrats had lost five. By 1900 Canadien Republicans had increased their number in those cities where they had been a majority five years earlier—Fall River, Lowell, Chicopee, and Northhampton. In Holyoke, Worcester, Marlboro, Pittsfield, and Fitchburg—where all ten Canadien councillors in 1895 were Democrats—nine of the ten in 1900 were Republicans. By 1900, in contrast to 1895, more than 80 percent of French Canadian city councillors were Republicans (see table 5.3).

The number and party affiliation of French Canadian candidates for state representative between 1896 and 1915 also reflected the expansion

Table 5.1

French Canadian officeholding in seventeen
Massachusetts cities, 1895, 1900, 1907, 1910

| | Number | | Percent |
	Total	French	French
1895			
City council	437	15	3.43
School committee	206	4	1.94
Governing boards	372	12	3.22
Administrative positions	182	3	1.65
Total	1,197	34	2.84
1900			
City council	453	30	6.62
School committee	218	5	2.29
Governing boards	463	18	3.89
Administrative positions	207	7	3.38
Total	1,341	60	4.47
1907			
City council	459	26	5.66
School committee	221	8	3.62
Governing boards	437	27	6.18
Administrative positions	210	8	3.81
Total	1,327	69	5.20
1910			
City council	454	34	7.49
School committee	201	5	2.49
Governing boards	455	27	5.93
Administrative positions	208	11	5.29
Total	1,318	77	5.84
Four years			
City council	1,803	105	5.82
School committee	846	22	2.60
Governing boards	1,727	84	4.86
Administrative positions	807	29	3.59
Total	5,183	240	4.63

Source: Massachusetts Yearbook, 1895, 1900, 1907, 1910.

Governing boards: board of health, overseers of the poor,
register of voters, assessors, park commission, license commission,
sinking fund commission, water commission.

Administrative positions: city clerk, auditor, marshall,
treasurer, collector, superintendent of streets, city engineer,
buildings inspector, sealer of weights and measures, superintendent
of water, solicitor, messenger, physician.

Cities: Fall River, Holyoke, Worcester, Lowell, New Bedford,
Lawrence, Chicopee, North Adams, Northhampton, Springfield, Taunton,
Pittsfield, Haverhill, Salem, Marlboro, Fitchburg, Lynn.

Table 5.2

Distribution of French Canadian officeholders
by relative size of the Canadien population,
1895, 1900, 1907, 1910

	Percent	Number of positions				
	Canadian[a]	All	City Council	School Comm.	Governing Boards	Administrative
Fall River	26.81	32	12	1	12	7
Holyoke	25.37	43	15	4	15	9
Marlboro	23.09	38	13	1	21	3
Chicopee	22.46	21	10	3	6	2
Lowell	20.60	17	10	3	4	0
North Adams	20.21	8	5	0	3	0
Fitchburg	20.01	7	6	0	1	0
New Bedford	19.98	19	9	7	3	0
		185	80	19	65	21
Salem	18.61	5	5	0	0	0
Lawrence	15.99	10	3	2	5	0
Northhampton	12.89	7	4	0	2	1
Haverhill	11.67	5	3	0	2	0
Taunton	11.21	6	3	0	3	0
Worcester	9.34	8	5	1	0	2
Springfield	8.12	5	0	0	3	2
Pittsfield	6.06	7	2	0	2	3
Lynn	4.14	2	0	0	2	0
		55	25	3	19	8

Source: Massachusetts Yearbook, 1895, 1900, 1907, 1910.

[a]Percent of the total population that was French Canadian in
1905.

of political activity among Canadiens and their shift to the GOP. Only
eighteen Canadien candidacies originated in seventeen cities between
1896 and 1900. Over the next five years, however, there were twice as
many, and about forty-eight in each of the two following five-year
periods. Although Democrats outnumbered Republicans eight to seven
between 1896 and 1900, thereafter Republicans held about a two to one
margin over Democrats. Of the 150 candidates who ran for the lower
house of the general court during the entire period, 53 percent were
Republicans while only 28 percent were Democrats, indicating a relatively strong relationship between French Canadians and the GOP (see
table 5.4). More telling still, nearly 90 percent of the Canadiens who
served at the state house were Republicans. Over a twenty-year span
Democratic candidates won only four times.[5]

Voting patterns in gubernatorial elections also point toward a substantial weakening of the tie between French Canadians and the Democratic party after 1895 in the seventeen cities considered. While reinforcing the hypothesis that many *Canadiens* established a closer relationship with the GOP after 1895, the pattern suggests that French Canadians remained nonetheless at least marginally Democratic in their voting habits. The correlation between French Canadians and the Democratic vote declined from a moderate mean of .53 between 1891 and 1895 to a relatively low .34 between 1896 and 1900 (see table 5.5). Through the first fifteen years of the twentieth century the relationship, while remaining positive, fluctuated widely. After reaching a peak of .63 in 1904, it dropped to a low of .14 in 1911. For the six primary cities alone, the same pattern was evident, although the decline after 1895 was steeper and prolonged. In addition, there was greater oscillation after 1900, suggesting that the on-again-off-again association between *Canadiens* and the Democratic party was more pronounced in these six cities (see table 5.6).

A comparison of French Canadian political patterns in the six primary cities indicates considerable diversity. *Canadiens* in these cites generally aligned themselves with the GOP by 1900, but the rela-

Table 5.3

Party affiliation of French Canadian
city councillors in seventeen Massachusetts
cities, 1895-1903[a]

		Number of French Canadian Councillors			Percent[b]	
Year	Total	Republican	Democrat	Unknown/ Other	Rep.	Dem.
1895	17	6	10	1	37.5	62.5
1896	14	7	7	0	50.0	50.0
1897	20	9	7	4	56.3	43.7
1898	32	16	10	6	61.5	38.5
1899	26	12	10	4	54.5	45.5
1900	30	22	5	3	81.5	18.5
1901	30	19	8	3	70.4	29.6
1902	25	15	3	7	83.3	16.7
1903	30	15	7	8	68.2	31.8
Total	224	121	67	36	64.4	35.6

[a]French Canadians were identified by name from city directories and the <u>Massachusetts Yearbook</u>, which often gives the party affiliation of the individuals.

[b]Percent Republican and percent Democratic of only those individuals whose party affiliation is known.

Table 5.4

Party affiliation of French Canadian
state representative candidates in
seventeen Massachusetts cities, 1896-1915

	Total	Republican	Democrat	Other[a]
Number				
1896-1900	18	7	8	3
1901-1905	36	19	9	8
1906-1910	49	26	14	9
1911-1915	47	28	11	8
Total	150	80	42	28
Percent				
1896-1900	100	38.9	44.4	16.7
1901-1905	100	52.8	25.0	22.2
1906-1910	100	53.1	38.6	18.3
1911-1915	100	59.6	23.4	17.0
Total	100	53.3	28.0	18.7

Source: Massachusetts, Public Document No. 43, 1896-1915.

[a]Includes Independents, Socialist Labor, Socialist,
Progressive, and Independence League candidates.

tionship differed from city to city, making it difficult to designate as typical the French Canadian political experience in any one of them. While discouraging facile generalizations, a comparative approach provides a basis for evaluating the patterns found by using case studies.

The diversity in political patterns may be illustrated by comparing the success of French Canadians in acquiring positions in urban government between 1890 and 1915. Canadiens generally expanded their influence during this period, but the timing and degree of political success varied from city to city. They were most successful in Holyoke and least successful in Worcester and Lawrence.[6] An analysis of Canadien city councillors, 1890–1915, shows that French Canadians in Holyoke enjoyed much early success, and maintained their position throughout this period even though their influence suffered some decline after 1895. This pattern contrasts sharply with that of New Bedford, where their influence increased steadily until 1915, and with that of Fall River, where their influence expanded rapidly between 1895 and 1900 and then leveled off. Elsewhere, an expansion in the number of French Canadian city councillors was followed by a decline. In Worcester and Lawrence, for example, Canadien influence peaked before 1900, while in Lowell, it peaked between 1906 and 1910 (see table 5.7).

An examination of French Canadian candidates for state representative in the primary cities reveals diversity from a different perspective. Given the relative success of the *Canadiens* in Fall River and Lowell in local politics, it is not surprising to find that they produced a fairly large number of candidates for the lower house and that many won. Despite their outstanding success on the local level in Holyoke, however, French Canadians had fewer candidates for state representative there than in Fall River or Lowell and the candidates were much less successful. In Worcester, where the number of *Canadien* councillors was quite small, there were an unexpectedly large number of state representative candidates, none of whom were successful. Differences such as these prove difficult to explain. A closer look at Holyoke, Fall River, and Worcester, however, permits a glimpse of the political dynamics that conditioned French Canadian political behavior in the cities of Massachusetts (see tables 5.8 and 5.9).

Holyoke: Republican Mayors, Democratic Aldermen

French Canadians of Holyoke were unusually successful in local politics early in the 1890s when the group was faring less well in other cities.[7] In the Paper City, unlike in Fall River or Worcester, French Canadians were densely settled in only two wards; by 1910 more than 75 percent of the city's *Canadiens* lived in Wards One and Two, forming

Table 5.5

Mean Pearsonian correlation coefficients (R) showing the association between the percent Democratic vote for governor and the percent French Canadian and percent Irish of the population in seventeen Massachusetts cities for five-year periods, 1891-1915

Variable 1	Percent Democratic	
Variable 2	Percent French Canadian	
Variable 3	Percent Irish	

	R_{12}	R_{13}
	Mean	Mean
1891-1895	.53	.54
1896-1900	.34	.61
1901-1905	.44	.57
1906-1910	.40	.46
1911-1915	.38	.59
1891-1915	.42	.55
1896-1915	.39	.56

Table 5.6

Pearsonian correlation coefficients (R) showing the
association between the percent Democratic vote for
governor and the percent French Canadian and
percent Irish of the population in seventeen
Massachusetts cities, 1891-1915

Variable 1   Percent Democratic
Variable 2   Percent French Canadian
Variable 3   Percent Irish

| | 17 cities | | | 6 primary cities | | | |
	R_{12}	R_{13}	$R_{12.3}$[a]	R_{12}	R_{13}	$R_{12.3}$[a]	R_{s12}[b]
1891	.58*	.33	.60*	.72	.38	.73	.77
1892	.49*	.46*	.52*	.66	.65	.77	.66
1893	.52*	.61*	.61*	.63	.65	.76	.43
1894	.51*	.67*	.64*	.61	.76*	.80	.46
1895	.57*	.65*	.70*	.61	.78*	.81*	.43
1896	.36	.51*	.39	.40	.80*	.50	.57
1897	.29	.57*	.32	.32	.81*	.36	.14
1898	.28	.70*	.34	.27	.75*	.26	.09
1899	.42*	.58*	.48*	.26	.78*	.25	.09
1900	.38	.67*	.46*	.29	.85*	.36	.09
1901	.51*	.69*	.66*	.35	.87*	.48	.14
1902	.27	.72*	.33	.37	.89*	.58	.37
1903	.36	.69*	.45*	.32	.82*	.38	.29
1904	.63*	.07	.63*	.57	-.24	.62	.43
1905	.41*	.67*	.51*	.40	.78*	.49	.31
1906	.45*	.35	.46*	.38	.35	.36	.14
1907	.26	.45*	.26	.65	.80*	.91*	.40
1908	.30	.37	.31	.11	.45	.06	-.09
1909	.51*	.44*	.55*	.39	.59	.40	.00
1910	.50*	.67*	.62* .	.36	.94*	.68	.34
1911	.14	.42*	.13	-.28	.50	-.40	-.34
1912	.48*	.63*	.58*	.41	.77*	.49	.54
1913	.47*	.64*	.57*	.34	.88*	.50	.03
1914	.44*			.28			
1915	.42*	.67*	.52*	.24	.71*	.21	.14

*Indicates significance at the .05 level of confidence.

[a]The correlation between percent French Canadian and percent
Irish of the population for the seventeen cities was .05 and for the
primary cities alone, .13. As might be expected, the partial
correlation coefficient ($R_{12.3}$), which controls for Irish, usually
higher than R_{12}.

[b]Using only six cases, Spearman's R is a more appropriate
statistic for the six primary cities. Pearson's R was used here for
comparative purposes. The results using Spearman's R are shown in
the last column and produce a similar pattern when graphed.

Table 5.7

French Canadian city councillors in
primary cities, 1891-1915

Number of French Canadian city councillors

	1891-1895	1896-1900	1901-1905	1906-1910	1911-1915	Total
Holyoke	27	16	16	12	16	87
Fall River	1	12	22	17	17	69
New Bedford	1	5	9	20	21	56
Lowell	9	10	10	21	4	54
Worcester	4	10	3	6	3	26
Lawrence	1	5	3	2	0	11
Total	43	58	63	78	61	303

Percent of quota[a]

	1891-1895	1896-1900	1901-1905	1906-1910	1911-1915	Total
Holyoke	76	60	60	45	60	62
Fall River	2	25	54	47	47	33
New Bedford	3	23	30	67	70	39
Lowell	24	27	27	57	37	34
Worcester	27	67	20	31	16	31
Lawrence	5	26	16	10	0	13

Sources: City directories, 1890-1915. French Canadian
councillors were identified by surname. Percent of quota was
calculated on the basis of the French Canadian population in 1905.

[a]The French Canadian quota equals the total number of city
council positions available multiplied by the percent of the city
population in 1905 that was French Canadian. Percent of the quota
equals the number of positions actually held by the Canadiens divided
by the quota.

a majority of the inhabitants in the latter (see tables 5.10 and 5.11).[8]
Partly because their concentration in Ward Two gave them control of
that ward, they were able to establish for themselves a political niche
early in Holyoke.

Early mobilization of French Canadian voters was another factor
contributing to quick success in municipal politics. In 1885, only 258
French Canadians in Holyoke were voters, about 6 percent of the city's
voters. Ten years later, eight hundred French-speaking voters made up
more than 12 percent of voters. As Peter Haebler shows, 40 percent of
all Canadiens who were naturalized in Holyoke between 1886 and 1906
did so before 1895.[9]

The rules of the political game also contributed to French Canadian
success in Holyoke. Before 1896 each ward elected an alderman and
three common councillors; French Canadians held between four and

Table 5.8

Distribution of French Canadian
state representative candidates
and city councillors in the
primary cities, 1891-1915

	City Councillors, 1891-1915		State Representative candidates, 1896-1915	
	#	%	#	%
Holyoke	87	29	10	11
Fall River	69	23	27	28
New Bedford	56	18	6	6
Lowell	54	18	19	20
Worcester	26	9	24	25
Lawrence	11	3	9	10
	303	100	95	100

Sources:　City directories, 1891-1915;
Massachusetts, Public Document No. 43, 1896-1915.

seven city council seats between 1890 and 1895. As Haebler points out, a change in the city charter after 1896 weakened French influence while strengthening the Republican party's position. The new charter provided for the election of one alderman from each ward and fourteen aldermen elected at large, making it more difficult for Canadiens to win as many council seats.[10]

Before 1898 French Canadians in Holyoke leaned toward the Democratic party and, despite some disputes, often cooperated with the Irish in city politics.[11] Until 1898 the heavily French Canadian Ward Two voted Democratic in mayoral races,[12] and in 1895 the French Canadians on the council were Democrats.[13] Due at least in part to a local political scandal, Canadiens veered towards the GOP in local politics after the alteration of the city charter.[14] By 1900 most Canadiens on the council were Republicans; between 1897 and 1904 more than half were Republicans.[15] Between 1898 and 1910 Precinct Two-A French Canadians supported Republican mayoral candidates and received appointive positions in local government from grateful Republican mayors.[16]

Political pragmatism underlay the French Canadian mayoral vote. The GOP, needing French voters to win the mayoralty, was more accommodating of Canadien demands for recognition. Besides appointing French Canadians to municipal boards, the Republicans, unlike the Democrats, offered them prestigious nomination for seats in the state

Table 5.9

Outcome of French Canadian candidacies
for state representative in
primary cities, 1896-1915

	Total	Number Won	Lost	Percent winning	Percent Republican of winning candidates
Fall River	27	16	11	59	93
Worcester	24	0	24	0	0
Lowell	19	8	11	42	87
Holyoke	10	1	9	10	100
Lawrence	9	2	7	22	0
New Bedford	6	1	5	17	100
Total	95	28	67	29	86

Source: Massachusetts, Public Document No. 43, 1896-1915.

house and senate. Save one, however, these nominees failed to win office. Election results for state representative contests in Precinct Two-A show that French Canadian Republican candidates did very well but that other GOP nominees did not attract French voters. When the Republicans did not run a *Canadien* for state representative, Precinct Two-A usually voted Democratic.[17] In alderman contests, moreover,

Table 5.10

Percentage distribution of the
French Canadian-born population
of four cities by ward, 1910

	Holyoke	Lowell	Fall River	Worcester
Ward 1	31.8	5.2	15.6	3.4
Ward 2	45.4	14.3	11.9	6.1
Ward 3	3.8	6.2	12.0	24.5
Ward 4	7.3	1.5	8.5	7.1
Ward 5	3.4	1.4	9.0	24.3
Ward 6	6.4	57.6	28.2	5.2
Ward 7	1.8	9.7	2.8	11.0
Ward 8	-	1.4	2.5	6.3
Ward 9	-	2.8	9.7	9.4
Ward 10	-	-	-	2.7
Total	100.0	100.0	100.0	100.0

Source: U.S. Bureau of the Census, Abstract of the
Thirteenth Census: 1910: 608-612.

Table 5.11

Percent French Canadian-born and Irish-born
of the population of four cities
by ward, 1910

| | Holyoke | | Lowell | | Fall River | | Worcester | |
	%FC	%IR	%FC	%IR	%FC	%IR	%FC	%IR
Ward 1	27.3	11.2	6.6	7.6	11.6	4.0	1.2	6.6
Ward 2	34.1	2.7	12.3	12.1	14.8	3.2	1.7	6.4
Ward 3	3.5	6.0	6.6	3.5	12.0	5.1	6.6	8.6
Ward 4	6.6	13.4	1.8	17.7	10.5	8.2	2.2	12.3
Ward 5	5.2	13.7	1.7	17.4	11.5	4.4	6.6	9.5
Ward 6	6.6	13.2	33.7	4.7	25.2	1.0	1.7	6.3
Ward 7	2.2	6.5	12.1	7.7	7.0	6.7	4.2	5.3
Ward 8	-	-	1.8	7.1	3.9	6.4	2.9	4.6
Ward 9	-	-	3.3	11.3	10.5	3.2	4.1	4.2
Ward 10	-	-	-	-	-	-	1.3	4.8
City	13.9	9.1	11.6	9.4	12.8	4.4	3.4	7.2

Source: U.S. Bureau of the Census, Abstract of the Thirteenth Census: 1910:   608-612.

that precinct usually preferred French Democrats over French Republicans, and it generally gave majorities to Democratic gubernatorial aspirants.[18] Mayoral politics aside, the voting pattern found in Precinct Two-A indicates a Democratic rather than a Republican tendency among French Canadians until 1910. The fractured nature of the voting record suggests that considerations of tactical political advantage loomed larger than party loyalty in French Canadian electoral preferences in Holyoke.

The hypothesis that French Canadians in the Paper City leaned toward the Democratic party until 1910, despite their mayoral vote and Republican patronage, is reinforced by a comparison with Fall River and Worcester, where the *Canadiens* appear more closely associated with the GOP. But French Canadian political behavior in these cities indicates, however, that their relationship with the Republican party, though more robust in some respects than in Holyoke, remained unstable. As in Holyoke, French Canadians in these cities displayed a remarkable flexibility in politics that won them few friends in an age when political men put much stock in party loyalty.

Fall River: Vicissitudes of a Franco-Republican Alliance

Fall River's textile boom had attracted some twenty-five thousand French Canadians by the turn of the century, the largest concentration outside Canada. Forming more than a fourth of the Spindle City's people, French-speaking immigrants distributed themselves widely throughout the city by 1910, creating pockets of *Canadien* culture on the steep hillsides overlooking dozens of granite factories. Unlike in Holyoke or Lowell where most could be found in just one or two wards, only 28 percent of the *Canadiens* in Fall River lived in Ward Six, where they were a majority of the voters.[19] By 1909 less than 30 percent of the city's French voters lived in that ward. Another 55 percent inhabited five other wards (Wards One, Two, Three, Five, and Nine), where they formed between 17 and 25 percent of the voters (see table 5.12).[20]

Because of their spatial distribution and because they were comparatively slower to mobilize, French Canadians in the Spindle City had gained less political influence before 1895 than in Holyoke. Although *Canadiens* comprised between 7 and 10 percent of the voters,[21] only one *Canadien* was elected to the city council in Fall River between 1891 and 1895, as compared with more than twenty-five in Holyoke.[22] In 1895 a single French Canadian sat on the thirty-six member council, and only two had been appointed to the city's governing boards (see tables 5.13 and 5.14).[23]

As the number of French-speaking voters increased rapidly after 1895, the group's influence in municipal affairs grew correspondingly.

Table 5.12

Percentage distribution of French Canadian
voters in Fall River by ward, 1887, 1909

	Percent French Canadian of registered voters		Percent of all French Canadian voters in Fall River in each ward	
	1887	1909	1887	1909
Ward 1	6.4	16.8	12.1	14.9
Ward 2	3.4	19.8	6.1	10.8
Ward 3	4.9	24.6	6.7	10.7
Ward 4	5.4	13.2	8.0	8.5
Ward 5	13.7	17.2	17.7	7.0
Ward 6	24.0	51.0	34.6	28.9
Ward 7	2.0	8.0	2.7	3.1
Ward 8	.3	6.5	.3	3.7
Ward 9	7.0	20.4	11.8	12.4
City	7.5	19.8	100.0	100.0

Calculated from data given in Philip Silvia, "The Spindle City: Labor, Politics, and Religion In Fall River, Massachusetts, 1876-1905," (Ph.D. diss., Fordham University, 1973), 863; and Massachusetts, Public Document No. 43, 1890, 1909.

Table 5.13

French Canadian candidates and officeholders
in Fall River, 1891-1915

	Candidates			Office Holders	
	R	D	O	R	D
1891-1895					
Ward 6	3	2		1	0
Other wards	4	0		0	0
Alderman at large	-	-		0	0
School committee	0	2		0	0
1896-1905					
Ward 6	20	1		22	0
Other wards	16	1	4	8	0
Alderman at large	3	4		3	0
School Committee	3	0		6	0
1906-1910					
Ward 6	5	1		10	0
Other wards	0	0		0	0
Alderman at large	2	3		4	3
School Committee	0	1		0	0
1911-1915					
Ward 6	6	2	2	10	0
Other wards	0	2		0	0
Alderman at large	2	3		4	3
School Committee	1	6		1	10

D-Democrat; R-Republican; O-Other

From about 600 in 1890, French voters multiplied to about 2,200 by 1899, and to about 3,000 ten years later. By 1909 nearly one in five voters was *Canadien*.[24] French Canadians held twelve city council seats between 1896 and 1900, and nearly twice as many over the next five years.[25] By 1900 seven *Canadiens* had been appointed to positions in city government, and by 1915, nine. Besides having established seats on the boards of health, overseers of the poor, and registrars of voters and on the water and park commissions, French Canadians usually served as city solicitors, city physicians, and in several minor posts by 1905. Although they were still considerably underrepresented in local government after 1910, their position had improved greatly from what it had been before 1895.

Canadien representation in city government expanded under Republican auspices, at least until 1904. They had supported Democratic candidates in the early 1890s when the party had nominated a number of their group for local offices. The Republican party captured much of the French vote after 1893 with offers of recognition and patronage. In 1894 and 1895 the GOP nominated Hercule Beauparland for state representative and other French Canadians for city council in three wards. Although all but one lost, the pattern that would prevail over the next decade was established.[26] Between 1896 and 1905 Republican *Canadien* candidates for municipal and state house offices far outnumbered Democrats and all *Canadiens* elected to such positions were Republicans (see tables 5.15 and 5.16).[27]

The Republican party courted the French vote in Fall River by giving them a free hand in Ward Six, where they constituted a majority of the voters. French Canadian Republicans from Wards Two and Nine were elected occasionally to the city council, but they dominated Ward Six. In 1897 only one of the four council positions from that ward was held

Table 5.14

French Canadians in appointive positions in city government, Fall River, 1895-1915

Position	1	2	3	4	5	6	7	8	9	10	11	12
1895	X	X				X						X
1896	X					X						X
1897	X	X				X						X
1898	X	X				X	X					X
1899	X	X				X	X					X
1900	X	X				X	X	X	X			X
1901	X	X				X		X	X			X
1902	X	X				X		X	X			X
1903	X	X	X			X	X	X				X
1904	X	X	X			X	X	X				X
1905	X	X	X			X		X				X
1906	X	X	X			X		X				X
1907	X	X	X	X		X		X				X
1908	X	2	X	X		X		X				X
1909	X	2	X	X		X		X				X
1910	X	X	X	X	X	X				X		X
1911	X	X	X	X	X	X						X
1912	X	X	X	X	X	X						X
1913	X	X	X	X	X	X				X	X	X
1914	X	X	X	X	X	X				X	X	X
1915	X	X	X	X	X	X				X	X	X

Source: Fall River *City Directory*, 1895-1916.

Position code: 1- registar of voters; 2- board of health; 3- assessors; 4- park commission; 5- water commission; 6- inspector of animals; 7- inspector of milk; 8- inspector of petroleum; 9- city solicitor; 10- school superintendant; 11- mayor's secretary; 12- city physician.

Table 5.15

Party affiliation of French Canadian
candidates, Fall River, 1891-1915

| | City council and school committee | | | | State representative and senator | | | |
	Total	R	D	O	Total	R	D	O
1891-1895	11	7	4	0	2	2	0	0
1896-1900	29	25	2	2	6	4	2	0
1901-1905	23	17	4	2	6	5	0	1
1906-1910	12	7	5	0	7	6	1	0
1911-1915	24	9	13	2	11	5	6	0
Total	99	65	28	6	32	22	9	1

Sources: Fall River Daily Globe, 1891-1915; Massachusetts, Public Document No. 43, 1895-1915.

by a *Canadien;* five years later they occupied all Ward Six seats. During this period nearly all French Canadian candidates for municipal offices were Republicans; a few ran as independents, but none as Democrats. French Canadian control of Ward Six persisted until at least 1915; all council members elected from that ward up to 1915 were *Canadien* Republicans.[28] In addition, no French Canadian candidate for one of three state representative seats elected each year in the Eleventh Bristol County District, which included Ward Six, lost an election during the twenty years after 1895. Only in five of these elections did the GOP fail to nominate a *Canadien;* only in those years did no French Canadian from the district sit in the lower house of the general court.[29]

In exchange for such ample Republican recognition, *Canadiens* strongly supported the GOP at the polls until 1902. The mean Democratic vote in Ward Six was 51 percent in gubernatorial and mayoral elections between 1889 and 1893 but fell sharply over the next nine years. In the more strongly French Precinct Six-A, the decline was even more pronounced, the mean vote for governor dropping to less than 20 percent and that for mayor to about 25 percent (see table 5.17).[30]

French Canadian voters contributed significantly to keeping Republican mayors in office in Fall River between 1896 and 1902 (see table 5.18).[31] In 1899, for example, French Canadian leaders such as Ward Six alderman Edmund Cote and state Rep. Hugo Dubuque backed Republican candidate John H. Abbott, who won citywide by 318 votes.[32] Democrats, who had expected a Republican majority of about 450 in Ward Six, were stunned by the accuracy of Cote's prediction that his ward would favor Abbott by 500 or more votes. According to Cote, French Canadian voters, who solidly backed Abbott, were responsible for Abbott's victory. Cote estimated that 95 percent of the 2,100 French who voted favored Abbott, and that without the French votes from Wards One, Two, and Five the Republican candidate would have lost. According to the *Fall River Daily Globe*, French Canadian leaders had reached an understanding with Abbott, who promised that they would receive the same or equivalent positions in city hall that they then occupied and that individuals recommended by *Canadien* leaders would be appointed.[33]

The Franco-Republican alliance, apparently solid between 1897 and 1899, began to weaken as early as 1900. As French Canadian political ambitions waxed, Republican willingness to accommodate their demands waned. Relations between the two soured. Alderman Cote quarrelled with Republican mayors in 1899 and 1900. Cote claimed credit for their election, a claim they could not deny. But when he demanded more patronage for his group and improvements for his ward, they balked. In the fall of 1900 the Democratic city convention offered Cote, who already had announced an independent candidacy, the mayoral nomination, hoping to exploit the rift between the *Canadiens* and their

Table 5.16

Party affiliation of French Canadian
officeholders, Fall River,
1891-1915

	City council and school committee			State representative		
	Total	R	D	Total	R	D
1891-1895	1	1	0	0	0	0
1896-1900	16	16	0	2	2	0
1901-1905	23	23	0	5	5	0
1906-1910	17	14	3	4	4	0
1911-1915	28	15	13	6	5	1
Total	85	69	16	17	16	1

Sources: Fall River Daily Globe, 1891-1915; Massachusetts, Public Document No. 43, 1895-1915.

Note: The number of French Canadian officeholders given is the number of offices held by French Canadians each year. Because some officials were elected for two- or three-year terms, these data are not strictly comparable to those concerning French Canadian candidates found in table 5.15.

Table 5.17

Mean percentage Democratic vote in
gubernatorial and mayoral
elections in Ward Six,
Fall River, 1889-1916

	#	Ward Six	Precinct Six-A	Precinct Six-B
Gubernatorial				
1889-1893	5	50.8	46.8	54.3
1894-1902	9	24.2	18.9	29.3
1903-1911	9	47.1	42.4	52.6
1912-1916	5	35.8	29.3	45.4
Mayoral[a]				
1889-1893	5	50.8	50.5	51.0
1894-1902	9	29.5	25.3	33.6
1904-1910	4	49.5	46.5	53.0
1912-1916	3	32.7	26.7	41.1

Source: <u>Fall River Daily Globe</u>, 1889-1916.

[a]Mayoral elections were biennial starting in 1902.

benefactors. Cote accepted, and later withdrew from the contest as the furious resistance to his candidacy from Irish Democrats and French Republicans proved insurmountable. Meeting again, the Democrats nominated James Holland in his stead. Cote and other French leaders such as Dubuque campaigned for incumbent Mayor Abbott. Their efforts, however, bore less fruit than in past contests.[34] A number of French voters bolted to Holland. Although Holland lost the election by 750 votes, the Republican majority in Ward Six was cut from an average of 450 (1897–99) to only 279.[35]

Relations between the *Canadiens* and the GOP worsened after 1900, in part because Republican rank and file voters undermined French candidates at the polls. They provided only half-hearted support for Hugo Dubuque's unsuccessful state senatorial candidacy in 1898.[36] In 1901, when Republicans chose Pierre F. Peloquin for state representative, they nominated James Buron, a one-term *Canadien* councillor, for a school committee seat. Buron, however, ran last in a four-way race for three seats, as Republican voters cut him out in favor of an independent woman's candidacy. Anger fulminated among French Canadian voters who have been "given to understand that if Mr. Buron accepted the

Republican nomination that he would be supported. Instead he was slashed right and left. . . ."[37] Wards Seven and Eight, the same wards that had "knifed" Dubuque three years earlier, cut Buron mercilessly. "It was," observed the Globe's editors, "like patting Mr. Buron on the back with one hand and reaching around with the other for a swing on his jaw."[38]

Dissatisfaction with the GOP had become manifest in Wards One and Nine earlier, in 1901, when Canadiens supported independent candidates for common council seats against Republican nominees. Discontent spread in 1902 as Republicans tried to contain and reduce French Canadian political influence in Fall River.[39] By 1902 French Canadians had secured all city council seats in Ward Six as well as a council seat in Ward Two. A new city charter, passed in 1902, threatened to reduce French influence in municipal affairs just as they had come into power. Under the old charter each ward elected an alderman and three common councillors. The new charter eliminated the common council entirely and provided for twenty-seven aldermen—nine elected by city-wide vote for two-year terms and two ward aldermen for each ward,

Table 5.18

Electoral majorities[a] in
mayoral elections
in Fall River, and in
Ward Six, 1896-1916

	City		Ward Six	
	R	D	R	D
1896	3121		665	
1897	561		438	
1898	66		402	
1899	318		512	
1900	751		279	
1901	5053		898	
1902	849		298	
1904		757	123	
1906		1009		73
1908		1340		32
1910		101	20	
1912	1820		597	
1914	3917		826	
1916	3411		265	

Source: Fall River Daily Globe, 1896-1916.

[a]Difference between Republicans and Democratic vote.

elected by each ward. With its passage, French Candians lost the aldermanic position in Ward Six that was assured them under the old
system.[40] The reform act received the support of the majority of the
city's voters. Republican precincts, excluding those with many French-
speaking voters, supported the measure more strongly than Democratic
precincts; not surprisingly, French Canadian precincts showed the least
enthusiasm for the new charter.[41]

Any suspicions the French Canadians may have harbored that their
role in city government was being curtailed were confirmed in the
municipal elections of 1902 and 1903. In the fall of 1902 Republicans
failed to renominate Frederic Gagnon, the three-term incumbent Republican common councillor from Ward Two. Gagnon nevertheless ran
as an independent against the GOP choice, and won by ninety-seven
votes.[42] The following year Republicans did nominate Gagnon. He won
again, but his lead was limited to ninety-two votes, leading him to
charge that some members of the Republican city committee had
worked for and provided campaign funds for the independent candidate opposing him.[43] The same year, Republicans, working under the
direction of Republican mayor George Grime, allegedly thwarted John
B. Nadeau's renomination for common council in Ward Nine.[44]

French Canadian discontent with the Republican party, having
brewed since 1900, came to a head in 1904, enabling the Democrats to
seize the mayoralty. Ward Six *Canadien* Republicans acridly disputed
among themselves whom they should back for the Republican mayoral
nomination. Some French leaders held the incumbent mayor Grime
responsible for Gagnon's troubles and Nadeau's demise.[45] In the end
Grime won the nomination of his party but could not redeem his
chair.[46] About two hundred Ward Six voters abstained from the mayoral
contest. Despite these defections, Grime carried the ward, but by a
much-trimmed majority.[47] While gratified that they had at least carried
Ward Six, Republican campaign managers admitted "they could do
nothing with the French voters in Wards One and Two," who spitefully
cast their ballots for John T. Coughlin, the Irish Democrat. Grime himself conceded that his defeat resulted from his "failure to keep the
French-American voters in line."[48]

For the next eight years Democrats kept the mayor's office with the
help of French Canadian voters. Ward Six twice returned majorities for
Coughlin, suggesting that the Democrats made significant inroads
among French voters.[49] However slim, Democratic majorities, or even a
close vote, amounted to victory in that ward where Republicans had
taken 70 percent or better of the vote during the formative years of the
Franco-Republican alliance. The mean Democratic vote in the four
elections between 1904 and 1910 rose to nearly 50 percent, practically

Table 5.19

Mean percentage Democratic vote in
gubernatorial and mayoral
elections in selected
French Canadian precincts,
Fall River, 1894-1916

	#	1-B	2-A	3-A	9-B
Gubernatorial					
1894-1902	9	33.5	27.8	64.7	30.8
1903-1911	9	63.0	41.5	68.2	39.0
1912-1916	5	47.6	37.9	63.1	33.2
Mayoral					
1894-1902	9	40.7	33.1	61.0	34.8
1904-1910	4	66.4	44.9	64.0	44.2
1912-1916	3	47.6	25.7	53.7	31.1

Source: Fall River Daily Globe, 1894-1916.

Note: In 1909 French Canadians formed 31 percent of the
potential voters in One-B; 29 percent in Two-A; 32 percent in
Three-A; and 32 percent in Nine-B.

twice as high as it had been during the nine previous races.[50] In 1908
French Canadians in Ward six reportedly were almost solid for
Coughlin.[51] Two years later Republicans blamed bolting French voters
in Wards One and Six for their loss.[52] The Democrats gained as well in
other precincts where Canadiens were a political force. Democratic
averages increased by 10 to 25 percentage points in three precincts—
One-B, Two-A, and Nine-B, which before 1900 had been quite strongly
Republican (see table 5.19).[53]

Officeholding as well as voting patterns denote a Democratic countertrend among French Canadians between 1902 and 1910. Democrats
abetted the strife between Canadiens and the GOP by competing more
vigorously for the French vote than they had from 1894 to 1901. They
had nominated no French Canadians for office between 1897 and 1901.
From 1906 to 1910, however, Democrats nearly matched the number of
Republican candidates for local office, and surpassed them, thirteen to
nine, over the next five years.[54] Consequently, French Canadian Democrats filled sixteen public offices between 1906 and 1915, whereas they
ahd filled none during the previous fifteen years.[55] Mayor Coughlin, for
his part, reappointed prominent Canadien Republicans to office or

filled their offices with other *Canadiens*, and gave the French Canadians positions on the park and water commissions.[56]

Democratic largesse enabled *Canadiens* to sidestep the potentially calamitous portents of the charter revision. Ward Six routinely returned French Republican aldermen to city hall after 1902, and the Republican party usually slotted a *Canadien* for alderman-at-large. Thus, French Canadians were assured at least two, and possibly three, positions on the city council. Starting in 1902 Democrats regularly ran a French Canadian for alderman-at-large as well, often in those years when no French Republicans were also running. Most *Canadien* candidates on the Democratic ticket lost, with the exception of Charles Lavoie. Lavoie, who coordinated his campaign with that of other Democrats, was elected to three two-year terms. Added to his Republican counterparts, Lavoie's seat gave the French Canadians plenty of voices around the council table.[57]

Although the Democratic vote in French Canadian precincts sagged in mayoral elections after 1910, the rapprochement between Irish Democrats and French Canadians was not defunct. Cooperation continued as the two groups united to seize control of the school committee, from which Catholics had long been excluded.[58] No French Canadian or Catholic had served on the school committee since the end of Pierre F. Peloquin's term in 1903. Although the Democratic ticket had included a *Canadien* for that board in 1908, he and other Democratic nominees suffered defeat as usual.[59] Three years later, however, Irish and French Canadian priests criticized the school committee, charging anti-Catholic prejudice. Until then, no Catholics had been appointed to the faculty of the city's high school. A new plan, requiring graduates of Catholic but not public grammar schools to undergo a qualifying examination before admission to the high school, especially irked the Catholic clergy. Determined to end the Protestant monopoly, Catholic voters joined forces in 1911. Their concerted action brought three Democrats—an Irishman and two *Canadiens*, including Rev. Jean Prevost—onto the school committee in 1912.[60] The following December, their numbers fortified by a legion of Catholic women voters, who were allowed to vote for school committee, Catholics once again prevailed, electing this time two Irishmen and a French Canadian to the nine-member board.[61] Constituting a majority on the school committee, the Catholics appointed a French Canadian as superintendent of schools and swiftly changed the complexion of the high school faculty.[62]

Cooperation between the Irish and French Canadians remained limited to the school issue, delaying for another decade the political ascendancy of the Catholic majority in Fall River. Unhappy with their treatment by Democratic Mayor Thomas Higgins, who succeeded

Coughlin in 1911 with the help of *Canadien* voters, French Canadians shifted their support to Republican mayoral candidate James Kay, as did some Irish voters. Kay, a popular mayor, easily overcame the challenge of a French Canadian Democrat, Edmond Talbot, to unseat him in 1916. Talbot lost badly, receiving the strong support he needed to win from neither Irish nor French Canadian voters.[63]

Compared with Holyoke, the French Canadians of Fall River appear more strongly Republican between 1896 and 1916. Ward Six, unlike Ward Two of Holyoke, returned Republican majorities in all presidential elections, and in nearly all gubernatorial and mayoral contests during that period. Ward Six, moreover, consistently elected French Canadian Republican representatives to city hall and to the state house in Boston. Within Ward Six the Republican-leaning electoral pattern was more pronounced in Precinct A, the more strongly French area. Voting patterns in Precincts Two-A and Nine-B, Republican precincts where *Canadiens* comprised 30 percent of the voters, essentially paralleled those of Ward Six, with Democratic candidates rarely receiving a majority.

Closer investigation, however, reveals that the Franco-Republican alliance in Fall River was actually less stable than these statistics suggest. No doubt many French Canadians were drawn into the Republican party after 1893 and many remained Republican-oriented until 1916. Just as conservative in economic matters as the Irish Democrats, with whom they aligned themselves in the early 1890s, the *Canadiens* disliked the free-silver doctrine that Democratic party leaders in Massachusetts espoused until 1900. However, unlike the Irish who controlled the party's political machinery and had far more to lose by bolting, the French Canadians had little to lose by abandoning that party after 1895. Guided by practical politicians like Edmund Cote, most *Canadien* voters favored GOP candidates in state and local elections from 1894 to 1902. In return, they received recognition and influence in municipal government and by 1900 had become an integral part of the Republican party machine.

Republican leaders soon sought to contain the political ambitions they had kindled among the *Canadiens*. Despite the leeway accorded them in Ward Six, French Canadians quarreled with their patrons. First in the outlying Wards One and Two and later in Ward Six, the solidly Republican French vote softened. After 1902, as the Democratic party began again to compete for *Canadien* support, French Canadian Democratic candidates and officeholders multiplied; French voters contributed to the mayoral victories of Irish Democrats and the Democratic vote in gubernatorial elections crept upwards in French precincts. Having first won substantial access to public office while aligned with the

GOP, the *Canadiens* maintained and increased their influence in local affairs in coalition with the Democrats. However, they never wholly severed the powerful Republican connection that provided them an important political base in Ward Six. Viewed from this perspective, the political patterns of French Canadians in Fall River appear to have been governed by a shrewd political pragmatism and little motivated by a bellicose anti-Irish grudge. While leaning more heavily on the Republican party as a source of political offices and often voting for GOP candidates, French Canadians in the Spindle City exhibited faint reluctance when political self-interest dictated cooperation with the local Irish Democrats.

Worcester: "Our People Have Nothing"

As in other large cities, political life in Worcester after 1890 centered on the conflict between two main antagonists—native-born American Republicans versus Irish Democrats—with other groups playing suporting but nonetheless crucial roles. Republicans easily controlled the city council and school committee, usually outnumbering Democrats by a two-to-one margin on both bodies. The GOP assured its dominion of the legislative branch by gerrymandering the bulk of Worcester's immigrant and Catholic inhabitants, who lived on the east side of the city, into three wards in which the Irish, more established if not more numerous, dominated politics.[64]

Although Republicans also sat in the mayor's chair in all but six years between 1886 and 1915, the party's control of that office was precarious.[65] To keep the mayoralty the GOP had to rely on both Swedish and French Canadian voters, in whose hands lay the balance of power by the 1890s. Disaffection among these two groups gave the Democrats an opportunity for victory. If united behind a popular candidate and duly attentive to the political sensitivities of the Swedes and *Canadiens*, the Democrats could win. Thus wedged between the leading contenders, French Canadians and Swedes, each comprising about 10 percent of the population, assumed a pivotal role in Worcester politics.

Most French Canadian voters probably had affiliated themselves with the Democratic party in Worcester before 1896, although the GOP had acquired a substantial following in Ward Three. Democrats had gained the favor of French voters largely because they had given the group the chance to gain representation in city government. Between 1887 and 1895 *Canadien* Democratic candidates for local office outnumbered Republicans eleven to four, and until 1896 all French Canadians on the city council were Democrats (see table 5.20).[66]

The election of a French Canadian Republican to the board of al-

Table 5.20

Party affiliation of French Canadian
candidates for city council and
school committee, Worcester,
1887-1912

	Candidates			Winning Candidates		
	R	D	Total	R	D	Total
1887	1	1	2	0	1	1
1888	1	0	1	0	0	0
1889	1	1	2	0	1	1
1890	0	1	1	0	0	0
1891	0	1	1	0	0	0
1892	0	0	0	0	0	0
1893	0	3	3	0	2	2
1894	1	1	2	0	0	0
1895	0	3	3	0	1	1
1896	3	3	6	1	1	2
1897	3	1	4	1	0	1
1898	3	0	3	2	0	2
1899	2	0	2	1	0	1
1900	2	1	3	1	0	1
1901	2	1	3	1	0	1
1902	3	1	4	0	1	1
1903	0	1	1	0	1	1
1904	0	1	1	0	0	0
1905	2	3	5	0	0	0
1906	4	0	4	0	0	0
1907	5	2	7	1	1	2
1908	4	0	4	1	0	1
1909	5	0	5	1	0	1
1910	2	1	3	0	0	0
1911	5	1	6	1	1	2
1912	5	1	6	0	0	0
Total	54	28	82	11	10	21

Source: _Worcester Evening Gazette_, 1887-1912.

dermen in 1896 marked the beginning of a new era. Intense competition for *Canadien* support characterized the next twenty years. Neither party proved entirely successful. As in Fall River, Republicans gained the upper hand at first but could not prevent the Democrats from enticing *Canadien* voters back to their ranks after 1902. Although many French Canadians remained identified with the GOP until 1915, officeholding and voting patterns indicate that the relationship was brittle and often cracked.

By 1895 French Canadian demands for additional recognition had soured relations with the Irish Democrats. Although *Canadiens* made up about 15 percent of the voters in Ward Three, Irish politicians refused to back John F. Jandron, a French Canadian Democrat, for one of three common council seats in that ward. Running as an independent Democrat, he swung French Republicans to his cause in 1893 and won. Two years later, although he and many *Canadien* voters supported the Democratic-Citizens' candidate for mayor, Jandron's bid for reelection was rejected, and the seeds of disaffection were sown.[67]

The Republican party, stung by the loss of the head of its ticket in 1895, perceived in Jandron's squabble with Ward Three Democrats the opportunity to recruit disgruntled *Canadiens* and regain the mayoralty. In 1896 the GOP therefore nominated Napoleon P. Huot, a Ward Three grocer long associated with the party, for the board of aldermen, hoping, as the *Worcester Evening Gazette* put it, "that this recognition will be appreciated by a return of Winslow Republican votes" in the mayoral contest.[68] Huot won. With the help of Republican voters, he became the first *Canadien* to serve on the alderman board. Republicans also nominated two additional French Canadians for common council seats in 1896, one of whom won, giving the French Canadians three seats on the city council the following year—two Republicans and one Democrat.[69]

A sustained effort by the GOP over the next few years welded much of the French vote to the Republican bloc. Between 1896 and 1901, French Canadian Republican candidates for municipal offices outnumbered Democrats fifteen to six. As a result, all French Canadians serving on the city council from 1898 to 1902 were Republicans. Each year a *Canadien* Republican sat on the board of aldermen.[70] Additionally, Republican mayor Rufus Dodge appointed C. Herbert DeFosse as sealer of weights and measures,[71] and W. Levi Bousquet gained admission to the city's Republican club, serving on its finance committee in 1900.[72] Predictably, Mayor Dodge received the full support of French Canadians in 1898 and 1899, and was elected both years.[73]

The Franco-Republican alliance reached its peak in the municipal election of 1900. That year the Republicans nominated two *Canadiens* for the board of aldermen—W. Levi Bousquet and John Rivard.[74] Because only six of the eight Republican nominees were expected to win and it was unlikely that both *Canadiens* would receive full rank and file backing, the French Canadians were forced to choose between the two candidates. They rallied around Bousquet, three-time president of the Ward Four and Five Naturalization Club and head of the advertising department of *L'Opinion Publique,* Worcester's French-language newspaper.[75] Following the lead of French Canadian community leaders, who viewed Rivard as the candidate of Ward Five Republicans "rather than as the candidate of the French people," the Republican city committee endorsed Bousquet as the preferred "choice of the French people as a class," and urged *Canadiens* to vote for him alone.[76] Bousquet, who had succeeded Huot as alderman in 1899, won. Rivard received less than half of the average vote given to other Republican aldermanic candidates and was the only GOP nominee for that position defeated in the election.[77] According to J. Arthur Favreau, editor of *L'Opinion Publique*, 75 percent of the city's *Canadien* voters had backed the Republican William A. Lytle over Irish Democrat Philip O'Connell in the mayoral contest.[78]

Bousquet's success in the municipal contest, and his election as president of the board of aldermen in 1901, symbolized the bond that had developed between French Canadians and the GOP by 1900. Underlying the relationship were two factors. First and foremost, because the Democrats had nominated no French Canadians for city council since 1897, the *Canadiens* had become dependent on the Republican party for representation in city government. Second, intense ethnic consciousness had been generated over a religious controversy between French Canadians in North Brookfield, a few miles west of Worcester, and Bishop Thomas Beaven, Irish head of the diocese of Springfield, which included Worcester County.

The North Brookfield incident, involving the formation of a French-language parish, had simmered in the late summer but came to a boil in October.[79] By then the French Canadian community of Worcester had become involved. Anti-Irish feeling abounded in St. Jean Baptiste hall where five hundred French Canadians gathered to hear their leaders expound their grievances and state the case for separate French-speaking parishes. One speaker, Dr. Felix Fontaine of Worcester, called upon them to

> . . . defend our rights and particularly, to obtain justly our due from the clerical authorities in this country. We have been oppressed and brow-beaten by bishops of other nationalities until it is impossible to bear it longer. Justice for the French-speaking Catholics is an un-heard-of-thing.[80]

Rev. Jean Berger, pastor of North Brookfield's rebellious French Canadian congregation and a principal figure in the dispute, put the issue more simply still:

> The whole question may be summed up in the following phrase: The Irish church for the Irish, the French church for the French. . . . It is a question of the French-speaking people and the Irish clergy.[81]

Such rhetoric no doubt helped to galvanize support among French Canadians for Bousquet's candidacy but probably did not help Democrat Philip O'Connell's bid for mayor in the municipal election held six weeks later.

No one, save perhaps himself, suspected young O'Connell of having any chance of becoming mayor of stolidly Republican Worcester. Only thirty years old, he was a political novice unknown outside of his party. "If the miracle happens, Phil will render good service," read the headline of the *Worcester Evening Post*, the city's traditionally Democratic news-sheet the day after his nomination. In its view, the Democrats had "nominated a dummy ticket, thus conceding in advance the election of the Republican candidate."[82] Despite the fact that O'Connell was the first Irish Catholic to run for mayor since 1887, the campaign generated little enthusiasm. Leaving him to plot his own course, the Democratic city committee sponsored none of the usual campaign rallies on his behalf. The day before the election the *Post* reported that "there is more interest centered in the tail of the ticket than in its head," and went on to explain the referenda issues before the voters without as much as mentioning O'Connell's name, never mind endorsing him.[83]

O'Connell won. So it seemed the morning after election day. Would-be Republican mayor-elect William Lytle went to bed on election night comforted by his forty-one vote victory. But by lunch time the next day, the discovery of an error in the tabulations had given O'Connell a nineteen-vote plurality. The ensuing tangle was the worst in Worcester's history. A recount, completed a week later, revealed a dead heat: 8,061 votes each for O'Connell and Lytle.[84] O'Connell sued the registrars of voters, claiming that three of his votes had been improperly disqualified. Once the state supreme court ruled against him, preparation for a February rematch began in earnest. Nearly a thousand new names were added to the voting lists during the brief but spirited campaign preceding the new election.[85]

The special election made Republicans glum and Democrats gleeful. Philip O'Connell became Worcester's first Irish Catholic mayor by 511 votes.[86] Irish Democrats, who turned out in record numbers, and 1,800 Republicans and ethnic voters had sidelined William Lytle.[87] French Canadians, Swedes, and Armenians split their vote, contributing to his defeat.[88] O'Connell, acknowledging his debt to Republican and ethnic voters, promised an administration dedicated to the interest of all the people and tried to alienate no group.[89] This policy soon put him at odds with regular Democrats, who believed that the spoils of office rightfully belonged to them. Within a month of being elected, O'Connell found himself embroiled in an acrid wrangle with the Democratic city committee over his appointments to the liquor commission.[90] The rift between the mayor and the Democrats had not been patched over before the municipal election in December 1901. A poor showing among Democratic voters defeated his bid for re-election.[91]

The defection of some French Canadian voters, mostly in Ward Five,

Table 5.21

French Canadian candidates for local offices[a]
by ward, Worcester, 1887-1912

	1887-1895		1896-1902		1903-1912	
	R	D	R	D	R	D
Alderman at large	0	0	7	2	3	3
Ward 3	4	2	5	0	12	0
Ward 4	0	0	2	0	6	0
Ward 5	0	4	3	3	9	2
Other wards	0	5	0	2	2	5
Total	4	11	17	7	32	10
Elected	0	5	7	2	4	3

Source: Worcester Evening Gazette, 1887-1912.

[a]Including alderman at large, alderman, councillor, and
school committee.

to O'Connell in the special election foreshadowed a serious falling out
between the *Canadiens* and the GOP between 1902 and 1906. While the
Republican leadership had given French Canadians an opportunity to
participate in city government between 1896 and 1901, the relationship
remained shallow. Republican rank and file voters consistently under-
cut *Canadien* Republican alderman candidates.[92] The GOP nominated
numerous *Canadiens* for seats on the common council and school
committee, but always in Irish-dominated wards where they were certain to lose rather than in safe Republican wards (see table 5.21).[93]
Consequently, the *Canadiens* usually had but a single seat on the city
council—an alderman-at-large—and none on the school committee.[94]
Only one French Canadian, moreover, had received a patronage plum
within the government.[95] In 1902 Republican voters changed the
charter, abandoning the selection of alderman by citywide vote that had
enabled French Canadians to be represented on that board, and providing for a return to ward-elected aldermen.[96] Because French-speaking
voters were dispersed throughout Worcester, they dominated no ward;
the new charter thus threatened to divest them of the only voice they
had on the city council (see table 5.22). As in Fall River, French Canadians in Worcester justifiably could suspect that the GOP had turned out
to be a somewhat less than magnanimous ally.

Meanwhile, Philip O'Connell's success had revitalized the Democratic party in Worcester by demonstrating that it could win. The

Table 5.22

Distribution of French Canadian voters in
Worcester by wards and selected
precincts, 1896-1906

Number	1896	1898	1900	1903	1906
Ward 1	48	70	90	94	78
Ward 2	81	113	102	141	125
Ward 3	329	345	445	555	412
Ward 4	197	248	281	335	183
Ward 5	297	316	426	512	395
Ward 6	221	224	254	345	122
Ward 7	126	138	146	144	183
Ward 8	108	98	101	86	149
Ward 9	--	--	--	--	204
Ward 10	--	--	--	--	94
Total	1407	1552	1845	2212	1945

Percent of the registered voters
who are French Canadians

	1896	1898	1900	1903	1906
Ward 1	2.2	3.5	3.8	3.6	3.3
Ward 2	3.4	4.7	3.6	4.7	7.2
Ward 3	14.9	16.9	19.1	21.0	27.1
Ward 4	8.3	10.2	10.2	10.9	10.8
Ward 5	12.9	13.4	15.6	17.3	23.4
Ward 6	9.3	9.2	9.0	11.1	6.5
Ward 7	5.2	6.1	5.3	4.9	10.9
Ward 8	4.8	4.4	4.2	3.5	8.8
Ward 9	-	-	-	-	12.7
Ward 10	-	-	-	-	5.6
Total	7.6	8.6	8.8	9.7	11.5
Precinct					
3-1	8.9	9.2	12.4	13.3	-
3-2	10.5	12.0	12.5	12.3	-
3-3	23.9	17.8	20.6	20.6	-
3-4	-	28.0	35.9	49.2	-
5-1	16.6	23.2	27.3	28.3	-
5-2	18.4	16.1	14.0	13.6	-
5-3	3.8	7.4	13.4	14.9	-
5-4	-	4.6	1.9	3.1	-

Sources: Le Worcester Canadien, 1896-1907; Massachusetts,
Public Document No. 43, 1896, 1898, 1900, 1902, 1906.

apparently solid Republican chain had at least a few weak links; with some effort the bond between the French Canadians and the GOP could be sundered. Early in 1902 O'Connell pointed the way. He astutely reappointed C. Herbert De Fosse as sealer of weights and measures, contrary to expectations, since De Fosse, a prominent Republican, had campaigned strongly against him.[97] The following year, as he tried to regain his old office, O'Connell was rumored to have offered now former alderman Bousquet a place on the liquor commission if he would help the ex-mayor to win.[98] The Democratic city committee continued O'Connell's initiatives towards the French Canadians, nominating six *Canadiens* for city council and school committee slots over the next several years.[99]

These efforts, coupled with the GOP's poor record of meaningful accommodation, brought French voters back to the Democratic fold. Louis A. Belisle was one of the usual three Democratic alderman candidates who won in 1902; John F. Jandron, one-time Democrat turned Republican, was turned out of office in the same election, badly mauled by French voters. According to the *Gazette,* Jandron's defeat signified that the "French vote throughout the city was with the Democracy."[100] In the mayoral contest nearly three hundred Ward Three *Canadiens* followed W. Levi Bousquet into the Democratic camp and voted for Philip O'Connell. Republican nominee Edward F. Fletcher was re-elected only because he received enough Irish Democratic votes to offset the defection of the French vote.[101] Voting patterns for French Canadian precincts suggest that *Canadiens* continued to vote for Democratic mayoral candidates David F. O'Connell and John T. Duggan during the next four years. With their support Duggan captured the office for the Democracy in 1905 and again in 1906.[102]

Distressed by the loss of the head of its ticket in two consecutive elections, the GOP in 1907 aimed to get the French vote back. The charter of 1902 had created a new position on the city council—alderman-at-large—elected by citywide vote as was the mayor. One cause of the falling out between the *Canadiens* and the GOP had been its failure to nominate Arthur B. Brunell, the *Canadien* choice, for that position in 1904.[103] The centerpiece of the 1907 strategy was, therefore, to make Brunell the Republican candidate for alderman-at-large while continuing to run *Canadiens* for other offices.[104] At the same time, many more French Canadians were brought into the party organization.[105] Predictably, *Canadiens* rallied to Brunell's side and Republican James Logan was swept into the mayor's office with their help.[106]

The strategy worked for three years but contained two fatal flaws. First, rank and file Republicans never gave Brunell the vote they accorded Logan, and they embittered Brunell by voting for an independent candidate against him in 1909.[107] Second, Brunell, an independent-minded and ambitious fellow, aimed to succeed Logan as mayor, much to the disenchantment of most Republicans. His ambition had become apparent by the municipal election of 1909.[108] By September of the next year he had already announced his candidacy for mayor against his three-year campaign companion.[109] Early in November Brunell launched a noisy and bitter battle for the Republican nomination. Speaking at enthusiastic outdoor rallies of French Canadians, he impetuously denounced Logan, charging him with corruption and "bossism," and did not forbear in unusually personal verbal assaults.[110] By the end of the month the war of words was over. Republican primary voters soundly repudiated the renegade *Canadien*, who received only 3,100 of more than ten thousand votes.[111] The shouting ended, that is, among all but the French Canadians.

The Democratic party prepared itself well for the inevitable outcome of Brunell's challenge. In November it had backed J. B. N. Soulliere's bid for sheriff and nominated Camille S. Trahan, a respected French Canadian businessman and long-time Democrat, for alderman-at-large, Brunell's old position.[112] Inflamed by Brunell's unceremonious dumping, French Canadian voters, among them many long-time Republican party activists, deserted the GOP in droves, promising to vote for the Democratic ticket.[113] Trahan, campaigning hand in hand with David F. O'Connell, the mayoral nominee, appealed pointedly to their severely bruised pride:

> Our city is composed of different elements or nationalities, resulting into groups, and each party is entitled to political rights. Each element should have some representation in the city government. The French population of Worcester is one-sixth and our people have nothing, no representation in the city government. Mayor Logan has treated the French population of Worcester shamefully. A man, Mr. Brunell, who could not be bossed by Logan, was turned out by the mayor. After the service Brunell had rendered to the Republican party, it was the duty of Mr. Logan to do something for us. Mr. Brunell had been disowned by the party, for which he labored so hard. But our time has come, Logan. We have joined hands with the Democratic party and on Tuesday next you will be displaced by Mr. O'Connell as mayor of Worcester, and French votes will help to do it.[114]

Election day substantiated only half of Trahan's prediction. French Canadians voted as a bloc for O'Connell and Trahan, but both lost.[115] The next year the Democrats persisted in their strategy: O'Connell teamed up with J. B. N. Soulliere. The French Canadian-Irish Democrat phalanx held firm, flanked by cadres of Swedish voters from Wards Two and Six. Both O'Connell and Soulliere won by substantial pluralities.[116]

However, David F. O'Connell's tenure in office was limited, like that of his predecessor Philip O'Connell a decade earlier, to a single year. O'Connell soon bickered with Camille Trahan, newly appointed liquor commissioner, over the distribution of licenses. Trahan resigned. The French Canadians railed that their confidence had been abused once again.[117] Soulliere was renominated the following December as was O'Connell, who again promised the *Canadiens* a seat on the liquor commission. But *Canadien* voters bolted. So did the Swedes. George Wright, a popular Republican, triumphed in 1912 and held the Republican coalition together for at least three years.[118]

As in Fall River and Holyoke, the French Canadians in Worcester remained strongly associated with neither political party from 1896 to 1915. Many *Canadien* leaders may have leaned more towards the GOP but both parties vied for and received at times the support of French voters. Given the political ambitions of the French Canadians and the limited resources of either party, however, alliances often had short, unstable lives. In electoral contests many *Canadien* voters remained independent, swinging from party to party as political currents changed. During the last five years of the nineteenth century, most French Canadian voters in Fall River and Worcester, and in other Bay State cities, strongly favored Republicans at the polling booth, encouraged partly by the willingness of the party to share some of the spoils of office. Seriously weakened by factional strife, the Democratic party had little to offer the *Canadiens* before 1900. When Bryanites lost their grip on the party, however, Democratic fortunes improved. During the first decade of the twentieth century the party gained French Canadian support in both local and state contests. Tension and suspicion between the French Canadians and the Irish no doubt existed, as the memories of religious controversies smoldered still and could be inflamed. Nevertheless, *Canadien* electoral behavior appears not to have been motivated primarily by anti-Irish feeling, powerful as such feeling may have been. Rather, political pragmatism led the French Canadians to vote for such Irish politicians as John T. Coughlin in Fall River and David F. O'Connell in Worcester. More often than not, practical political considerations proved more salient than the legacy of ill will in determining French Canadian political choices.

6

Franco-Democrats and Partisan Politics: A Two-Town Case Study, 1896–1915

French Canadians in the manufacturing towns of central Massachusetts followed a course in politics similar to that in the cities except in one important respect. As in the cities they mobilized to secure greater influence in local government after 1895 and aligned themselves with political parties with an eye to the accommodation of their demands for recognition. In most towns, however, the *Canadiens* maintained closer ties with the Democratic party from 1895 to 1915 despite some Republican inroads after 1900. Case studies of two towns—Spencer and Southbridge—during these two decades provide evidence to support this hypothesis.

Officeholding and Voting Patterns in Towns

French Canadian influence in town government, measured in terms of officeholding, expanded significantly after 1895. In 1895 French Canadians held only nine local offices in twenty-two towns where they formed at least 20 percent of the population. By 1901 the number of *Canadien* officeholders had nearly quadrupled and the percentage of offices held by French Canadians had risen from 2 percent to nearly 7 percent. By 1910 *Canadien* officials had doubled in number. Compared with urban *Canadiens* French Canadians in towns were more successful during the first decade of the twentieth century (see table 6.1).[1] By the end of that decade French Canadians commonly held public offices in the towns, though they had achieved proportional representation in few localities. As in the cities, their success in local politics varied widely. Southbridge and Spencer, which contained about 25 percent of the *Canadien* population of all the towns, accounted for 40 percent of all French Canadian officeholders. Although at least one *Canadien* held office in nearly every town between 1895 and 1910,

128

Table 6.1

Number of French Canadian officeholders
in twenty-two towns by type of office,
1895-1910

	1895	1898	1900	1901	1903	1907	1910	Total
Clerk	0	0	0	0	0	0	0	0
Selectman	1	1	2	2	5	4	5	20
Treasurer	0	0	0	0	0	0	0	0
Auditor	0	1	1	4	6	7	7	26
Assessor	1	3	2	3	5	5	6	25
Collector	1	0	0	0	0	1	2	4
Overseer of the Poor	1	4	5	5	8	10	9	42
Constable	4	10	12	15	15	21	26	103
Water Board	0	0	0	1	2	3	3	9
Sinking Fund	0	1	1	1	1	4	4	12
Board of Health	1	1	2	3	3	8	7	25
Canadians	9	21	25	34	45	63	69	266
Total Number of positions	435	491	504	504	507	517	517	3475
Percent Canadian	2.1	4.3	5.0	6.8	8.9	12.2	13.3	7.7

Source: Massachusetts Yearbook, 1895, 1898, 1900, 1901, 1903, 1907, 1910. For a list of the twenty-two towns included in the table see table 3 in the appendix.

three-quarters of the towns had fewer than ten over the fifteen-year period (see table 6.2).[2]

The party affiliation of *Canadien* candidates for the Massachusetts General Court as well as voting patterns each indicate that French Canadians in the towns were more closely associated with the Democratic party than *Canadiens* in urban areas. Between 1896 and 1900, for example, all six French Canadians running for the lower house were Democrats. Although fourteen Republican candidates ran over the next fifteen years, Democrats outnumbered them two to one over the entire twenty-year period—the opposite trend than found among French Canadian state representative candidacies in the cities (see table 6.3).[3] Voting patterns also suggest that the French Canadians in towns leaned more toward the Democratic party. The mean correlation between the Democratic vote and the presence of French Canadians for sixty towns between 1896 and 1915 was .45, as compared with .39 for 17 cities, and

Table 6.2

Number of French Canadian officeholders in
twenty-two towns by town, 1895-1910

	Number Seven years[a]	Three years[b]	Percent of quota filled in three years[c]
Southbridge	63	22	61.1
Spencer	47	19	54.3
Montague	37	15	83.3
Ware	24	7	30.4
Adams	16	6	46.2
Webster	10	8	47.1
Grafton	9	2	13.3
Dudley	7	0	0
Millbury	6	3	18.8
Northboro	6	1	9.1
North Brookfield	6	2	11.8
Gardner	5	2	15.4
Warren	5	2	14.3
Palmer	4	2	20.0
Auburn	4	3	42.9
Oxford	4	3	21.4
Sutton	4	2	7.7
Douglas	3	1	7.7
Sturbridge	3	2	14.3
Harwick	2	1	7.7
Northbridge	1	1	6.3
Ludlow	0	0	0
	266	104	24.2

Source: Massachusetts Yearbook, 1895,1898,1900, 1901, 1903, 1907, 1910.

[a]1895, 1898, 1900, 1901, 1903, 1907, 1910.

[b]1895, 1900, 1910.

[c]The percent of the quota of offices filled was derived by estimating the number of offices in three years (1895, 1900, 1910) that would have been filled by French Canadians had they had the same proportion of offices as their proportion of the town's population in 1905, and dividing that estimate by the actual number of Canadien officeholders.

Table 6.3

Party affiliation of French Canadian
candidates for state senate and
state representative originating
in towns, 1896-1915

	Total	Republicans	Democrats	Other
Senators				
1896-1900	1	0	1	0
1901-1905	4	0	3	1
1906-1910	0	0	0	0
1911-1915	3	0	3	0
Total	8	0	7	1
Winning	0	0	0	0
Representatives				
1896-1900	6	0	6	0
1901-1905	13	5	8	0
1906-1910	13	3	7	3
1911-1915	12	6	6	0
Total	44	14	27	3
Winning	24	8	16	0

Source: Massachusetts, Public Document No. 43, 1896-1915.

the pattern in the towns was more stable (see tables 6.4 and 6.5).[4] Similarly divergent patterns emerge when the voting patterns of ten central towns with high concentrations of French Canadians are compared with those of the primary cities (see tables 6.6 and 6.7).[5]

A closer look at the political behavior of French Canadians in Southbridge and Spencer, where they were especially successful in local politics, reveals the different ways in which they interacted with political parties. French Canadians had settled in both towns, located in south Worcester County, in sizeable numbers before 1870. By 1885 *Canadiens* were the dominant ethnic group, numerically, in each town, forming between 35 and 50 percent of the population, while the Irish constituted less than 15 percent. French Canadians in both towns began holding local offices in the 1880s and by the early 1890s were aligned with the Democratic party. In response to their diminished role in town government during the mid-1890s, French Canadians mobilized, determined to regain and expand their voice in town affairs. The Democratic party served as the vehicle to realize this goal in both cases. Thereafter, the *Canadiens* remained closely connected to that party. In both South-

Table 6.4

Mean Pearsonian correlation coefficients (R)
showing the association between the percent
Democratic vote for governor and the
percent French Canadian for sixty towns
compared to seventeen cities, 1896-1915

Variable 1 Percent Democratic
Variable 2 Percent French Canadian
Variable 3 Percent Irish

| | Towns | | Cities | |
	R_{12}	R_{13}	R_{12}	R_{13}
1896-1900	.47	.56	.35	.61
1901-1905	.43	.58	.44	.57
1906-1910	.46	.55	.40	.46
1911-1915	.44	.62	.38	.59
1896-1915	.45	.58	.39	.56

bridge and Spencer, however, there were French Canadian Republicans; their demands for recognition helped to increase the number of *Canadien* officeholders after 1900. Thus, though more Democratic-leaning than their counterparts in the large cities of the Bay State, French Canadians in small manufacturing towns exhibited the same pragmatic approach to politics found in such places as Fall River and Worcester.

Spencer: French Canadian Unity and Factionalism

French Canadians in Spencer began to play a significant role in town politics in the 1880s, much earlier than in most cities and towns. Indeed a few *Canadiens* had held office in Spencer earlier, but after 1880 they became much more active.[6] Two related forces propelled them into the local political arena. First, the state's implementation of a local option law requiring an annual plebescite on the sale of alcoholic beverages aroused the concern of both the Irish and the *Canadiens*, most of whom opposed prohibition. Second, both groups, who together formed nearly half of the town's electorate, wanted more representation in town government.

The liquor law deeply divided the voters of Spencer. Not only did the law create pro- and anti-liquor factions, it also divided particular groups and crosscut political parties, erecting a patchwork of political factions. On the local level the Citizens or pro-license caucus was in fact the organization of the Democrats. The no-license caucus, organized and led by prohibitionists, was not the Republican party caucus,

Table 6.5

Pearsonian correlation coefficients (R)
and coefficients of determination
(multiple R^2) for gubernatorial
elections for sixty towns
in central Massachusetts,[a]
1895-1915

Variable 1 Percent Democratic
Variable 2 Percent French Canadian
Variable 3 Percent Irish

| | R_{12} | R_{13} | Multiple R squared | |
			Irish and French Canadian	French Canadian alone
1895	.41	.53	.47	.19
1896	.38	.58	.51	.17
1897	.42	.55	.51	.20
1898	.58	.51	.63	.37
1899	.52	.52	.57	.30
1900	.45	.65	.66	.24
1901	.44	.60	.58	.22
1902	.42	.55	.50	.20
1903	.36	.58	.49	.16
1904	.46	.56	.55	.24
1905	.48	.60	.62	.26
1906	.53	.54	.60	.30
1907	.41	.39	.33	.18
1908	.39	.66	.60	.17
1909	.43	.61	.59	.21
1910	.56	.53	.63	.34
1911	.52	.57	.61	.29
1912	.49	.60	.63	.27
1913	.41	.61	.56	.20
1914	.41	.66	.62	.19
1915	.37	.66	.59	.16

[a]The sixty towns included here are all the towns of Worcester County and those towns outside of Worcester County in which French Canadians formed at least 20 percent of the population in 1895.

Table 6.6

Mean Pearsonian correlation coefficients (R) showing
the association between the percent Democratic vote for
governor and the percent French Canadian for ten
central towns compared to six primary cities, 1891-1915

	Central towns	Primary cities
1891-1895	.29	.65
1896-1900	.52	.31
1901-1905	.59	.40
1906-1910	.58	.38
1911-1915	.28	.20
1891-1915	.45	.39

however, as a significant proportion of Republicans, particularly French Canadian Republicans, did not favor prohibition. Until 1904 the Republican party, itself split on the issue of licensing, took no official stand on the issue and did not nominate candidates for local office. To add to the confusion, a few Irish and French Canadians favored prohibition and associated themselves with the no-license caucus and the Republican party, although they could be weaned from these affiliations temporarily.

The immediate and probably most important consequence of the local option law's implementation in 1882 was the mobilization of Catholic voters in Spencer. In the spring of 1882 Irish and French Canadians held separate caucuses to nominate candidates for local offices—the first ethnic group caucuses in the town. More importantly, the Irish and *Canadiens* then met jointly "to unite on some plan to carry into the Regular Town Caucus" where final nominations would be made. The explicit purpose of the joint Catholic caucus was to gain greater recognition for both groups. John O'Gara, the leading Irish Democrat of the town, made this clear, saying "that the Irish and the French ought to be represented on each town board."[7] A committee, formed at the joint caucus meeting and composed of representatives from both groups, was charged with preparing one ticket of Irish and French Canadian choices for submission to the Regular Town Caucus which, unlike the Regular Citizens' Caucus or the Prohibition Caucus, was willing to accept both pro- and anti-liquor Irish and *Canadien* nominations.[8]

The concerted action of the Irish and French Canadians in 1882 opened a new era in town politics in which ethnicity and liquor played vital roles. Although the two groups never again met jointly, each

Table 6.7
Correlation coefficients showing the association between percent Democratic and percent French Canadian in presidential and gubernatorial elections for ten towns in central Massachusetts, 1890-1916

	Presidential R	Presidential R_s	Gubernatorial R	Gubernatorial R_s
1890			.32	.27
1891			.41	.38
1892	.24	.27	.29	.36
1893			.35	.39
1894			.21	.21
1895			.21	.31
1896	.61*	.56*	.65	.59*
1897			.41	.43
1898			.44	.38
1899			.50	.49
1900	.48	.53	.62*	.69*
1901			.72*	.72*
1902			.59*	.62*
1903			.62*	.66*
1904	.59*	.67*	.54*	.59*
1905			.46	.51
1906			.63*	.50
1907			.73*	.66*
1908	.47	.61*	.48	.49
1909			.44	.43
1910			.62*	.66*
1911			.17	.38
1912	.42	.50	.49	.39
1913			.20	.37
1914			.30	.37
1915			.24	.37
1916	.81*	.87*		

[a]The ten towns included are; Southbridge, Sutton, Spencer, Ware, Dudley, Ludlow, Sturbridge, Millbury, Grafton, and Palmer. French Canadians made up at least 25 percent of the population of each of these towns in 1895. In only ten cases, R_s (Spearman's correlation coefficient) is more appropriate. R (Pearson's correlation coefficient) is provided to make comparisons with other data feasible.

*Indicates significance at .05 level of confidence.

continued to convene separately and submit their caucus choices to the Regular Town Caucus, which until the 1890s was controlled by local Yankee Democrats. While approving of representation for both groups—at a count of three Americans, one Irish, and one *Canadien*—Yankee Democrats, led by Judge Luther Hill, objected to the assertiveness of the new ethnic political leaders.[9] Consequently, from 1884 to 1888 the Democrats remained divided. With the so-called Hill party at odds with the O'Gara party, a coalition of pro-liquor Irish and French Canadians, the local Democrats remained out of power.[10]

The editor of the *Spencer Sun*, the town's only newspaper, deplored the rise of parties in town politics and found "the introduction of racial lines into local affairs . . . both unwise and reprehensible." "If our politics have sunk to this narrow-minded and degraded state," he concluded, "it is time for our people, at least the patriotic portion of them to plant themselves on the principles enunciated by the founders of the Republic."[11] The editor's call for a halt to ethnic politics was ignored. The month he spoke out saw the formation of a short-lived so-called American caucus in response to separate ethnic caucuses, which continued to meet.[12]

A united Catholic vote conceivably could win control of local political life with the help of some Yankee Democrats. Just as ethnic Democrats did not see eye to eye with Yankee Democrats, however, French Canadians themselves were divided. Prominent French Canadians were active in both parties during the mid-1880s, and, French Republicans, like other Republicans, were divided on the liquor issue and were willing to cooperate with the prohibitionists in order to gain influence in town government. French Canadian Republican candidates on the no-license ticket, who did not usually have the endorsement of the French caucus, often won because the Democrats remained divided. Between 1886 and 1888, for example, thirty-four French Canadian candidates ran for local office in Spencer, but only sixteen won. All but three of the successful candidates were Republicans; twelve of the nineteen losers were Democrats who had the approval of the French caucus (see table 6.8).

By 1890, when most French Canadian voters rallied behind the popular Democratic gubernatorial nominee William Russell, the fortunes of French Canadian Democrats improved. Of sixteen *Canadiens* winning local office from 1890 to 1893, eleven were Democrats; all but four of thirteen *Canadien* Republican candidates met defeat.[13]

French Canadian gains in local government were undermined, however, when Russell's coalition began to falter. The defection of French-speaking Republicans to Russell and to local Democratic candidates angered no-license men, who then refused to back pro-license French

Canadian Republicans for town offices. Since Irish Democrats also refused to support French Republicans nominated by French caucus, only two Canadiens, both anti-liquor men, won office in 1893. The next few years proved just as bad for the French Canadians in Spencer. Of twenty Canadien candidates between 1894 and 1897 only four won offices; of these, three were elected constables, the lowest-ranking elected position in the town. As a result Canadien influence in town government declined dramatically (see tables 6.8 and 6.9).[14]

The French Naturalization Club, founded in the spring of 1896, reversed this trend and spearheaded the growth of French Canadian political power by reunifying the Canadiens. Organized by French Democrats, the club's primary purpose, according to Eugene D. Marchessault, its first president, was to seek recognition of the French Canadians in Spencer. Some 350 French-speaking voters lived in the town, he pointed out, but they had no representation on the three most important governing boards—selectmen, assessors, and overseers of the poor—as they had earlier had. The club intended to recruit additional French voters and sponsored a bipartisan caucus to select and support French Canadian candidates.[15]

The new French caucus successfully promoted the interests of the French Canadians as a group by sidestepping the liquor issue and crosscutting party lines. The caucus met each year the week before the regular caucus meetings, starting in 1897, and endorsed a slate of French Canadian candidates who would be presented to both the liquor and anti-liquor caucuses. These candidates were "considered as the candidates of the French people of the town."[16] If either regular caucus refused to adopt them, no other French Canadians would be put on the ballot. The French caucus expected, moreover, that its candidates would be "supported by every French voter."[17] By thus unifying the French vote, the French Naturalization Club could force both regular caucuses to accept its candidates since the exclusion of its choices by either would drive the Canadiens en masse to the other.

While not always successful in maintaining a solid French voting bloc, the French Naturalization Club nonetheless increased the number of French voters and public officials. In 1892 about 320 French voters had formed about 20 percent of the town's registered voters. Between 1892 and 1895 about ten French voters had been added yearly. In 1896 alone, the first year of operation of the club, forty-six of the 170 new registrations—or about one-third—were French Canadians. Within three years, about 150 new French-speaking voters were enlisted, bringing the total to about five hundred, about 33 percent of Spencer's voters. Over the next twenty years, from 1896 to 1916, about a third of all newly registered voters were Canadiens, so that by 1910 nearly four in

Table 6.8

French Canadian candidates and local officeholders,
Spencer, 1884-1912

	Candidates			Officeholders			#[a]	Percent French Canadian of all officeholders[a]
	R	D	O	R	D	O		
1884	4	3	0	3	3	0	6	15.4
1885	5	2	0	3	2	0	5	12.8
1886	6	5	0	5	1	0	6	15.4
1887	5	3	0	4	1	0	5	12.8
1888	7	7	1	4	1	0	5	12.8
1889	-	-	-	3	2	1	6	15.4
1890	4	5	1	1	4	1	6	15.4
1891	2	8	1	1	3	0	4	10.3
1892	4	4	0	2	2	0	4	10.3
1893	3	4	0	0	2	0	2	5.1
1894	2	4	0	0	1	0	1	2.6
1895	0	1	0	0	0	0	0	0.0
1896	1	5	0	0	1	0	1	2.6
1897	4	2	1	1	1	0	2	5.1
1898	2	5	1	2	4	1	6	15.4
1899	2	4	1	2	3	1	6	15.4
1900	3	3	2	3	3	1	7	17.9
1901	3	4	1	3	3	1	7	17.9
1902	4	7	0	3	4	0	7	17.9
1903	9	6	0	5	5	0	8	20.5
1904	4	5	0	4	6	0	10	25.6
1905	4	5	2	4	5	0	10	25.6
1906	6	7	1	6	7	1	11	25.6
1907	6	6	1	5	6	1	11	28.2
1908	5	6	4	5	5	4	12	30.8
1909	4	5	6	4	5	4	11	28.2
1910	5	6	3	4	5	3	12	30.8
1911	3	6	5	3	6	4	14	35.9
1912	3	5	6	3	5	6	15	38.5

R-Republican; D-Democrat; O-Other

Source: Spencer Sun-Leader, 1884-1912; Spencer Town Records, 1884-1912. No data for 1889.

[a]Including only the following offices: selectman, treasurer, auditor, assessor, collector, overseer of the poor, constable.

Table 6.9

French Canadian officeholders in town
government, Spencer, 1884-1915

Positions	1	2	3	4	5	6	7	Totals
1884	1	0	0	1	0	1	3	6
1885	1	0	0	1	0	1	2	5
1886	1	0	0	1	0	1	3	6
1887	1	0	0	1	0	1	2	5
1888	1	0	0	1	0	1	2	5
1889	1	0	0	1	0	1	3	6
1890	1	0	0	1	0	1	3	6
1891	1	0	0	0	0	1	2	4
1892	0	0	0	1	0	1	2	4
1893	0	0	0	0	0	1	1	2
1894	0	0	0	0	0	0	1	1
1895	0	0	0	0	0	0	0	0
1896	0	0	0	0	0	0	1	1
1897	0	0	0	1	0	0	1	2
1898	1	0	0	1	0	1	3	6
1899	1	0	0	1	0	1	3	6
1900	1	0	0	1	0	1	4	7
1901	1	0	0	2	0	1	3	7
1902	0	0	1	2	0	1	3	7
1903	1	0	0	2	0	1	4	8
1904	1	0	0	2	1	1	5	10
1905	1	0	0	2	1	1	5	10
1906	1	0	0	2	1	1	6	11
1907	1	0	0	2	1	1	6	11
1908	1	0	0	2	1	2	5	11
1909	1	0	0	2	1	3	6	12
1910	1	0	0	2	1	2	6	12
1911	2	0	0	2	1	2	7	14
1912	2	0	0	2	1	2	8	15
1913	2	0	0	2	1	2	7	14
1914	2	0	0	2	1	2	6	13
1915	2	0	0	2	1	2	6	13

Source: Spencer Town Records, 1884-1915.

Code: 1, selectman (5); 2, treasurer (1); 3, auditor (1);
4, assessor (5); 5, collector (1); 6, overseer of the poor (3);
7, constable (13).   The number between parentheses indicates the
number of persons holding that position each year.

ten of the town's voters were French Canadian. Together, they and the Irish made up between 55 and 60 percent of the town's electorate and were thus in a position of controling its political fate.[18]

The impact of the French Naturalization Club on officeholding became evident within a few years of its founding. By 1900 French Canadians had gained representation on the boards of selectmen, assessors, overseers of the poor, and constables as well as on the park commission. The number of French Canadian officeholders rose from none in 1895, to seven in 1900, and to twelve by 1910. By 1910 French Canadians occupied a third of all positions and had acquired representation proportional to their voting strength on the key governing boards of the town.

Success did not come immediately, however. The first effort of the French caucus to have *Canadiens* elected in the spring of 1897 failed. Save for one *Canadien* candidate, who ran unopposed for the board of assessors, all the caucus's candidates were defeated, due in part to factionalism within French Canadian ranks. Rather than agree on one candidate to be presented to both caucuses as the sole choice for selectman, the caucus instead submitted a list of four choices. One of these was chosen by the license caucus and another by the no-license caucus, splitting the French vote and causing both French Canadian candidates to be defeated.[19] Suspicion of the French caucus activities also contributed to the defeat of the *Canadiens* in 1897. Although the French Naturalization Club itself took no position on the liquor issue, many of the voters it recruited were expected to favor the sale of alcohol.[20] Prohibition voters therefore voted against *Canadien* candidates, fearing that the French Canadian mobilization ultimately would make Spencer wet. License Democrats, on the other hand, questioned the motives of the French caucus, criticizing especially its practice of submitting its choices to both caucuses. Finally, a number of pro-license Republicans resented the efforts of French Democrats to defeat a pro-license Republican and voted against *Canadien* candidates.[21] The alienation of every other important voting bloc—no-license voters, license Democrats, and license Republicans—combined with the failure of the French caucus to unify French voters behind one selectman candidate doomed its first effort.

The French caucus proved more successful the next year. In 1898 it presented only one choice for selectman—a man acceptable to both regular caucuses—and its other candidates, with the exception of one, also received the nomination of both caucuses. The result: seven of the eight *Canadien* candidates were elected.[22] Using the same strategy over the next several years, French Canadians gained substantial representation in local government.

The French Naturalization Club brought newly mobilized *Canadien* voters into a closer alliance with the local Democratic party, marking the formation of a cooperative relationship between all the town's Catholics that challenged the hegemony of Yankee Republicans. The ascendancy of the Catholic anti-prohibition alliance was revealed in the results of the local option vote. During thirteen of the sixteen years between 1882 and 1897 Spencer had remained dry. Once the *Canadiens* were fully mobilized, after 1897, liquor was sold legally in the town during thirteen of the next fifteen years.[23]

In large measure this reversal was due to the union of Irish and French Canadian voters. The fears of prohibitionists in 1897—that the infusion of the French as a separate political force would tilt Spencer into the license column—were realized. The park commissioner elections of 1897 and 1898 revealed the strength of the combined Catholic vote. In 1896 the three members of the park commission opposed Sunday openings of the cafe in the town's public park; but strict observance of the Sabbath in a town where ethnic Catholic inhabitants were a majority was an affront to the traditions and customs of more than half the population and could not be sustained for long once the Catholic voters were mobilized. Thus, in 1897, a candidate with more tolerant views regarding the use of the park was elected over one of the conservatives running for re-election. The next year another conservative "who abhorred Sunday sacred concerts and clambakes" in the park lost to a French Canadian, giving the cultural liberals a two to one majority on the commission.[24]

The effect of the *Canadien* mobilization was felt also in the state representative elections. From 1886 to 1897 the voters of the Sixth Worcester County District usually had returned a Republican to the general court. The Democratic party helped win over French Canadian voters when the French Naturalization Club was formed in 1896 by choosing Alfred Arsenault as the Democratic candidate for state representative. Although Arsenault lost, a Democratic nominee, Eugene D. Marchessault, won two years later, tightening the bond between the French Canadians and the Democratic party. As a result, the state representative for the Sixth Worcester County District between 1898 and 1912 was usually a Democrat who benefited from a strong French vote (see table 6.10).[25]

Marchessault ran for state representative four times but won only twice. In 1898 he won because *Canadiens* and Democrats gave him solid support and because the Republican vote was split.[26] The following year he lost in part because the Republicans rallied behind one candidate. The race was close, however, and revealed how important the French vote was to Democratic victory. Marchessault lost in the

Table 6.10

Results of state representative contests for the district
including Southbridge and Spencer, 1876-1915

	Spencer						Southbridge					
	R	R	D	D	O	O	R	R	D	D	O	O
1876	W	W					W	W				
1877	W	W					W	W				
1878	W	W					W	W				
1879	W	W					W	W				
1880	W	W					W	W				
1881	W	W					W	W				
1882	W				W		W					W
1883	W	W					W	W				
1884	W	W					W	W				
1885	W		W				W		W			
1886	W								W			
1887	W								W			
1888	W						W					
1889			W*						W			
1890			W*				W					
1891	W*								W			
1892	W						W		*			
1893	W						W		*			
1894	W						W					
1895	W						W					
1896	W		*				W	W				
1897	W						W	W				
1898			W*				W		W			
1899	W		*				W		W			
1900	W		*				W		W	*		
1901			W*				W		W*			
1902			W					*	W*	W		
1903			W					*	W*	W		
1904			W				W	W				
1905			W				W*		W			
1906	W*							*	W*			
1907	W*								W*			
1908			W				W					
1909			W*						W*			
1910			W*						W*			
1911			W						W*			
1912			W						W*			
1913			W						W*			*
1914			W						W*			
1915	*	W						*	W			

Sources: Southbridge Journal, 23 October 1885; Worcester Evening Gazette, 1885-1889; Massachusetts, Public Document No. 43, 1890-1915.

Code: R, Republican; D, Democrat; O, other; W, winning candidate; *, French Canadian candidate.

district by only thirty-four votes, losing Spencer itself by a mere fifteen. Crucial to his defeat was the defection of some fifty French Canadian voters, led by Dr. Marc Fontaine, a prominent *Canadien* Republican, to Charles Allen, the Republican candidate. In 1900 Marchessault won Spencer with strong *Canadien* support but lost again in the district because of higher Republican turnout in the district rural towns, typical of presidential-year politics. Marchessault again won handily in 1901, however, when the Franco-Democratic phalanx held and Republican rural voters did not turn out.[27]

Marchessault's Democratic candidacies brought French Canadian voters solidly into the Democratic column. Non-French Democratic candidates over the next four elections continued to receive strong support in Spencer and won. The GOP recaptured the seat only by running a *Canadien* candidate, as they did in 1906 and 1907. Although these Republican victories clearly showed the strength of ethnic loyalties among Spencer's *Canadien* voters, they represented only a temporary aberration. Democratic majorities were restored in 1908 and substantially increased when Alfred Arsenault once again ran on the Democratic ticket in 1909 and 1910.[28]

Although most French Canadian voters supported Marchessault's bids for the state house, not all were Democrats. Of about five hundred *Canadien* voters in 1900, about 60 percent were Democrats who favored licensing.[29] Because the election of *Canadiens* to local office depended on the inclusion of their names on both license and anti-license tickets and a unified French vote, however, French Democrats had to accommodate the French Republican faction as well as maintain discipline among the *Canadien* voters, candidates, and potential candidates.

The French caucus tried to keep the peace among the French Canadian factions by dividing its endorsements fairly evenly among French Democrats, French Republicans, and French independents. In 1899, for example, seven individuals received the endorsement of the caucus— three Republicans, two Democrats, and two independents—and all but one also received the backing of both regular caucuses despite their differing views on the liquor question.[30]

Besides balancing its ticket, the French caucus also had to persuade French voters that only its chocies should be accepted as the true choices of the French people. To do so sometimes required disciplining the political ambitions of particular *Canadiens*, as exemplified by caucus actions towards Marc Fontaine and Emory Arbour, who resisted its authority.

In the spring of 1899, for example, Fontaine was elected overseer of the poor with the backing of the French caucus. The next fall, however, Fontaine campaigned against the re-election of Eugene Marchessault to the state legislature. Because of his efforts on behalf of the Republican candidate, Marchessault lost. Fontaine's behavior angered many French Canadians who the next spring denied Fontaine their endorsement for the position of overseer of the poor and never again backed him for a local office.[31]

At the same caucus meeting at which Fontaine was first punished for his delinquency, some opposition arose among Democrats to the re-nomination of L. N. Hamelin for selectman. Emory Arbour, a Democrat like Hamelin, challenged Hamelin for the position. Hamelin dutifully pledged himself to abide by the choice of the caucus. Arbour would not do so, however, and lost the contest by a two-to-one margin. Arbour sought to win the citizen's caucus nomination later the same week but failed. Refusing to defer to the choice of either caucus, Arbour then ran for selectman as an independent candidate. As president of the largest French Canadian society in Spencer, the six hundred-member St. Jean Baptiste Society, Arbour's candidacy potentially could have split the French vote, leaving Hamelin with insufficient votes for re-election. It did not, however; for the influence of the French caucus prevailed among *Candien* voters as well as among license Democrats. Hamelin won; Arbour received the lowest vote of the eight candidates. Despite his prominence within the French community, Arbour never again received the backing of the French caucus for an important post in local government.[32]

After 1900 more serious fissures within the French Canadian com-munity surfaced, fracturing along party lines the unity that had existed since 1896. From 1896 to 1901 the French caucus had been dominated by French Canadian license Democrats. While accommodating French Republicans with a share of political offices, the Democrats had re-served for themselves the most prestigious and powerful position in town government—selectman. By 1902 French Republicans, after hav-ing cooperated with the French Naturalization Club for several years, revolted against Democratic predominance and sought an expanded role for themselves within the French caucus and in town politics. By 1906 the French Republican faction was ascendant. Although the Re-publican dissenters jeopardized the group's unity and its gains in local government, their aggressiveness ultimately increased the number of *Canadiens* in local offices. By 1911 two French Canadians sat on the board of selectmen—one Democrat and one Republican.

Rumblings of dissatisfaction with the operation of the French caucus had been articulated nearly from its beginning. Criticism originated primarily among French Republicans and French prohibition advocates who viewed the caucus as a vehicle for promoting the interests of Democrats and liquor men. Opposition arose in 1897, for example, when Marc Fontaine denounced the club's practice of defraying the cost of naturalization for its members. Fontaine claimed that such a practice was a "system of indirect bribery" and argued that "if a man is not enterprising enough himself to pay for his own naturalization, he is hardly fit to become an American citizen." "Good citizens are not bought," he proclaimed.[33]

By 1902 resentment of the French caucus was voiced by others who viewed it, quite accurately, as asking favors of both the license and no-license caucuses because it demanded that its choices and no other Canadiens receive caucus support. One critic, in a letter signed simply "A Native," complained:

Why should the French caucus expect the Citizen's caucus to adopt a no-license French candidate? Why should the no-license caucus be expected to endorse the candidate of the French caucus if that candidate is out-and-out a license man?[34]

Discontent with the French caucus came to a head in 1902. Despite the best efforts of prohibitionists, the majorities in favor of license had risen as the number of French voters increased. Until 1902 the French caucus had chosen Hamelin, a pro-license Democrat, for selectman. Anti-license Canadiens and French Republicans had supported Hamelin in the interest of group unity, and had persuaded the no-license caucus to endorse him, expecting that a French Republican would eventually be chosen by the French caucus to even the score. In 1902, however, the Democratic leadership of the French caucus once again guided it away from a French Republican candidate for selectman. Joseph Richard, an "out-and-out liquor man" was endorsed instead.

French Republicans bolted and ran their own candidate, who received the backing of the no-license caucus. Richard, unlike his predecessor, received only the approval of the license caucus. As might have been expected, the French voters split and neither French Canadian won. The Canadiens were left with no representation on the board of selectmen.[35]

Over the next few years the rift among French Canadians grew bitter. French Republicans called for the termination of the French caucus, charging that it was "useless agitation" and "un-American." Aiming to undermine its role in local affairs French Republicans called for conducting town elections on regular party lines. Responding to their initiative, the GOP called the first of four municipal caucuses in 1904. Republican candidates did poorly at the polls, however, partly because no-license advocates resented being sidelined by the Republicans. French Canadian Democrats, for their part, continued to defend the caucus as the only way to ensure the election of *Canadiens* to local office. Most French-speaking voters agreed; they returned Joseph Richard to the board of selectmen, leaving the French Canadian Republican candidates out in the cold.[36]

Fraternal wrangling among French Canadians reached a peak in 1906 when French Canadian Republicans seized control of the French caucus. Having failed to win public office by changing the rules of town politics, they threatened to fracture the French bloc by forming a separate French Republican caucus. This new caucus met a week before the regular French caucus. At its first and only meeting, *Canadien* Republican leaders explained its purpose. "In the past," said one, "the French people had been represented by Democrats and the Republicans had to take a back seat" and would have to as long as the "present leaders are in control of the French vote." Explained another, "We have learned from the past that we got nothing. . . . We want a Republican representative once in a while and that is why we have called this caucus."[37]

The French Republican caucus endorsed J. Ulric Dufault for selectman over Napoleon O'Coin, both Republicans, by a vote of thirty-five to five. But the vote settled nothing; for the meeting was attended by the small, no-license faction of French Republicans whose opinions were out of step with most *Canadiens* in Spencer. Proof of their minority standing came at the regular French caucus, which was heavily attended despite a blizzard. Republicans outnumbered Democrats at the meeting by about two to one. Despite its Republican leadership and majority, the caucus could not decide on a French Canadian candidate for selectman. Dufault, a no-license man favored by French Canadian prohibition voters, could not carry a majority at the regular French caucus. A spirited contest developed between him and Napoleon O'Coin, who favored license and was treasurer of the Republican town committee. Neither man expressed a willingness to abide by the decision of the caucus. Dufault argued that he was the choice of the French Republican caucus and proposed that the Republican town caucus should decide between himself and O'Coin as both were Republicans. O'Coin rejected this solution, claiming that several "Yankee Republicans" had told him that the French must settle the matter themselves. Besides, he added, he intended to get the nomination of the Democratic town caucus and did not intend to attend that of the Republicans. Hopelessly divided—Democrats versus Republicans, license Republicans versus no-license Republicans—the French caucus adjourned without having chosen a candidate for selectman.[38]

When it met, the Republican town caucus, attended largely by French voters, many casting a Republican ballot for the first time that night, gave O'Coin its nomination. So did the Democratic caucus. With the endorsement of both regular caucuses, O'Coin won a seat as selectman. The following year he defeated Dufault, who ran as an independent against him. O'Coin, a license Republican, had emerged as the most suitable compromise candidate, satisfying the French Republicans who wanted recognition for their faction as well as the majority of license Democrats. Only the no-license French Republicans remained dissatisfied with O'Coin.[39]

O'Coin sat on the selectmen's board for six years, receiving strong French support at the polls. French Republicans strengthened their control of the French caucus during this period, assisted by the GOP, which nominated Frank Colette Jr., a leading French Republican, for state representative.[40]

By 1910 party fissures among the French Canadians had been sealed over and the French caucus, once again unified and confident, nominated two *Canadiens* for selectmen, seeking to elect both. According to one spokesman, the French in Spencer comprised two-thirds of the town's inhabitants and two-fifths of its voters, and thus had "a right to have two selectmen" on the five-man board. Eugene Marchessault, whose influence had declined with the rise of the French Republican faction, warned that such a demand was premature and would alienate both the Irish and the Yankee Republicans of the town, leaving the French Canadians without allies. His words, however, failed to persuade the ambitious caucus. While the first attempt to elect two *Canadien* selectmen failed in 1910, the effort was successful the next year when Hamelin, a four-year veteran Democrat on the board, joined O'Coin.[41]

The relationship between French Canadians and the political parties in Spencer indeed was by no means simple and straightforward. As in most cities, the *Canadiens* of Spencer were divided between the two major parties between 1884 and 1915, although overall they tended to have Democratic leanings after 1890, unlike in the cities. Some *Canadiens* had aligned themselves with Irish Democrats during the 1880s; but most French Canadian voters shifted toward the Democratic party during its heyday in the early 1890s. Coincidental with this shift, however, the *Canadiens* lost much of the influence they had gained earlier in town government. Unlike French Canadians in larger cities, those of Spencer remained closely tied to the Democratic party after 1896 as they mobilized to expand their role in local affairs.

Led by French-speaking Democrats who organized the French Naturalization Club in 1896, the *Canadiens* unified themselves. By pragmatically subordinating party and factional differences, *Canadiens* increased their share of local offices, from less than 5 percent (between

1893 and 1897) to about 20 percent by 1902. As in Fall River, though, the French bloc in Spencer splintered after 1902. Factional disputes re-emerged, pitting French Democrats against French Republicans as both groups vied for control of the French caucus and a larger share of the honors of office. Ironically, internal divisions did not adversely affect the French Canadians in local politics. Rather, factionalism actually increased their share of offices.

Southbridge: Franco-Democrats and the Fruit of Competition

French Canadians first arrived in Southbridge before the Civil War. Although they constituted about half of the town's population as early as 1875, fewer than fifty were voters and they had little role in town government. The efforts of a committee formed in 1875 to encourage naturalization increased the number of *Canadien* voters to seventy by 1879, but not until the 1880s did the French Canadians become a significant political force in Southbridge. Between 1879 and 1890 French-speaking voters nearly quadrupled; consequently, *Canadiens*, began to gain access to the town's governing boards.[42] From 1884 to 1887, for example, eighteen French Canadians ran for local office but only five won. Over the five years following 1887, the number of *Canadien* candidates doubled and officeholders tripled (see tables 6.11 and 6.12).

French Canadians forged a close association with the Democratic party during the early phase of their mobilization. A few *Canadien* Republicans were nominated for local offices, but the Democratic party attracted most French Canadian voters because it was willing to offer them a position on the board of selectmen. While French Canadians won a seat on that board only three times before 1897, their nomination by the local Democrats welded the *Canadien* vote to that party. Not only did the Democrats give the French Canadians more prestigious nomina-tions, they also gave them more nominations for other town offices. Of the eighty-three French Canadian candidates for local office between 1884 and 1896, 80 percent were Democrats, as were 90 percent of the thirty-five *Canadien* officeholders.[43]

French Canadians remained closely tied to the Democratic party between 1897 and 1902. During this period they doubled their repre-sentation in local government and began as well to receive nominations for state representative. While retaining or increasing their representa-tion on the boards of assessors, overseers of the poor, and constabulary, they also gained secure seats on the boards of selectmen and auditors. By 1902 they were firmly entrenched on the key governing boards of the town. Although 22 percent of French Canadian candidates were Re-

Table 6.11

French Canadian candidates and local officeholders,
Southbridge, 1884-1914[a]

	Candidates		Wins	
	R	D	R	D
1884	0	3	0	0
1885	0	3	0	3
1886	2	5	0	2
1887	0	5	0	0
1888	1	7	1	3
1889	4	4	0	1
1890	2	5	2	4
1891	1	5	0	2
1892	1	7	0	3
1893	1	6	0	3
1894	1	7	0	2
1895	1	5	0	3
1896	0	7	0	3
1897	1	6	1	2
1898	1	7	1	4
1899	3	7	1	5
1900	3	7	1	6
1901	-	-	1	6
1902	2	8	1	6
1903	3	10	1	10
1904	3	10	3	7
1905	4	11	3	7
1906	6	11	2	9
1907	5	11	2	9
1908	6	12	2	9
1909	5	10	4	5
1910	8	12	3	12
1911	4	13	1	10
1912	6	14	0	13
1913	7	14	0	14
1914	6	14	2	12

R-Republican; D-Democrat

Source: Southbridge Journal, 1884-1914. No data for 1901.

[a]Includes the offices of selectman, treasurer, auditor, assessor, collector, overseer of the poor and constable.

Table 6.12

French Canadian officeholders in town government,
Southbridge, 1884-1914

Positions	1	2	3	4	5	6	7	Total	Percent Canadien of all officeholders
1884	0	0	0	0	0	0	0	0	0
1885	0	0	1	1	0	0	1	3	14.3
1886	0	0	0	1	0	0	1	2	9.5
1887	0	0	0	0	0	0	0	0	0
1888	1	0	0	1	0	0	2	4	19.0
1889	0	0	1	0	0	0	0	1	4.7
1890	1	0	1	1	0	1	2	6	28.6
1891	0	0	0	1	0	0	1	2	9.5
1892	1	0	0	0	0	1	1	3	14.3
1893	1	0	1	0	0	0	1	3	14.3
1894	0	0	0	1	0	0	1	2	9.5
1895	0	0	0	1	0	1	1	3	14.3
1896	0	0	0	1	0	1	1	3	14.3
1897	0	0	0	1	0	1	1	3	14.3
1898	0	0	1	1	0	2	1	5	23.8
1899	1	0	1	1	0	2	1	6	28.6
1900	1	0	1	1	0	2	2	7	33.3
1901	1	0	1	1	0	2	2	7	33.3
1902	1	0	0	1	0	2	3	7	33.3
1903	2	0	1	2	0	2	4	11	52.4
1904	1	0	2	2	0	2	3	10	47.6
1905	1	0	2	2	1	2	2	10	47.6
1906	1	0	1	2	1	2	4	11	52.4
1907	1	0	1	2	1	2	4	11	52.4
1908	1	0	1	2	1	2	4	11	52.4
1909	1	0	2	0	1	2	3	9	47.4
1910	3	1	3	1	1	3	3	15	78.9
1911	2	1	2	0	1	2	3	11	57.9
1912	2	1	3	1	1	2	3	13	68.4
1913	2	1	3	1	1	2	4	14	73.7
1914	3	1	3	1	1	2	4	15	78.9

Source: Southbridge Town Records, 1884-1915.

Code: 1, selectman (3); 2, treasurer (1); 3, auditor (3); 4,
assessor (3); 5, collector (1); 6, overseer of the poor (3); 7,
constable (7). From 1909-1914 there was only one assessor. The
number in parentheses indicates the number of persons holding that
position each year.

Table 6.13

French Canadian candidates for local offices by party
affiliation, Spencer and Southbridge,
1884-1912

| | Spencer | | | | Southbridge | | |
	T	R	D	O	T	R	D
Number							
1884-1889	48	27	20	1	34	7	27
1890-1896	49	16	31	2	49	7	42
1897-1902	49	18	25	6	45	10	35
1903-1912	135	49	58	28	164	50	114
Total	218	110	134	37	292	74	218
Percent							
1884-1889	100	56	42	2	100	21	79
1890-1896	100	33	63	4	100	14	86
1897-1902	100	37	51	12	100	22	78
1903-1912	100	36	43	21	100	30	70
Total	100	39	48	13	100	25	75
Winning candidates							
Number							
1884-1889	33	22	10	1	10	1	9
1890-1896	18	4	13	1	22	2	20
1897-1902	36	14	18	4	35	6	29
1903-1912	121	43	55	23	112	21	91
Total	208	83	96	29	179	30	149
Percent							
1884-1889	100	67	30	3	100	10	90
1890-1896	100	22	72	6	100	9	91
1897-1902	100	39	50	11	100	17	83
1903-1912	100	36	45	19	100	19	81
Total	100	40	46	14	100	17	83

T-Total; R-Republican; D-Democrat; O-Other

Based on data in tables 6.8 and 6.11.

publicans during this period, 83 percent of *Canadien* officeholders were Democrats (see table 6.13).

Underlying these gains was the growth of the French Canadian electorate. There had been about 330 French voters in Southbridge by 1895, approximately 25 percent of the town's voters. Over the following five years *Canadien* voters were added to the voting list at a rapid clip, as in Spencer. By 1900 the French electorate was nearly twice as large. Numbering about six hundred by the fall election of 1900, French Canadian voters formed more than 35 percent of Southbridge's registered voters. Most of the newly registered voters were Democrats, so that by 1900 French Democrats probably outnumbered French Republicans by a margin of three to one.[44]

The close tie between the *Canadiens* and the Democratic party was reflected also in their strength within the party organization. In the fall of 1900, for example, the Democrats of the town selected about fifty delegates to various party conventions. More than half the delegates were French Canadians, as were half the members of the party's town committee, whose chairman, Alexis Boyer Jr., was the only *Canadien* chairman of a local committee of either party in the state that year. In striking contrast, only four of the forty-six delegates selected by the local GOP in 1900 were French Canadians (see table 6.14).[45]

The frequent choice of French Canadians for the prestigious office of the state representative strengthened the relationship between the *Canadiens* and the Democratic party after 1900. Before 1900 most of the representatives from the district including Southbridge had been Republicans. Between 1900 and 1914, however, two-thirds were Democrats. In large measure the change in Democratic fortunes was due to its practice of nominating French Canadians for that office. Nearly half the Democratic candidates after 1900 were *Candiens;* between 1906 and 1914, all but one was *Canadien.*[46]

Despite the strong association between them and the local Democracy, not all French Canadians were Democrats. French Democrats had gained offices between 1897 and 1902 with the support of French Republicans who were willing to vote for Democrats in order to have *Canadiens* elected to office. The GOP sought to counteract this trend after 1900 by offering French Canadians more recognition. As French Democrats began to win representative seats away from regular Republicans, the GOP also began to run French Republicans against them, albeit with little success. Only in 1905, when the Democrats failed to run a French Canadian, did a French Republican win a seat in the house of representatives in Southbridge.

The Republican party gave the French Canadians more local nominations as well once they had become a significant force in town politics.

Table 6.14

French Canadian delegates to party
conventions, Southbridge,
1896-1907

	Total number of delegates[a]		Number of French Canadian delegates		Percent French Canadian of all delegates	
	R	D	R	D	R	D
1896	50	63	2	13	4.0	20.6
1898	50	33	4	6	8.0	9.1
1900	46	51	4	27	8.7	52.9
1904	51	42	10	23	19.6	54.8
1905	45	53	9	27	20.0	50.9
1906	54	53	9	25	16.7	47.2
1907	49	57	10	29	20.4	50.9
Total	345	352	48	150	13.9	42.6

Sources: Worcester Daily Spy, 11, 17 September 1896, 28
September 1898; Southbridge Journal, 4 October 1900, 1 October
1904, 30 September 1905, 29 September 1906, 21, 28 September 1906.

[a]The totals shown here include all delegates to congressional,
state, councillor, county, senatorial, and representative
conventions as well as the town committee.

Between 1897 and 1902, roughly 10 percent of Republican candidates
for local offices were *Canadiens,* while among Democratic candidates
the proportion was closer to one-third. After 1902 French Canadians
comprised about a quarter of the GOP candidates and about half of the
Democratic office seekers. Increasingly, French Democrats faced off
against French Republicans and the election of a French Canadian from
either party became more likely than ever before. From 1890 to 1902,
for example, a *Canadien* Democrat usually had won a place on the
three-man board of assessors. Starting in 1903 a French Canadian Republican also ran for that board, resulting in the election of two *Canadiens,* giving the group a majority.

Party competition for French voters thus significantly increased the
number of French Canadian candidates and the number of *Canadien*
officeholders as well. Between 1897 and 1902 roughly ten French Canadians ran for local offices annually; about one in four were Republicans.

Between 1903 and 1914 the annual average rose to sixteen and about one in three were Republicans. Consequently, the proportion of French Republican officeholders rose from 15 percent before 1902 to 25 percent afterwards, and French Canadians, who had held about a third of local offices between 1897 and 1902, won more than half between 1903 and 1910.

The political mobilization of the French Canadians in Southbridge differed from that in Spencer in that the Southbridge *Canadiens* leaned even more heavily towards the Democratic party than those in Spencer and by 1915 had secured for themselves a larger role in town government. As in Spencer, French Canadians had little say in local affairs before 1884 despite their relatively early arrival in those towns. As the *Canadien* electorate grew during the 1880s, French Canadians assumed a larger political role. By 1890, when *Canadiens* in most communities formed closer ties with the Democratic coalition led by Gov. William Russell, they had acquired a larger proportion of town offices in both Spencer and Southbridge than in most cities. As the Russell coalition declined, however, these advances wilted, particularly in Spencer.

In sharp contrast with the *Canadiens* in most cities, French Canadians in Southbridge and Spencer remained associated with the Democratic party after 1895. Just as the Republican party in Fall River or Worcester enabled the *Canadiens* to gain more political influence, the Democratic party in Southbridge and Spencer helped to increase the number of French Canadian officeholders in these towns. Coincidentally, the Franco-Democratic alliance gave the Democratic party a competitive edge in electoral contests, compelling the GOP to pay greater heed to *Canadien* demands for recognition lest it be swamped at the polls. Although French Canadians in both towns remained mostly Democratic until 1915, both parties competed for their support. As in the cities, French Canadians benefited from the competition. Using their pivotal voting power to its best advantage, French Canadians in Southbridge and Spencer pragmatically played both parties off each other, and thus they greatly expanded their influence in town affairs. Given the close relationship between the *Canadiens* and the Democratic party in these towns, Franco-Irish rivalry probably had less influence in shaping *Canadien* political behavior in Southbridge and Spencer than in such cities as Fall River and Worcester.

7
Conclusion

Unless we can break this compact foreign vote, we are gone and the
grand chapter of the old Massachusetts is closed.
　　　　—Senator George Frisbie Hoar to Henry Cabot Lodge, 1883

And why should it not be so? The American nation is a composite of
racial elements with perhaps individual customs and ways of thinking, but nevertheless united in their allegiance to the government
they helped to build. . . . The time has come when all the racial
elements that make up our nation should have a voice in government. . . . This is real Americanism."
—Edmond Talbot, Democratic candidate for lieutenant governor,
1926, responding to the *Springfield Republican's* criticism of the
Democratic practice of ethnically balancing its ticket

Between the Civil War and the Great Depression the twin forces of
immigration and industrialism transformed the Commonwealth of Massachusetts. The arrival of large numbers of immigrants during these
decades altered the social composition of the Bay State. In the short
term, immigration posed many new and difficult social and economic
problems. In the long term, the immigrants had a dramatic impact on
politics. The opening quotations illustrate the change in Massachusetts's political culture between 1880 and 1930. As Senator Hoar's
statement suggests, many native white Americans viewed immigrants
as a threat to Anglo-Saxon, Protestant culture and sought to contain that
threat.[1] By the 1920s the political changes attending the Great Immigration had become manifest and Yankee political hegemony was eclipsed.
Primary among these changes were the development of ethnic politics—a new style of politics illustrated by Talbot's statement—and the
alignment of the New Immigrants with the Democratic party, resulting
in the critical election of 1928.

At first glance, however, politics in Massachusetts appears quite
stable; through these decades the Republican party retained its
hegemony.[2] No Democratic candidate won 50 percent of the popular
vote for president in the fifteen presidential elections between 1868 and

1924. The Democrats received the state's electoral votes, for the first time in history, in 1912 primarily because Woodrow Wilson faced a deeply divided Republican party.[3] On the state level the GOP usually controlled all branches of government until 1932. Only in six years before 1900 and six years between 1900 and 1932 did Democrats occupy the governor's chair.[4] The contrast with the period since 1924 is striking indeed, particularly in presidential contests. From 1928 to 1980 no Republican candidate save Dwight D. Eisenhower captured 50 percent of the popular vote.[5] Most governors have been Democrats, and the Democratic party has controlled the legislature since the end of World War II.[6]

The seeds of political change were no doubt sown in the last decades of the nineteenth century and blossomed in the 1920s, as J. Joseph Huthmacher argued in his *Massachusetts People and Politics, 1919– 1933*, with the formation of the Democratic coalition that swept Franklin D. Roosevelt to the presidency and supported the programs of the New Deal. According to Huthmacher, the transition of Massachusetts from a Republican stronghold to a Democratic state may be traced to the new Democratic coalition formed during the 1920s. The fruit of this coalition was first evident in the Walsh revolution of 1926 when Irish Democrat David I. Walsh won a second term in the senate. The Walsh revolution preceded the Smith revolution of 1928, when Al Smith become the first Democratic presidential candidate to win 50 percent of the popular vote.[7] In Huthmacher's words, "The 1920s was the period in which the political effects of [the] Newer American culture became most evident."[8] That new American civilization was, in his terms, "urbanized, industrialized, and immigrantized," and given the social and economic structure of Massachusettts by 1920, the Commonwealth is an ideal state in which the study the emergence of the New Deal coalition during the 1920s.

According to Huthmacher, the essential element of the emergent Democratic coalition was the welding of large numbers of new immigrant voters to the Irish mainframe of the Democratic party. In his view immigrants joined the Democratic ranks in the 1920s for several reasons. First, the state shoe and textile industries in which thousands of new immigrants found employment did not enjoy the fruits, as Huthmacher puts it, of the "Coolidge prosperity, relieving new immigrant voters of their formerly strong belief in the magical powers of Republican economic doctrine." Second, the identification of the GOP with prohibiton, 100 percent Americanism, Ku Kluxism, and immigration restriction led new immigrants to view the Democratic party as the party of cultural liberalism. Finally, and most important, new immigrant groups grew aware of their political strength in the 1920s and their demands for recognition intensified. Recognition politics in the 1920s itself came to mean more than patronage jobs rewarding past loyalty.[9] As Huthmacher explained, "It meant acknowledgement that the ethnic group involved was capable and worthy of sharing in running the government. . . ."[10] The GOP's reluctant and clumsy attempts to placate ethnic demands for recognition pushed new immigrant groups from it while the Democratic party's sympathetic understanding of demands for recognition and its more adept practice of the delicate art of ethnic politics pulled them closer into its orbit.

This study of French Canadian political assimilation in Massachusetts shows that the developments identified by Huthmacher as critical to the 1920s were foreshadowed during the Progressive Era. It reveals the complex and changing relationship between ethnicity and politics during the late nineteenth and early twentieth centuries. French Canadian voting behavior suggests that they began to question Republican economic doctrine before World War I and the the Democratic party attracted immigrant votes by espousing cultural liberalism. More importantly, an analysis of French Canadian politics on the local level demonstrates that the development of recognition politics was well under way in Massachusetts during the first two decades of the twentieth century, a factor overlooked in other works concerning Massachusetts politics during this period.[11]

Most analysts of French Canadian political behavior have agreed on several points.[12] First, they have usually agreed that the group's political assimilation, judged in terms of the percentage of adult males who became naturalized, was comparatively slow compared with that of other groups. Second, most have agreed that since the 1920s French Canadian voters have leaned toward the Democratic party and that French Canadians have been more active in the Democratic party than in the GOP. Finally, most analysts have argued that the Democratic leaning among French Canadians after the 1920s represented a shift away from the Republican party, with whom they had identified from the mid-1890s. Little controversy exists over the first two claims. Whether French Canadians were Democrats or Republicans between 1892 and 1920, however, is a point of disagreement as are the causes of their political alignment.

The controversy over French Canadian political alignment from the 1890s to 1920 is essentially two-sided. Duane Lockard, in New England State Politics, agreed that language, clannishness, and slow assimilation retarded the entry of French Canadians into politics, but pointed out that when they did so, "they . . . came largely into the Democratic party."[13] According to Lockard, the Democratic party attracted immigrant voters partly because its close association with the Irish had tempered anti-Catholic and anti-immigrant attitudes within it. While he emphasized the Democratic leanings of Catholic immigrants, Lockard cautioned that "the entry of these groups into the Democratic party was far from automatic."[14] Irish domination of the party and economic conflict between them and later immigrants led "both Italians and French Canadians . . . to vote with the Republicans in various areas."[15] In the end, however, the more liberal position of the Democrats on economic issues drew in many working-class immigrant voters like French Canadians before 1920.[16]

According to David Walker, however, most French Canadians in New England probably voted for Democratic presidential candidates between 1880 and 1892 but from 1892 to 1928 "favoured the Republican presidential candidates—in large measure for ethnic and religious reasons."[17] In his view, the realignment in 1896 resulted from "a culturally rooted sense of fiscal orthodoxy" and a dislike of Bryan's fundamentalist, agrarian Protestantism. After 1896 Theodore Roosevelt's popularity among *Canadiens* as well as religious and economic antagonisms between them and the Irish kept them in Republican columns until the 1920s. The candidacy of Al Smith and the onset of the Great Depression reversed this trend, inaugurating a new political era during which most *Canadiens* moved into and remained within Democratic ranks.[18]

Walker qualified his generalizations in two ways. First, he pointed out the French Canadian voting was not uniform throughout New England; the *Canadien* vote varied from state to state, and from locality to locality. This divisive pattern he attributed primarily to Franco-Irish hostilities. Where the Irish were stronger, as in Rhode Island, the GOP attracted French voters. Where the Irish Democratic party was weaker and the "more nativist, Yankee Republican party" stronger, as in Maine and New Hampshire, French Canadians tended to be Democrats. French Canadian voting in Massachusetts, where "a wholly confusing pattern" prevailed, fit neither of these types before 1896.[19] Second, he pointed out the *Canadiens* became more active politically after 1896 and that this increased activity coincided with a rapprochement between them and the Irish Democrats.

> Due to a decline of Irish strength in some areas and a warmer relationship with them in others, the regional group generally displayed stronger Democratic tendencies in state and local elections than had previously been the case.[20]

Thus, while French Canadians were "leaning Republican" in national politics between 1896 and 1924, a "Democratic countertrend" evolved, resulting in a "larger Democratic municipal vote" and more French Canadian Democratic candidates.

The simplicity of Duane Lockard's interpretation is its strength: most French Canadians, like other Catholic immigrant groups, have been more inclined to be Democrats from the start, though deviations from that rule existed due to the occasional political and economic conflicts with the Irish. Lockard used analyses of both voting and officeholding patterns to determine party preferences in the period after 1920. For the earlier period, however, he relied exclusively on officeholding patterns in four New England states. Close examination of his evidence shows that French Canadian Democrats actually outnumbered Republicans only by the slimmest of margins in three states and were a minority in the other. The total number of French Canadian state legislators in the four states was twenty-one—ten Republicans and eleven Democrats. Although Lockard's evidence was on surer footing by mid-century, when Democrats outnumbered Republicans by four to one, it is less convincing for the turn of the century.[21]

By postulating that French Canadian party preferences on the state and local level depended on the relative strength of the Irish in the Democratic party, Walker's interpretation may seem to better explain the nearly even split of Canadien legislators between the two parties at the turn of the century. A rapprochement between the Canadiens and the Irish conceivably could account for a drift towards the Democratic party on the state and local level between 1896 and 1920, measured in terms of the number of Canadien officeholders. But if this were the case, it would be difficult to accept Walker's view that Franco-Irish antagonisms helped to keep the French Canadians Republican in presidential contests during the same period. While it is plausible that the French Canadians had dichotomous voting patterns on different levels of politics, it seems unlikely that the divergent patterns could have the same cause—their relationship with the Irish. If ethnic conflict pushed the Canadiens away from the Democratic party between 1896 and 1920, would it not have also pushed them into Republican ranks on the local level where ethnic conflicts were more salient? The ambiguity of Walker's argument, especially regarding the effect of ethnic antagonisms on party preferences, weakens his interpretation of French Canadian politics during this period. While Lockard's conclusion that the French Canadians were mostly Democrats appears uncorroborated by his evidence, Walker's explanation of his observation that most French Canadians voted Republican in national politics between 1896 and 1920 appears at odds with his explanation of the simultaneous "Democratic countertrend" he observed on the state and local level.

Which of these views best characterizes the relationship between French Canadians and the political parties between 1892 and 1920? Both interpretations, it should be emphasized, point to divisions among French Canadian voters and assume that antagonisms between the *Canadiens* and the Irish had some bearing on their party preferences. Lockard, however, views such conflict as secondary, leading to local deviations from the essentially pro-Democratic orientation expected of working-class Catholic immigrants. Walker, on the other hand, views the Franco-Irish conflict as crucial to French Canadian party preferences on the national as well as other levels.

Most analysts of French Canadian political behavior during this period have followed Walker's lead. As articulated by Walker and others, the conventional interpretation contends that religious and economic animosities between the Irish and French Canadians played a central and determinative role in shaping the *Canadiens'* relationship with the political parties. These rivalries were compounded, according to some observers, by the political selfishness of the Irish, who proved unwilling to share the rewards of politics with newcomers.[22] Repulsed from the Democratic party by the Irish, the French Canadians reputedly turned to the Republican party after 1896 because it offered the group more recognition—in the form of nominations and offices—and because its conservative high-tariff doctrine appealed to them as the employees of protected industries.[23]

This study of French Canadians in Massachusetts before 1920 reexamines and modifies the conventional interpretation of their political behavior. Political pragmatism, I believe, rather than Franco-Irish animosity, best describes the political style developed by French Canadians and the relationship between them and the political parties. The religious and cultural rivalry between *Canadiens* and the Irish affected politics at times but was not the central determinate of their behavior. Poised equidistantly between Irish Democratic and Yankee Republican elements in the Bay State, French Canadians throughout this period sought political opportunities by which to enhance the prestige and status of their group. Theirs was a style that subordinated party loyalty and intergroup frictions to the psychic rewards and practical gains derived from recognition politics.

The development of political pragmatism had its origins in the national identity that *Canadien* immigrants carried with them from the fields and farms of Quebec to the factories of New England and in their efforts to preserve their culture. The ethos of *la survivance* shaped the group's perception of itself and contributed heavily to the formation of Little Canadas, where French Canadian culture nourished its ethnic identity. The pattern of concentrated settlement in industrial cities and towns facilitated the continuity of culture but isolated the great mass of transplanted *habitants*. The cultural conflicts with native Yankees and

Irish Catholics that arose from the French Canadians' efforts on behalf of *la survivance* fortified their sense of alienation. Their pre-immigration experience and the conditions of life in New England thus enhanced the minority mentality that French Canadians arrived with, and inclined them to assume an essentially defensive posture towards other groups.

Outbursts of cultural conflict between the French Canadians, Yankee Protestants, and Irish Catholics also influenced the development of political pragmatism. Catholic community-building evoked the concern of native-born and foreign-born Protestants during the late 1880s, precipitating a flood of anti-immigrant and anti-Catholic sentiment that overflowed into Bay State politics. The identification of the Republican party with prohibition and anti-Catholic feeling pushed many newly mobilized French Canadian voters away from the GOP between 1888 and 1892. Meanwhile, the Democratic party, under Gov. William Russell's leadership, improved its appeal among *Canadiens* by emphasizing its defense of Catholic minority rights and by making special efforts to extend to French Canadians the political recognition they desired, especially at a time of heightened insecurity. Voting patterns suggest that the initial alignment of French Canadians with the Democratic party persisted long afterwards, albeit weakened by Republican inroads after 1895.

The Democratic party gained electoral support among French Canadians for a variety of reasons. The salience of ethnocultural issues diminished between 1896 and 1900 as the GOP made an effort to attract ethnic voters who were disenchanted by the Democratic party's association with Bryan and the cause of free silver. During the early years of the twentieth century, however, cultural issues regained their salience. The prohibition movement in Massachusetts, for example, peaked in 1907–08 when 267 cities and towns in the state voted for local prohibition, including Worcester, the largest city in the nation to vote itself dry. The effort to restrict state aid to Catholic charitable organizations inflamed religious tensions during this period and contributed to the calling of a state constitutional convention. In 1913 immigration restriction further fanned ethnoreligious embers when the Republican gubernatorial candidate made this issue the centerpiece of his campaign.[24]

Too narrow a focus on ethnocultural issues overlooks the positive economic and political incentives that the Democratic party gave to immigrant, working-class groups. While the Democrats' defense of Catholic immigrant minority rights benefited the party in the early 1890s, so did the party's emphasis on tariff reform in national and state campaigns. From 1888 to 1893, for example, the Democrats under the leadership of Governor Russell in Massachusetts emphasized reciprocity with Canada and lower tariffs on imported raw materials. Both positions carried potent overtones for French Canadians, who strongly supported Democratic candidates like Russell and Grover Cleveland. Tariff reductions on wool and leather promised job protection for many *Canadien* voters who worked in woolen textile and boot and shoe factories; reciprocity meant not only lower prices for food products imported from Quebec but also a boost to the farmers of Quebec with whom French Canadians of New England remained in close contact. The Democrats coupled their tariff proposals with a program of labor reforms from which many working-class immigrants might expect to benefit and French Canadians often voted for Democratic labor legislators.[25]

After 1900 the Democratic party continued to advocate tariff and labor reform. The 1904 election of William Douglas, the first twentieth-century Democratic governor of the Bay State, was due primarily to the Democratic emphasis on reciprocity.[26] Internal divisions within the party and the personal popularity of Republican governor Curtis Guild weakened the party's electoral support between 1906 and 1908, but Democratic candidates such as Henry M. Whitney, the most prominent pro-reciprocity businessman in the state, kept the issue before the voters, as did the emphasis on that issue by Sir Wilfrid Laurier and the Liberal party in Canada in the general elections of 1904 and 1908.[27] Democratic fortunes began their upward swing in 1909 when Eugene Foss, the state's leading advocate of reciprocity, switched parties and received the Democratic nomination for lieutenant governor. Foss lost in 1909 but led the Democratic party to victory in the next three elections. David Walsh, Foss's lieutenant governor and who, like Foss, stressed progressive tariff and labor reforms, succeeded Foss as governor in 1913 and 1914.[28] Given the Democratic party's defense of their economic interests as well as their religious and cultural rights, it is not surprising that it attracted many ethnic, working-class voters, as V.O. Key, Duane Lockard and John Buenker have previously suggested.[29]

The Democratic party practice of recognition politics, above all, strengthened its attraction to French Canadians. Twenty years before Edmond Talbot was nominated for lieutenant governor, French Canadian names were commonly visible among Democratic candidates for statewide executive offices such as state auditor or treasurer. Between 1900 and 1920 the Democratic state ticket included French Canadian names in twelve of twenty annual elections.[30] Unlike its counterpart in Rhode Island, which sponsored the election of a French Canadian governor early in the twentieth century, the GOP in Massachusetts failed to nominate any French Canadians for statewide elective offices until the 1930s.[31]

Yet the Republican party did compete vigorously for French Canadian support in local politics. The development of ethnic recognition politics on the local level was especially important in giving the GOP a base among French Canadians that countered the advantages of the Democratic party in state elections. After the election of 1896 the Republican party recruited *Canadien* political activists and sponsored their movement into local government in a number of Massachusetts cities like Worcester and Fall River. Exploiting the rift between the Democratic rank and file and its free silver leadership as well as the latent tensions between the constituent ethnic groups of the Democratic coalition, this strategy was quite successful. In 1895 two-thirds of the seventeen French city councillors in Massachusetts were Democrats; by 1903 two-thirds of thirty city concillors were Republicans.[32] Between 1896 and 1900 only 38 percent of the eighteen French Canadian candidates for the state legislature were Republicans; between 1901 and 1905, 53 percent were Republicans.[33]

The GOP might have preserved and increased its gains among French Canadians had it been willing and able to continue accommodating their demands for a greater role in municipal affairs or had it nominated French Canadians for statewide offices. It did neither. Confronted with French Canadian demands for more recognition after 1900, the GOP leadership balked, alienated *Canadien* voters, and enabled the Democrats to drive a wedge between the two by offering the French Canadians alternative political opportunities on the state and local level.

Although Democratic candidates for state offices stood little chance of winning, such recognition contributed to the prestige and self-respect of the group, which was, by virtue of the ethos of *la survivance*, its experience in Quebec, and its position in New England, self-conscious about its status within the American community and sensitive to slights, real or imagined.[34] Recognition politics thus helped to keep many French Canadians in Democratic columns in state and national elections. As might be expected, the Democratic tendency was less pronounced in those communities where the GOP had gained the most ground among French Canadians before 1900. The relationship between French Canadians and the political parties remained fragile on the municipal level, particularly as recognition politics became increasingly important to political alignments.

The antipathy between French Canadians and their Irish co-religists affected the development of their political style but may not have been as potent or pervasive an influence in politics as earlier studies have suggested. Anti-Irish feeling probably reduced the level of Democratic partisanship among *Canadiens* and led them to favor Republican candidates under certain conditions, as Duane Lockard suggested.[35] But analyses of French Canadian political activities in Fall River, Worcester,

Spencer, and Southbridge show that French Canadians often collaborated with Irish Democrats in local politics despite their differences. The relationship between the French Canadians, the Irish, and the political parties varied from community to community and, therefore, should be considered within specific contexts.[36]

Political pragmatism had a larger role than ethnic animosity in determining French Canadian partisan preferences on the local level. Inclined to favor the Democratic party like other Catholic groups, French Canadians often placed ethnic loyalty above party loyalty. In practical terms this meant getting political offices that at once satisfied their desire for recognition and gave them some influence in the political process. Political parties, likewise guided by pragmatism, sought to gain the allegiance of *Canadien* voters by accommodating their aspirations. Having only limited resources, however, neither political party could fully satiate the French Canadian political appetite. Political alliances remained fragile and often short-lived, being subject to the vagaries of local ethnic politics. Thus, before 1920 French Canadians became adept at playing each party off the other in an effort to expand the group's influence in politics. Their relationship with the political parties might best be characterized as one of mutual exploitation in which the exchange of votes and offices loomed larger than adherence to political principles or ethnic prejudices.[37]

This pragmatic approach to politics is evident in such cities as Fall River and Worcester where the *Canadiens* tended to be less Democratic in their voting. As elsewhere, French Canadians in these cities aligned themselves with the Democratic party in the early 1890s. They gravitated towards the Republican party after 1895 largely because the GOP offered them more recognition than the Democrats, divided and out of power, could give them. By 1900 the French Canadians appeared solidly welded to the Republican party. As case studies of Fall River and Worcester show, however, the knot tying *Canadiens* to the GOP was not as tight as it seemed. After 1900, French Canadians grew increasingly dissatisfied with their treatment by the Republicans. Recovering from the devastation wrought by Bryanism, the Democratic party began once again to court French Canadian voters. As the Democrats improved their practice of the delicate art of ethnic politics, the seemingly solid Franco-Republican bond weakened. Over the next decade and a half many French Canadian voters often swung into Democratic columns, supporting *Canadien* Democratic candidates and also helping to elect Irish Democratic mayors, councillors, and school committeemen.[38] In both cities political pragmatism dulled the sharp edge of ethnic prejudice as French Canadians collaborated with Irish Democrats in order to improve their own position in community politics.

In the smaller towns of central Massachusetts, where French Canadians formed a larger proportion of the total population than in the cities, Franco-Irish hostility had even less impact on politics, and cooperation between the two groups was closer. As in the cities, French Canadians mobilized in the 1890s to expand their influence in government. In these towns, however, the Democratic party proved more accommodating of *Canadien* desires for recognition than the GOP. French Canadians associated themselves closely with the Democratic party after the demise of Governor Russell's Democratic coalition and by 1900 remained aligned with the Democrats, unlike in the cities.

The differences in the relationships between the French Canadians, the Irish, and the Democratic party in large cities and small manufacturing towns in Massachusetts reflected important differences in the assimilation processes among immigrant groups relative to the size of communities. In large cities residential segregation and the larger size of ethnic populations enhanced ethnic group consciousness and insularity, resulting in sharper boundaries between social groups and, perhaps, greater intragroup differentiation and intergroup conflict. The physical and social context of the smaller towns may have, on the other hand, encouraged more face-to-face relationships among members of the same ethnic groups as well as with persons belonging to other groups. Given the relatively large French Canadian and small Irish populations of these towns, it is conceivable that cooperation among Catholics was encouraged by greater Protestant-Catholic polarization. Finally, it should be noted that French Canadians had been settled in towns such as Southbridge and Spencer since the 1850s and had by the 1880s developed a solid core of middle-class businessmen and professionals respected enough by their own group as well as by the larger community to entrust them with the reins of local government.[39]

A comparison of Southbridge and Spencer shows that the relationship between the *Canadiens* and Democrats was stronger in Southbridge. In that town French Canadian Democratic candidates and officeholders far outnumbered Republicans. The very strength of the relationship forced the Republicans to offer French Canadians greater recognition after 1900, enabling the *Canadiens* to increase substantially their share of local offices.

Although most French Canadian political activists in Spencer were Democrats, the French Canadian voters in that town were more evenly divided between the parties. Partisan divisions probably hindered the growth of French Canadian political influence in the mid-1890s, leading French Canadians to unify and mobilize themselves after 1895. Led by French-speaking Democrats, the *Canadiens* successfully organized their own party, or caucus. Wedging themselves between the contending local parties, they extracted from both the recognition they wanted. By 1900 French Canadians filled nearly one in five of key town offices. The success of the French caucus lay in its ability to balance its slate to satisfy both its Democratic and Republican factions and in its persuading *Canadiens* to vote as a bloc. This was no easy task. Factional disputes fractured group solidarity after 1902 as both factions struggled for control of the caucus. Internal divisions, ironically, benefited French Canadians in Spencer; for, as in Southbridge, interparty competition gave them a larger voice in both parties and increased the proportion of French Canadians among local officeholders.

The traditional emphasis on Franco-Irish religious tension as the primary stimulus for anti-Democratic political behavior appears exaggerated in light of a Democratic voting tendency among French Canadians in Massachusetts and their cooperation with Irish Democrats in certain communities. Certainly such tension formed part of each group's political culture and affected its politics. The impact, however, varied from community to community. In Southbridge, where French Canadians formed a majority of the townspeople and were securely established, anti-Irish feeling did not preclude *Canadiens* from aligning themselves with the Democratic party, which opened political opportunities for them. In Fall River, the Flint Affair (1884–85) steered the *Canadiens* toward the GOP but did not hinder them from supporting Democratic candidates in the early 1890s. During the early years of the next century mutual political and cultural interests again moderated the influence of ethnic hostility even in Ward Six, where many French Canadian leaders remained closely tied to the Republican city organization. In Spencer, the North Brookfield religious controversy in 1900 caused hardly a flurry, disturbing not in the least the newly formed Franco-Democratic alliance. In Worcester, however, where French Canadians lived as a political minority in Irish-dominated wards, the controversy stirred up a storm of anti-Irish rhetoric. Venting deeply-felt frustration, it rallied *Canadiens* behind a French Canadian Republican aldermanic candidate and damaged the prospects of the Irish Democratic mayoral candidate. The tempest quickly spent itself and left little lasting impact, for soon afterwards many French Canadians supported Irish mayoral candidates. In sum, although relations between the French Canadians and the Irish could not properly be described as harmonious, mutual interests and political pragmatism prevailed over prejudice in these communities.

The efforts of the Democrats and Republicans to attract French Canadian voters reflected the importance of ethnicity and religion in the political life of the Commonwealth during the late nineteenth and early twentieth centuries. The continuing immigration of *Canadiens,* the rapid growth of their institutions, and the rising political power of the Irish in the state's major cities during the 1880s all signaled the beginning of the decline of Yankee-Protestant, Republican hegemony in Massachusetts, a long process that would not culminate until decades later. The social changes transforming Massachusetts in the nineteenth century manifested themselves in politics during the 1880s as ethnoreligious issues grew in significance, polarizing Catholics and Protestants. By the end of that decade the mobilization of large numbers of French Canadian voters enlarged the mass base of the Democratic party, enabling it to win a series of narrow electoral victories. William Russell's successes revealed the potency of a heavily immigrant and Catholic Democratic coalition that, of political necessity, advocated a pluralistic view of America. The emergent new majority frightened the GOP, which by the late 1890s began to undermine the Democratic coalition. While trying to minimize its association with militant anti-Catholicism, particularly the APA movement in Massachusetts, the Republican party also recruited French Canadians, largely by offering them what they wanted most and what the Democratic party could not as easily accord them—recognition and a share in local government.

The Republican strategy implied an acceptance, however reluctant, of ethnic and cultural differences in American society and marked the transition from the highly-charged and divisive politics of culture of the late nineteenth century to the politics of recognition and accommodation more typical of twentieth-century urban politics. As earlier, ethnocultural issues remained important in Massachusetts after 1895 but ethnic and interest group politics, with its bargaining and compromising, increasingly came to dominate Bay State politics. Coincidentally the instability of urban coalitional politics—resulting from each party's difficult, if not impossible, task of satisfying the often conflicting demands of its constituent groups—accelerated the loosening of party loyalties that had begun during the political upheavals of the 1890s.

The espousal of pluralism by the Republican as well as the Democratic party symbolized an important step in the political acculturation of the French Canadians. From the late 1880s French Canadian proponents of *la survivance* had adopted a pluralistic model of the American Republic that incorporated a tolerance of separate group development and in which immigrants like themselves could become loyal Americans while remaining loyal *Canadiens.* In their view, naturalization permitted French Canadians to become legal citizens of the United States without requiring of them a change of heart, a forfeiture of their faith and language. Their hope was that the political mobilization of French Canadians could serve to protect and preserve the group's cultural heritage by enhancing the group's prestige and by giving it a say in the creation of public policy proportional to its population.[40]

The pragmatic efforts of both political parties to adjust to the rapidly changing demographic, social, and political realities in Massachusetts no doubt pleased the French Canadians but probably disappointed others who did not share a pluralistic vision of American society. Indeed, early critics of the French Canadians and their emphasis on *la survivance* might have seen in the intensification of ethnic group politics the decline of the virtuous Republic in which all feelings of religion and race were subordinated for the sake of the common good. From their point of view, Albert Bartlett's prediction that the arrival and survival of ethnic groups portended a future in which America would become "a heterogeneous collection of different nationalities with diverse allegiance" and American political life "reduced" to mutual group jealousies and suspicions had been realized, to no one's advantage.[41]

The politics of recognition widened the avenues of political participation for the French Canadians who used their strategic position in many Bay State communities to gain social and political concessions from both parties while identifying strongly with neither. The expansion of their political influence under Republican auspices in many cities between 1895 and 1900 thus represented a pragmatic response to newly opened political opportunities more than it signified a conversion to Republicanism motivated by a change in principle among French Canadians or a sudden surge of Franco-Irish hostility.

For French Canadians, participation in American political life (in the long run an important first step in their assimilation) represented one of several aspects of *la survivance*. The politics of recognition suited them well because it accepted the group basis of politics and because interparty competition for their votes gave them a foothold in politics on their own terms. Equally wary of both the Yankee-dominated GOP and the Irish-dominated Democratic party, the French Canadians exhibited a spirit of political independence that probably typified many other ethnic groups during the chaotic transitional years between the third and fourth electoral systems, when deeply rooted party identifications waned.[42] In light of their consistent, albeit marginal Democratic voting pattern in Massachusetts, French Canadians appear to have been less exceptional among Catholic ethnic groups than other analysts have suggested. To some extent, Franco-Irish animosity contributed to the Republican party's inroads among the *Canadiens* in some localities, but the instability of the urban Franco-Republican alliances and the cooperation between the *Canadiens* and Irish Democrats in urban and town politics suggest that pragmatism superseded other forces as an influence on local politics.

Appendix

Table 1 French Canadian population of localities in Massachusetts having at least 1,000 French Canadians, first and second generation, 1895.

	Total population (1895)	French Canadians			Percent of population in state (1895)		
		1885	1895	1905	All	FC	Cumulative
Fall River	89,203	10,640	24,212	28,357	3.57	13.41	13.41
Lowell	84,367	8,412	17,768	19,549.	3.57	9.84	23.25
Holyoke	40,322	7,099	10,006	12,668	1.61	5.54	28.79
Worcester	98,767	5,673	9,156	11,962	3.95	5.07	33.86
New Bedford	55,251	2,830	7,744	14,856	2.21	4.29	38.15
Lawrence	52,164	2,567	6,465	11,202	2.09	3.58	41.73
Salem	34,473	1,990	5,334	7,003	1.38	2.95	44.68
Fitchburg	26,409	1,256	4,603	6,607	1.06	2.55	47.23
Haverhill	30,209	2,140	4,308	4,416	1.21	2.39	49.62
Southbridge	8,250	3,187	4,217	5,649	.33	2.33	51.95
Springfield	51,522	2,678	4,176	5,973	2.06	2.31	54.26
North Adams	19,135	1,778	3,575	4,477	.77	1.98	56.24
Marlboro	14,977	1,853	3,462	3,250	.60	1.92	58.16
Chicopee	16,420	1,903	3,271	4,535	.66	1.81	59.97
Boston	496,920	1,538	3,022	3,914	19.88	1.67	61.64
Spencer	7,614	3,684	3,017	2,619	.30	1.67	63.31
Ware	7,651	1,826	2,895	2,909	.31	1.60	64.91
Northhampton	16,746	1,371	2,311	2,573	.67	1.28	66.19
Taunton	27,115	1,275	2,060	3,470	1.08	1.14	67.33
Gardner	9,182	1,531	1,945	2,722	.37	1.08	68.41
Cambridge	81,643	1,180	1,882	2,540	3.27	1.04	69.45
Lynn	62,354	685	1,719	3,186	2.49	.95	70.40
Palmer	6,858	1,122	1,705	1,367	.27	.94	71.34
Adams	7,837	1,860	1,647	2,852	.31	.91	72.25
Sutton	3,420	1,253	1,647	1,530	.14	.91	73.16
Pittsfield	20,461	805	1,572	1,515	.82	.87	74.03
Webster	7,799	1,744	1,511	2,345	.31	.84	74.87
Millbury	5,222	933	1,389	1,240	.21	.77	75.64
Gloucester	28,211	59	1,301	151	1.13	.72	76.36
Grafton	5,101	1,068	1,271	1,148	.20	.70	77.06
Montague	6,058	1,094	1,207	1,293	.24	.67	77.73
West Boylston	2,968	948	1,206	86	.12	.67	78.40
Amesbury	9,986	285	1,100	1,348	.40	.61	79.01
Attleborough	8,288	628	1,035	1,943	.33	.57	79.58
Northbridge	5,286	611	1,032	1,914	.21	.57	80.15
N. Brookfield	4,635	779	1,010	277	.19	.56	80.71

Tables 1-7 are based on the published volumes of the state censuses of Massachusetts, 1885, 1895, and 1905.

Table 2 Summary table comparing three types of French Canadian centers of settlement.

	Mean: Total Population	Mean: French Canadian population	Mean: Amount of capital in in manufacturing	Mean: Capital in manufacturing per capita ($)	Mean: Average annual earnings of wage earners
Primary cities	70,012	12,559	27,000	421	393
Secondary cities	33,455	3,189	7,197	247	461
Secondary towns	5,246	1,340	1,459	267	392

	Cumulative percent of state	Cumulative percent of FC state population	Mean percent of FC of population in place	Mean percentage of FC population of which is first generation
Primary cities	16.9	41.7	18.1	66.1
Secondary cities	16.3	21.2	12.6	55.5
Secondary towns	5.0	17.9	25.6	52.5

Percent of the French Canadian-born male workforce in selected occupations, 1885

	White collar	Trades	Textiles and shoes	Common and farm laborers
Primary cities	6.7	16.6	37.0	10.9
Secondary cities	4.3	13.4	35.1	9.1
Secondary towns	2.8	7.1	47.2	13.8

1905	French Canadians	Irish	British	English Canadians
Rank	1 2 3 4	1 2 3 4	1 2 3 4	1 2 3 4

Number of localities in which the specified group has a given rank

	French Canadians	Irish	British	English Canadians
Primary cities	2 3 1 0	4 0 2 0	0 2 3 1	0 0 0 1
Secondary cities	4 4 2 2	8 4 0 0	0 0 6 5	0 3 2 0
Secondary towns	21 3 0 0	2 14 5 2	0 0 12 6	0 0 1 12

Table 3   Economic profile of French Canadian centers of settlement, Massachusetts, 1895.

	Total population	FC population	Capital invested in manufacturing $(000)	Capital per capita	Average annual earnings of wage earners	% of total manufacturing workforce (1885) employed in: Textiles	Boots & Shoes
Primary cities							
Fall River	89,203	24,212	43,851	494	341	81.4	.5
Lowell	84,367	17,768	29,967	355	367	67.0	1.2
Holyoke	40,322	10,006	21,609	536	410	41.3	.5
Worcester	98,767	9,156	22,767	230	472	6.7	13.3
New Bedford	55,251	7,744	22,480	407	380	49.4	4.7
Lawrence	52,164	6,465	26,323	505	385	68.6	.7
Secondary cities							
Salem	34,473	5,334	4,834	230	472	19.6	42.3
Fitchburg	26,409	4,603	8,079	306	439	31.3	2.5
Haverhill	30,209	4,308	4,601	152	494	1.8	68.2
Springfield	51,522	4,176	10,541	205	494	10.7	.9
North Adams	19,135	3,575	10,060	527	428	54.0	19.1
Marlboro	14,977	3,462	1,898	126	466	-	84.2
Chicopee	16,420	3,271	7,175	437	440	62.5	.5
Northhampton	16,746	2,311	3,047	182	393	34.7	.8
Taunton	27,115	2,060	7,112	262	450	32.1	1.0
Cambridge	81,643	1,882	14,053	172	500	-	-
Lynn	62,354	1,719	11,047	177	513	-	68.3
Pittsfield	20,461	1,572	3,917	191	437	44.4	8.1

Table 3 (continued)

	Total population	FC population	Capital invested in manufacturing $ (000)	Capital per capita	Average annual earnings of wage earners	% of total manufacturing workforce (1885) employed in: Textiles	Boots & Shoes
Secondary towns							
Southbridge	8,250	4,217	2,744	335	394	63.8	-
Spencer	7,614	3,017	1,015	134	510	10.3	72.6
Ware	7,651	2,895	2,066	272	324	81.5	1.8
Gardner	9,182	1,945	1,886	207	523	-	-
Palmer	6,858	1,705	1,969	285	358	76.6	-
Adams	7,837	1,647	3,245	416	366	81.4	-
Sutton	3,420	1,647	876	258	317	78.0	3.8
Webster	7,799	1,511	1,714	220	337	76.8	10.6
Millbury	5,222	1,389	1,075	207	387	62.0	2.7
Grafton	5,101	1,271	1,798	353	348	52.4	30.2
Montague	6,058	1,207	2,222	363	424	10.7	.7
Amesbury	9,986	1,100	2,091	209	438	42.4	.8
Attleborough	8,288	1,035	2,659	320	480	14.4	-
Northbridge	5,286	1,032	2,095	395	422	46.3	18.6
North Brookfield	4,635	1,010	601	131	433	-	87.2
Dudley	3,203	994	1,178	368	327	83.2	4.8
Ludlow	2,562	782	n/a	n/a	n/a	80.5	-
Warren	4,430	882	1,289	293	437	59.2	3.1
Oxford	2,390	572	222	92	380	49.3	29.5
Hardwick	2,655	554	1,290	477	362	86.3	-
Douglas	2,026	477	533	266	384	20.4	-
Sturbridge	1,910	523	726	382	371	65.5	2.6
Auburn	1,598	318	155	97	314	49.3	15.4
Northboro	1,940	434	102	54	393	49.3	3.8

Table 4 Dominant industry and number of boot and shoe, cotton, and woolen textile establishments in French Canadian centers of settlement, Massachusetts, 1895.

	Dominant Industry (1885)	Number of establishments (1895)		
		Boot & Shoe	Cotton	Woolen
Primary cities				
Fall River	Cotton goods	28	51	0
Lowell	Cotton goods	37	10	6
Holyoke	Paper goods	8	4	4
Worcester	Metal goods	94	5	9
New Bedford	Cotton goods	63	13	1
Lawrence	Worsted goods	21	5	5
Secondary cities				
Salem	Boots & shoes	70	1	0
Fitchburg	n/a	6	8	0
Haverhill	Boots & shoes	289	0	1
Springfield	n/a	20	7	0
North Adams	n/a	9	5	2
Marlboro	Boots & shoes	10	0	0
Chicopee	Cotton textiles	1	2	0
Northhampton	n/a	1	0	0
Taunton	Cotton textiles	20	6	0
Cambridge	n/a	38	0	0
Lynn	Boots & shoes	284	0	0
Pittsfield	Woolen goods	0	0	4
Secondary towns				
Southbridge	Boots & shoes	2	1	1
Spencer	Boots & shoes	9	0	2
Ware	Woolen goods	0	1	2
Gardner	n/a	5	0	0
Palmer	Cotton goods	0	1	1
Adams	Cotton goods	0	4	0
Sutton	Cotton goods	1	2	3
Webster	Woolen goods	4	1	1
Millbury	Cotton goods	1	3	5
Grafton	Cotton goods	5	4	1
Montague	Metal goods	2	1	0
Amesbury	Boots & shoes	3	1	0
Attleborough	Metal goods	1	2	0
Northbridge	Cotton goods	1	3	1
North Brookfield	Boots & shoes	2	0	0
Dudley	Worsted goods	0	0	4
Ludlow	n/a	-	-	-
Warren	Cotton goods	1	2	1
Oxford	Boots & shoes	1	1	3
Hardwick	Paper goods	0	0	1
Douglas	Woolen goods	0	0	1
Sturbridge	Cotton goods	0	1	0
Auburn	Worsted goods	0	0	2
Northboro	Woolen goods	2	0	2

Table 5 Demographic profile of French Canadian centers of settlement, 1895.

	% of total state population in locality	% of total FC in state	% FC of total population of locality	% of FC who are immigrants	Rate of growth of the FC population 1885-95	Rate of growth of the FC population 1895-1905
Primary cities						
Fall River	3.6	13.4	27.1	70.5	128	17
Lowell	3.4	9.8	21.1	72.3	111	10
Holyoke	1.6	5.5	24.8	63.4	41	27
Worcester	4.0	5.1	9.3	46.1	61	31
New Bedford	2.2	4.3	14.0	72.8	174	92
Lawrence	2.1	3.6	12.4	71.7	152	73
Secondary cities						
Salem	1.4	3.0	15.5	69.7	168	31
Fitchburg	1.1	2.6	17.4	63.0	266	43
Haverhill	1.2	2.4	14.3	54.7	101	2
Springfield	2.1	2.3	8.1	53.4	56	43
North Adams	.8	2.0	18.7	51.4	101	25
Marlboro	.6	1.9	23.1	40.5	87	- 6
Chicopee	.7	1.8	19.9	60.4	72	39
Northhampton	.7	1.3	13.8	46.5	69	11
Taunton	1.1	1.1	7.6	66.9	62	25
Cambridge	3.3	1.0	2.3	57.6	59	35
Lynn	2.5	.9	2.3	60.2	171	85
Pittfield	.8	.9	7.7	41.9	95	- 4

Table 5 (continued)

	% of total state population in locality	% of total FC in state in locality	% FC of total population of locality	% of FC who are immigrants	Rate of growth of the FC population 1885-95	Rate of growth of the FC population 1895-1905
Secondary towns						
Southbridge	.3	2.3	51.1	48.1	32	34
Spencer	.3	1.7	34.6	39.6	-18	-13
Ware	.3	1.6	37.8	64.7	58	1
Gardner	.4	1.1	21.2	55.5	27	40
Palmer	.3	.9	24.9	54.2	52	-20
Adams	.3	.9	21.0	52.8	-11	73
Sutton	.1	.9	48.2	53.5	31	-7
Webster	.3	.8	19.4	55.0	-14	55
Millbury	.2	.8	26.6	50.6	41	-11
Grafton	.2	.7	24.9	50.9	23	-10
Montague	.2	.7	19.9	51.5	-10	7
Amesbury	.4	.6	11.0	63.4	211	23
Attleborough	.3	.6	12.5	54.3	37	88
Northbridge	.2	.6	19.5	64.6	53	85
North Brookfiled	.2	.6	21.8	36.1	10	-72
Dudley	.1	.6	31.0	53.9	25	-2
Ludlow	.1	.4	30.5	64.8	15	21
Warren	.2	.5	19.9	51.8	15	6
Oxford	.1	.3	23.9	46.1	98	43
Hardwick	.1	.3	20.9	64.6	-25	31
Douglas	.1	.3	23.5	41.5	- 1	23
Sturbridge	.1	.3	27.4	47.4	10	5
Auburn	.1	.2	19.9	45.0	41	15
Northboro	.1	.2	22.4	49.3	34	-17

Table 6 Percent of the French Canadian-born male labor force in selected occupations, 1885.

	White collar	Trades	Textiles	Boots & Shoes	Laborers	Farm laborers	Other	Total
Primary cities								
Fall River	6.8	8.8	49.3	1.1	5.0	1.6	8.7	81.3
Lowell	6.9	16.2	36.7	5.6	8.9	4.2		78.5
Holyoke	7.7	18.2	23.4	-	10.9	1.3		73.9
Worcester	5.7	26.5	8.6	14.7	3.3	1.5	12.4	66.3
New Bedford	7.2	10.4	54.0	2.0	8.9	1.9	6.0	84.4
Lawrence	6.0	19.4	25.9	.9	9.0	4.3		65.5
Secondary cities								
Salem	4.2	5.9	39.8	13.9	5.7	.8		70.3
Fitchburg	2.4	14.4	8.4	1.6	10.2	3.0	15.0	54.0
Haverhill	5.3	11.6	.4	64.0	3.8	1.3		86.4
Springfield	7.4	16.8	20.0	1.6	2.9	1.1	13.4	63.2
North Adams	5.0	15.0	20.5	21.4	11.9	1.9		75.7
Marlboro	4.4	5.4	-	72.6	2.7	1.7		86.8
Chicopee	5.8	20.8	34.7	-	2.6	10.6		74.5
Northhampton	4.0	16.2	6.4	1.8	2.6	6.4		49.8
Taunton	4.3	18.1	18.9	-	15.0	.8		61.8
Cambridge	.9	4.2			7.7	1.3	26.2	34.1
Lynn	3.3	5.2	-	60.0	1.9	-		70.4
Pittsfield	4.5	26.6	13.4	3.1	10.8	4.0		61.4

Table 6 (continued)

	White collar	Trades	Textiles	Boots & Shoes	Laborers	Farm laborers	Other	Total
Secondary towns								
Southbridge	5.1	9.6	27.0	-	8.1	6.1	18.2	74.1
Spencer	7.2	7.3	3.3	55.9	5.5	2.3		81.5
Ware	3.6	8.2	51.7	3.6	8.2	6.1		81.4
Gardner	2.9	8.4	-	-	16.7	1.9	51.9	81.8
Palmer	5.2	3.8	67.1	-	6.9	4.1		87.1
Adams	3.5	8.7	38.6	-	21.5	3.7	9.5	85.5
Sutton	1.7	4.8	50.8	1.7	-	16.7		75.7
Webster	3.9	5.7	49.4	8.5	8.5	4.8		80.8
Millbury	5.6	19.7	28.2	3.8	13.4	2.3		73.0
Grafton	2.6	6.0	36.3	17.1	13.7	4.3		80.0
Montague	2.5	16.8	6.1	6.1	12.9	1.4	16.5	62.3
Amesbury	1.0	8.3	44.7	-	3.1	1.0	27.0	85.1
Attleborough	1.0	5.8	23.6	-	7.3	19.9	20.4	78.0
Northbridge	1.0	7.0	49.7	1.5	5.0	11.0		75.2
North Brookfield	7.2	5.4	-	63.2	-	1.8		77.6
Dudley	.0	5.1	52.0	5.6	-	17.3		80.0
Ludlow	1.3	2.6	57.9	-	-	15.8		77.6
Warren	5.7	16.5	43.7	3.4	6.3	4.0		79.6
Oxford	1.3	1.3	30.3	32.9	-	6.6		72.4
Hardwick	1.4	3.8	69.5	-	5.2	5.2		85.1
Douglas	2.3	7.0	11.7	-	7.0	1.6	55.5	85.1
Sturbridge	.1	3.3	54.2	1.6	10.0	7.5		76.7
Auburn	.0	4.3	34.8	26.1	7.2	10.1		82.5
Northboro	.0	1.3	64.9	6.5	-	9.1		81.8

Table 7 Ethnic composition of French Canadian centers of settlement, showing the percent of the total population comprised by the four largest foreign stock groups in each locality, Massachusetts, 1905.

Rank	First		Second		Third		Fourth		Total
Primary cities									
Fall River	FC	26.8	BR	21.9	IR	17.5	PT	8.7	74.9
Lowell	IR	28.6	FC	20.6	BR	8.0	CO	5.9	63.1
Holyoke	IR	27.3	FC	25.4	BR	8.0	GR.	6.7	67.4
Worcester	IR	23.8	SW	10.5	FC	9.3	BR	5.4	49.0
New Bedford	FC	20.0	BR	15.9	PT	15.8	IR	10.2	61.9
Lawrence	IR	24.6	FC	16.0	BR	15.3	GR	6.7	62.6
Secondary cities									
Salem	IR	23.3	FC	18.6	CO	6.6	BR	3.4	51.9
Fitchburg	FC	20.0	IR	17.8	FI	8.1	BR	7.3	53.2
Haverhill	IR	14.4	CO	13.7	FC	11.7	BR	4.5	44.3
Springfield	IR	22.1	FC	8.1	BR	6.1	GR	3.2	39.5
North Adams	FC	20.2	IR	16.5	BR	9.5	IT	4.5	50.7
Marlboro	FC	23.1	IR	21.7	CO	7.2	BR	2.3	54.4
Chicopee	FC	22.5	IR	19.7	AU	13.3	PL	7.5	63.0
Northhampton	IR	21.2	FC	12.9	BR	5.6	GR	3.3	43.0
Taunton	IR	22.1	FC	11.2	BR	8.2	PT	7.6	49.1
Cambridge	IR	30.0	CO	13.5	BR	6.5	FC	2.6	52.6
Lynn	IR	19.4	CO	13.5	BR	6.5	FC	4.1	43.5
Pittsfield	IR	23.5	GR	6.7	FC	6.1	BR	5.9	42.2
Secondary towns									
Southbridge	FC	51.4	IR	8.9	BR	4.5	CO	1.6	66.4
Spencer	FC	38.9	IR	12.0	BR	3.1	CO	2.1	56.1
Ware	FC	33.8	IR	16.4	PL	13.9	BR	2.7	66.8
Gardner	FC	22.7	FI	10.5	IR	9.8	CO	5.2	48.2
Palmer	AU	19.7	FC	17.6	IR	16.0	BR	4.5	57.8
Adams	FC	22.8	AU	15.4	GR	12.2	BR	10.7	61.1
Sutton	FC	48.2	IR	3.4	BR	3.0	CO	2.0	56.6
Webster	FC	23.4	GR	19.3	PL	12.8	IR	11.0	66.5
Millbury	FC	26.8	IR	16.3	BR	7.6	CO	3.4	54.1
Grafton	FC	22.7	IR	16.5	BR	9.0	CO	6.3	54.5
Montague	FC	18.4	IR	14.3	GR	10.3	PL	6.5	49.5
Amesbury	IR	19.6	FC	15.2	BR	7.6	CO	6.5	48.9
Attleborough	FC	15.3	IR	11.2	BR	11.0	CO	6.5	44.0
Northbridge	FC	25.9	IR	21.5	BR	6.9	CO	3.5	57.8
North Brookfield	IR	26.3	FC	10.6	BR	3.9	CO	3.9	44.7
Dudley	FC	25.4	PL	19.1	IR	12.5	AU	5.1	62.1
Ludlow	FC	24.4	AU	17.9	BR	13.5	IR	7.7	63.5
Warren	FC	21.7	IR	15.3	GR	6.5	BR	6.0	49.5
Oxford	FC	28.0	IR	6.6	BR	3.2	CO	3.2	41.0
Hardwick	FC	22.3	IR	18.5	AU	11.7	BR	6.0	58.5
Douglas	FC	27.7	AU	9.4	IR	6.4	SW	3.4	46.9
Sturbridge	FC	27.7	IR	12.5	BR	3.6	--	-	43.8
Auburn	FC	18.2	SW	11.4	IR	8.9	CO	7.6	46.1
Northboro	FC	18.5	IR	9.0	CO	6.5	BR	5.5	39.5

Code: AU, Austrian; BR, British; CO, Canadian, other than French; FC, French Canadian; FI, Finnish; GR, German; IR, Irish; IT, Italian; PL, Polish; PT, Portuguese; SW, Swedish.

Notes

Chapter 1. Introduction

1. See Richard Hofstadter, *The Age of Reform* (New York: Vintage, 1955), pp. 9, 181–85; Edward C. Banfield and James Q. Wilson, *City Politics* (New York: Vintage, 1963), pp. 116–27; John M. Allswang, *Bosses, Machines, and Urban Voters*, 2d ed. (Baltimore: Johns Hopkins University Press, 1986).

2. For a negative assessment of the rise of interest group liberalism, see Theodore J. Lowi, *The End of Liberalism: Ideology, Policy, and the Crisis of Public Authority* (New York: Norton, 1969).

3. J. Joseph Huthmacher, *Massachusetts People and Politics, 1919–1933* (Cambridge: Harvard University Press, 1959); Alec Barbrook, *God Save the Commonwealth: An Electoral History of Massachusetts* (Amherst: University of Massachusetts Press, 1966); Richard M. Abrams, *Conservatism in a Progressive Era; Massachusetts Politics 1900–1912* (Cambridge: Harvard University Press, 1964); Geoffrey Blodgett, *The Gentle Reformers: Massachusetts Democrats in the Cleveland Era* (Cambridge: Harvard University Press, 1966).

4. Huthmacher, *Massachusetts People*; Hofstadter and Lubell offered a similar viewpoint in their observations about national politics. See Hofstadter, *Age of Reform*, pp. 298–301, and Samuel Lubell, *The Future of American Politics*, 3d ed. (New York: Harper, 1965), pp. 34–35; see also Raymond Wolfinger, "The Development and Persistence of Ethnic Voting," *American Political Science Review* 59 (December 1965): 896–908.

5. Lawrence H. Fuchs, ed., *American Ethnic Politics* (New York: Harper Torchbooks, 1968), pp. 4–7. For examples of the political styles developed by other ethnic groups, see the first seven essays in Fuchs and Edgar Litt, *Ethnic Politics in America* (Glenview, Il.: Scott, Foresman, 1970).

6. See Michael Parenti, "Ethnic Politics and the Persistence of Ethnic Identification," *American Political Science Review* 61 (September 1967): 717–26.

7. See Raymond E. Wolfinger, "The Development and Persistence of Ethnic Voting," *American Political Science Review* 59 (December 1965): 896–908. Although the ethos of *la survivance* may have exaggerated this tendency among the *Canadiens*, the tendency to place ethnic loyalty above party loyalty is common among American ethnic groups. As Robert Lane points out, party loyalty among ethnic voters is "often a derived loyalty, receiving its emotional charge from the primary ethnic loyalty and dependent upon an ethnic-party identification for its direction," *Political Life: Why People Get Involved in Politics* (New York: Free Press, 1959), p. 243. Lane adds that in most cases ethnic party identification hinges on recognition, pp. 239, 249. See also Litt, *Ethnic Politics*, pp. 20, 24.

8. Mason Wade, *The French Canadians, 1760–1967*, rev. ed. (Toronto: Macmillan, 1968), pp. xiii, 47–8.

9 See Richard S. Sorrell, "The *survivance* of French Canadians in New England (1865–1930): History, Geography, and Demography as Destiny," *Ethnic and Racial Studies* 4 (1981): 91–109.

10. See, for example, Alexandre Bélisle, *Histoire de la presse franco-américaine et des canadiens-français aux Etats-Unis* (Worcester: L'Opinion Publique, 1911); Josaphat Benoit, *L'Ame franco-américaine* (Montreal: Jouve, 1935); Felix Gatineaux, *Historique des Convention des Canadiens-Français aux Etats-Unis, 1865–1901* (Woonsocket, R.I.:

L'Union Saint-Jean-Baptiste d'Amérique, 1927); and especially Robert Rumilly, *Histoire des franco-américains* (Montreal: L'Union Saint-Jean-Baptiste d'Amérique, 1958).

11. See Dyke Hendrickson, *Quiet Presence; Histoires de Franco-Américains en New England* (Portland, Maine: Guy Gannett Publishing Co., 1980), pp. 25–78, for a sketch of the history of French Canadians in New England. The term "quiet presence" refers to the lack of recognition received by French Canadians. Despite their sizeable population, the history of French Canadians is not widely known and they have received little publicity through the media or in politics.

12. See Edouard Hamon, *Les Canadiens-français de la Nouvelle Angleterre* (Quebec: Hardy, 1891); Robert Rumilly, *Histoire des franco-américains*; Herve B. Lemaire, "French Canadian Efforts on Behalf of the French Language in New England," in *Language Loyalty in the United States*, ed. Joshua Fishman (London: Mouton, 1966), pp. 253–79; and Richard S. Sorrell, "The *survivance* of French Canadians in New England (1865–1930): History, Geography, and Demography as Destiny," *Ethnic and Racial Studies* 4 (1981): 91–109.

13. The neglect of French Canadians, as well as other ethnic groups until the 1960s, stemmed also from the belief prevailing among many scholars that ethnicity was a declining force in American life during the latter half of the twentieth century. A revival of interest among social scientists and historians in the "ethnic factor" and a raising of popular awareness in America's ethnic heritage began in the 1960s. Over the last two decades historians have significantly advanced our knowledge and understanding of the place of ethnicity in American society, in the past as well as in the present. See Robert Kelly, "Ideology and Political Culture from Jefferson to Nixon," *American Historical Review* 82 (1977): 531–62, and Ronald P. Formisano's "Comment," ibid.: 567–77.

The literature devoted to the study of ethnicity and minority groups is voluminous and growing. For a sampling of this work, refer to the bibliographies in: John Bodnar, *The Transplanted: A History of Immigrants in Urban America* (Bloomington: Indiana University Press, 1987); Leonard Dinnerstein and David M. Reimers, *Ethnic Americans: A History of Immigration and Assimilation* (New York: Dodd, Mead & Co., 1975); James Stuart Olson, *The Ethnic Dimension in American History*, 2 vols. (New York: St. Martin's Press, 1979). See also Michael Novak, *The Rise of the Unmeltable Ethnics; Politics and Culture in the Seventies* (New York: Macmillan, 1972), and Andrew M. Greeley and William C. McCready, *Ethnicity in the United States: A Preliminary Reconnaissance* (New York: Wiley, 1974).

14. As a starting point for the study of French Canadians, see Pierre Anctil, *A Franco-American Bibliography: New England* (Bedford, N.H.: National Materials Development Center, 1979); Stanley L. Freeman and Raymond J. Pelletier, *Initiating Franco-American Studies: A Handbook for Teachers* (Orono, Maine: University of Maine, 1981); Madeleine Giguere, ed., *A Franco-American Overview*, III (Cambridge, Mass: National Assessment and Dissemination Center, 1981); and Claire Quintal and André Vachon, eds., *Situation de la Recherche sur les Franco-Américains* (Worcester: French Institute/Assumption College, 1980); Claire Quintal, ed., *The Little Canadas of New England* (Worcester: French Institute/Assumption College, 1983).

15. Greeley and McCready, *Ethnicity*, and Fuchs, *American Ethnic Politics*.

16. By comparing the effect of ethnicity in different communities, this study follows the perspective suggested by Ronald P. Formisano and Paul Kleppner, who warned historians against the danger of treating the ethnocultural perspective as another frontier thesis and of substituting ethnocultural for economic determinism. See Ronald P. Formisano, "Comment on Robert Kelley's 'Ideology and Political Culture from Jefferson to Nixon,' " *American Historical Review* 82 (1977): 567–77; and the last chapter of Paul Kleppner, *The Third Electoral System, 1853–1892: Parties, Voters, and Political Cultures* (Chapel Hill: University of North Carolina Press, 1979). Both historians have pointed out the need to analyze ethnicity and religion within specific sociopolitical contexts. Ethnic and religious identifications, in their view should be considered as variables (Formisano, p. 571), and historians should not assume that such identifications "had the *same* partisan effects in *all* contexts and under *all* conditions," (Kleppner, p. 362). The political

roles that ethnoreligious groups played, as Formisano explained, changed over time and varied from one community to another, because ethnocultural values acquired their political salience as they interacted with particular political events and social structures.

17. Lee Benson, *The Concept of Jacksonian Democracy: New York as a Test Case* (Princeton: Princeton University Press, 1961); Ronald P. Formisano, *The Birth of Mass Political Parties: Michigan, 1827–1861* (Princeton: Princeton University Press, 1971); Richard J. Jensen, *The Winning of the Midwest: Social and Political Conflict, 1888–1896* (Chicago: University of Chicago Press, 1971); Paul Kleppner, *The Cross of Culture: A Social Analysis of Midwestern Politics, 1850–1900* (New York: Macmillan, 1970), and *Third Electoral System.* See also Michael Holt, *Forging a Majority: The Formation of the Republican Party in Pittsburg, 1848–1860* (New Haven: Yale University Press, 1969); Frederick C. Luebke, *Immigrants and Politics: The Germans of Nebraska, 1880–1900* (Lincoln: University of Nebraska Press, 1969); Samuel T. McSeveney, *The Politics of Depression: Political Behavior in the Northeast, 1893–1896* (New York: Oxford, 1972); Melvyn Hammarberg, *The Indiana Voter: The Historical Dynamics of Party Allegiance during the 1870s* (Chicago: University of Chicago Press, 1977). For critical evaluations of the new political history, see Robert P. Swierenga, "Ethnocultural Political Analysis: A New Approach to American Ethnic Studies," *Journal of American Studies* 5 (April 1971); 55–79; Samuel T. McSeveney, "Ethnic Groups, Ethnic Conflicts, and Recent Quantitative Research in American Political History," *International Migration Review* 7 (1973): 14–33; Richard L. McCormick, "Ethnocultural Interpretations of Nineteenth Century American Voting Behavior," *Political Science Quarterly* 89 (1974): 351–77; and James E. Wright, "The Ethnocultural Model of Voting: A Behavioral and Historical Critique," *American Behavioral Scientists* 16 (1973): 35–56.

18. Gerhard Lenski, *The Religious Factor: A Sociological Study of Religion's Impact on Politics, Economics, and Family Life* (Garden City, NY: Doubleday, 1961); Samuel Lubell, *The Future of American Politics*, 3d ed., (New York: Harper, 1965).

19. Kleppner, *Third Electoral System*, pp. 144, 367.

20. See Formisano, *Birth of Mass Political Parties*, pp. 137–39; Jensen, *Winning of the Midwest*, pp. 58–76; Kleppner, *Third Electoral System*, pp. 180–97.

21. Paul Kleppner, "Partisanship and Ethnoreligious Conflict: The Third Electoral System, 1853–1892," in *Evolution of American Electoral Systems*, ed. Paul Kleppner et al. (Westport, Conn: Greenwood, 1981), pp. 132–33; and "Political Confessionalism: The Ethnoreligious Roots of Partisanship," chap. 5, pp. 143–97 in Kleppner's *Third Electoral System.* Republicans drew voting support among the following native-stock groups: Baptists, Congregationalists, Episcopalians, Free Will Baptists, Methodists, Presbyterians, and Quakers. They also drew support among the following immigrant groups: British-stock voters, English Canadians, less ritualistic German Lutherans, German Sectarians, Norwegian and Swedish Lutherans. Highly confessional Germany Lutherans, German Reformed groups, Southern-stock Baptists, Methodists and Presbyterians, and most Catholics tended to support the Democratic party.

22. Kleppner, *Third Electoral System*, p. 144.

23. For example, see Kleppner's discussion of German-born voters in his *Third Electoral System*, pp. 153–58.

24. Ibid., pp. 149–53.

25. Kleppner, "Partisanship and Ethnoreligious Conflict," pp. 132–33 and *Third Electoral System*, pp. 149–51.

26. Kleppner, "Partisanship and Ethnoreligious Conflict," p. 133. As Kleppner pointed out, however, the hostility between the two groups was at times muted in the face of a common enemy. Late in the 1880s, for example, the intrusion of ethnocultural issues—prohibition and the parochial school question—into state politics polarized Protestants and Catholics in Massachusetts and carried French Canadians into the Democratic party during the early 1890s. See his *Third Electoral System*, pp. 348–52.

27. For the best treatment of the traditional view of the French Canadians, see David B. Walker, *Politics and Ethnocentrism: The Case of Franco-Americans* (Brunswick, Maine: Bowdoin College, Bureau for Research in Municipal Government, 1961), and "Presidential Politics of Franco-Americans," *Canadian Journal of Economics and Politi-*

cal Science 28 (August 1962): 353–63; Philip T. Silvia Jr., "The Spindle City: Labor, Politics, and Religion in Fall River, Massachusetts, 1870–1905," (Ph.D. diss., Fordham University, 1973); and Peter Haebler, "Habitants of Holyoke: The Development of the French Canadian Community in a Massachusetts City, 1865–1910," (Ph.D. diss., University of New Hampshire, 1976). This view is also expressed in Richard M. Abrams, *Conservatism in a Progressive Era: Massachusetts Politics, 1900–1912* (Cambridge: Harvard University Press, 1964), pp. 50–51; Mary H. Blewett, "The Mills and the Multitude: A Political History," in *Cotton was King: A History of Lowell, Massachusetts,* ed. Arthur L. Eno (Lowell: Lowell Historical Society, 1976), p. 175; John D. Buenker, *Urban Liberalism and Progressive Reform* (New York: Scribner's Sons, 1973); pp. 8–10, Donald B. Cole, *Immigrant City: Lawrence, Massachusetts, 1845–1921* (Chapel Hill: University of North Carolina Press, 1963), p. 158; Constance McLaughlin Green, *Holyoke, Massachusetts: A Case Study of the Industrial Revolution in America* (New Haven: Yale University Press, 1939), p. 338; Granville T. Prior, "The French Canadians in New England," (Master's thesis, Brown University, 1932), p. 294; Silvie Rimbert, "L'immigration franco-canadienne au Massachusetts," *Revue Canadienne de Géographie* 8 (1954), p. 84; Robert Rumilly, *Histoire des franco-américains* (Montreal: L'Union Saint-Jean-Baptiste d'Amérique, 1959), pp. 85, 174; and Norman Sepenuk, "A Profile of Franco-American Political Attitudes in New England," in *A Franco-American Overview,* vol. 3, ed. Madeleine Giguere (Cambridge: National Assessment and Dissemination Center, 1981), p. 175.

Chapter 2. *La Survivance* and the Little Canadas of Massachusetts

1. Hubert Guindon, "The Social Evolution of Quebec Reconsidered," in *French-Canadian Society,* vol. 1, ed. Marcel Rioux and Yves Martin (Toronto: McClelland & Stewart, 1964), pp. 137–61; Mason Wade, *The French Canadians, 1760–1967,* rev. ed. (Toronto: Macmillan, 1968), vol. 1, chap. 1–3. Ferdinand Ouellet, *Histoire économique et sociale du Québec, 1760–1850* (Montreal and Paris: Fides, 1966), and Jean-Pierre Wallot, "Religion and French-Canadian Mores in the Early Nineteenth Century," *Canadian Historical Review* 52 (March 1971): 51–91, stress the continuity between the eighteenth- and nineteenth-century history of French Canada.

2. Marcel Séquin, "Le régime seigneurial au pays de Québec, 1760–1854," *Revue d'histoire de l'Amérique française* 1 (March 1948): 119–32; Ralph D. Vicero, "Immigration of French Canadians to New England, 1840–1900: A Geographical Analysis," (Ph.D. diss., University of Wisconsin, 1968), chap. 1, especially pp. 13–23.

3. Guindon, "Social Evolution," p. 142.

4. For descriptions of traditional French Canadian society, see Léon Gérin, *Le Type économique et social des Canadiens,* 2d ed. (Montreal: Bibliothèque Economique et Sociale, 1948); Everett C. Hughes, *French Canada in Transition* (Chicago: University of Chicago Press, 1943). The nature and evolution of French Canada's rural society, as viewed by these scholars, has been disputed by Philippe Garigue but defended by other French Canadian sociologists. For a summary of this controversy, see Rioux and Martin, *French-Canadian Society.*

5. Wallot, "Religion and French-Canadian Mores," pp. 85–87, 90. The changing role of the church in French Canada remains a controversial subject. Recent interpretations argue that it had a more restricted role before 1840 than earlier scholars (such as those listed in note 4) suggested. There appears to be a consensus that it gained importance after 1840.

6. Guindon, "Social Evolution," p. 154.

7. About 65,000 French lived in Canada at the time of the conquest; by 1851 their descendants numbered ten times that figure and nine in ten lived in a rural environment. See Jacques Henripin, "From Acceptance of Nature to Control: The Demography of the French Canadians since the Seventeenth Century," in *French-Canadian Society,* p. 209; and Vicero, "Immigration of French Canadians," pp. 10–13. Gerald Fortin, "Socio-Cultural Change in an Agricultural Parish," in *French-Canadian Society,* pp. 92–96,

emphasizes the isolation of rural life. Winning the struggle for cultural survival by outreproducing the English-speaking Canadians was called "the revenge of the cradle" by French Canadians, and was a key strategem in their pursual of *la survivance*. See Ouellet, *Histoire*, for detailed demographic data.

8. The term "tribal ethnicity" is taken from Cynthia H. Enloe, *Ethnic Conflict and Political Development* (Boston: Little Brown, 1973), pp. 23–27. Enloe distinguishes three different types of ethnicity on the basis of "origins of their separate identities." "*Tribal ethnicity* is characterized by cultural and communal boundaries derived from bonds of kinship . . . Tribes are likely to have their own languages and customs; this is what makes them ethnic groups, not merely extended families. Their high levels of integration together with their kinship bonds make their ethnicity especially hard to break down" (pp. 23–24). "*National ethnicity* is characterized by communal identity having its roots in association with a foreign country," according to Enloe, while "*racial ethnicity* is characterized by values and bonds stemming from physical and biological distinctions" (pp. 24–25). Thus, within French Canada the French Canadian ethnic identity may best be viewed as tribal, at least in terms of its origins. After migration to the United States, it became a sort of national ethnicity.

9. Wade, *The French Canadians*, vol. 1, chaps. 2–7 trace the history of the French Canadian struggle for national survival. Wade's work is primarily a constitutional and political history, but it offers a psychological interpretation of the French Canadians that stresses the "basic loneliness and insecurity" that motivates *la survivance*; see especially pp. xiii, 47–48.

10. Marcel Rioux, "Ideologie et crise de conscience du Canada francais," *Cite Libre* 14 (December 1955): 1–29, quoted in Fernand Dumond, "The Systematic Study of the French Canadian Total Society," in *French-Canadian Society*, p. 392. See also Jacques Dofny and Marcel Rioux, "Social class in French Canada," *French-Canadian Society*, pp. 307–18, for an interpretation of French Canadian group consciousness that stresses the tension created by their minority-group status within Canada.

11. Dofny and Rioux, "Social Class," in *French Canadian Society*, pp. 308–11; Jean-Claude Falardeau, "The Role and Importance of the Church in French Canada," ibid., pp. 342–57; Fernand Dumont, "Idéologies au Canada français (1850–1900)," *Recherches sociographiques* 10 (1969): 145–56. See also Pierre Savard, "La vie du clergé Québecois au XIXᵉ siècle," *Recherches sociographiques* 8 (1967): 253–73; Michel Brunet, "L'Eglise catholique du bas-Canada et le partage du pouvoir à l'heure d'une nouvelle donne (1837–1854)," Catholic Historical Association, *Historical Papers*, (1969): 37–51.

12. Falardeau, "The Role and Importance of the Church," p. 350.

13. Falardeau, "Les Canadiens francais et leur ideologie," in *Canadian Dualism*, ed. Mason Wade (Toronto: University of Toronto Press, 1960), pp. 26–31. Falardeau stresses the importance of this identification of language and religion in alienating French Canadians not only from English-speaking Protestants but also from non-French-speaking Catholics, who were viewed as *les étrangers* in French Canada.

14. Fortin, "Socio-Cultural Changes," pp. 90–91; Falardeau, "Les Canadiens francais," p. 30; the term "demographic contradiction" is Guindon's, "Social Evolution," pp. 142–54. See also Fernand Dumont, "La Representation idéologique des classes au Canada français," *Recherches sociographiques* 6 (1965): 9–22.

15. Hughes, *French Canada in Transition*, p. 8.

16. This description of Quebec's economy relies on Ouellet, *Histoire*; Vicero,"Immigration of French Canadians," chap. 1; and R. Cole Harris and John Warkenten, *Canada Before Confederation* (New York: Oxford, 1974), chap. 3.

17. Ibid.

18. An extensive literature now exists on the immigration of the French Canadians to the United States. Ralph D. Vicero, "Immigration of French Canadians," is the best analysis of the movement to New England. See also Marcus Lee Hansen, "The Second Colonization of New England," *New England Quarterly* 2 (1929): 539–60; Marcus Lee Hansen and John B. Brebner, *The Mingling of the Canadian and American Peoples* (New Haven: Yale University Press, 1940); James P. Allen, "Migration Fields of French Canadian Immigrants to Southern Maine," *Geographical Review* 62 (1972): 366–83; Leon E. True-

sdell, *The Canadian Born in the United States* (New Haven: Yale University Press, 1943); Albert Faucher, "L'Emigration des canadiens-français aux Etats-Unis au XIXᵉ siècle: Position du problème et perspectives," *Recherches sociographiques* 5 (1964): 277–317; Gilles Paquet, "L'emigration des canadiens-français vers la Nouvelle-Angleterre, 1870–1910: prises du vue quantitatives," *Recherches sociographiques* 5 (1964): 319–70; Yolande Lavoie, *L'emigration des Canadiens aux Etats-Unis avant 1930: Mesure du Phenomene* (Montreal: Presses de l'Université de Montreal, 1972); Silvie Rimbert, "L'Immigration Franco-Canadienne au Massachusetts," *Revue Canadienne de Géographie* 8 (1954): 75–85.

19. Truesdell, *The Canadian Born*, pp. 77–81.

20. Vicero, "Immigration of French Canadians," p. 2.

21. Truesdell, *The Canadian Born*, p. 77.

22. Niles Carpenter, *Immigrants and their Children, 1920* (Washington, D.C.: Government Printing Office, 1927), pp. 123–29.

23. See Vicero, "Immigration of French Canadians," chap. 4; Jeffrey Williamson, *Late Nineteenth Century American Economic Growth: A General Equilibrium Model* (Cambridge: Cambridge University Press, 1974); Brinley Thomas, *Migration and Economic Growth* (Cambridge: Cambridge University Press, 1954).

24. Vicero, "Immigration of French Canadians," chaps. 2–5 provides a very detailed discussion of the changing patterns of French Canadian settlement in New England. For more detail on the distribution of the French Canadian population in New England from 1840 through 1930, see Ronald A. Petrin "Ethnicity and Political Pragmatism: The French Canadians in Massachusetts, 1885–1915," (Ph.D. diss., Clark University, 1983), table 1.2.

25. Estimates of the French Canadian population vary. Vicero's estimate of 270,000 includes the third generation. Truesdell's figure (250,024) is closer to my calculation from the federal census for 1920 (246, 773). See U.S. Bureau of the Census, *Twelfth Census of the United States: 1900, Population*, vol. 1, pt. 1, pp. 732–35, 814, 822, 830, for the distribution of *Canadiens* by state. A total of 513,314 French Canadians lived in New England in 1900 (61.7 percent of the national total). Massachusetts had 246,773 *Canadiens* (48.1 percent of the total in New England). See also Petrin, "Political Pragmatism," table 2.1.

26. U.S. Bureau of the Census, *Twelfth Census of the United States: 1900, Population*, vol. 1, part 1, pp. 732–35, 814, 822, 830. By 1900 French Canadians made up 8.8 percent of the population of Massachusetts, compared with New Hampshire (18.0), Rhode Island (13.1), and Vermont (11.8). See also Petrin, "Political Pragmatism," table 2.3.

27. Massachusetts, Bureau of Statistics of Labor, *Census of Massachusetts: 1905*, vols. 1, 25; *Census of Massachusetts: 1915*, p. 290; See Petrin, "Political Pragmatism," tables 2.4 and 2.5.

28. Oscar Handlin, *Boston's Immigrants: A Study in Acculturation*, rev. and enl. ed. (New York: Atheneum, 1977), chap. 3.

29. Massachusetts Bureau of Statistics of Labor, *Census of Massachusetts: 1885*, vol. 1, pt. 2, pp. 36, 614–19. See tables 2.6–2.9 in Petrin, "Political Pragmatism" for a summary of occupational patterns for French Canadians.

30. Ibid.

31. Massachusetts Bureau of Statistics of Labor, *Census of Massachusetts: 1885*, vol. 1, pt. 2, pp. 612–17; *Census of Massachusetts: 1905*, vol. 2., p. 9; *Report* (1903), "Race in Industry"; U.S. Bureau of the Census, *Special Reports, Occupations at the Twelfth Census*, 1900, pp. 300–304. For details, see Petrin, "Political Pragmatism," tables 2.10–2.14.

32. From a report of the seventh census of Canada (1931), cited in Iris S. Podea, "From Quebec to 'Little Canada': The Coming of the French Canadians to New England in the Nineteenth century,:" *New England Quarterly* 23 (September 1950): 367.

33. U.S. Senate, Immigration Commission, *Immigrants in Industries*, 61st sess., S. Doc. 633, 1911, vol. 10, p. 7; Vicero, "Immigration of French Canadians," pp. 316–32; Massachusetts, Bureau of Statistics of Labor, *Report* (1910), pt. 3, "Living Conditions in Massachusetts," p. 320. See also Jeremiah W. Jenks and W. Jett Lauck, *The Immigration Problem*, 4th ed. (New York: Funk & Wagnalls, 1917), especially chaps. 9–11; Isaac A.

Hourwich, *Immigration and Labor; The Economic Aspects of European Immigration to the United States* (New York: G. P. Putnam's Son's, 1912), chap. 18, for the effect of immigration on wages in the textile industry, and Herbert J. Lahne, *The Cotton Textile Worker* (New York: Farrar & Rinehart, 1944), chaps. 3, 6, and 8.

34. Lahne, *Cotton Textile Worker*, chaps., 8–12, Vicero, "Immigration of French Canadians," pp. 316–32. U.S. Senate, Immigration Commission, *Immigrants in Industries*, vol. 10, pp. 99, 101, 104, 107. See also Massachusetts, *Report of the Commission on the Cost of Living*, 1910, House Doc. 1750, pp. 77–78, for a comparison of the yearly average earnings of workers in various industries from 1886 to 1909. Tables 2.15–2.17 of Petrin, "Political Pragmatism," summarize the evidence in support of this point.

35. For supporting evidence see Petrin, "Political Pragmatism," tables 2.18–2.22.

36. These forty-two communities include all but three of the thirty-six places where French Canadians, first and second generation, numbered a thousand or more, and all but two of the places where they formed 20 percent or more of the total population in 1895. Boston, having more than three thousand *Canadiens* in 1895, was excluded because they formed less than 1 percent of the city's total population. Gloucester and West Boylston, each having between 1,200 and 1,300 French Canadians, were excluded because the *Canadien* population had been greatly reduced by 1905—in the case of Gloucester to 151, and in that of West Boylston, to only 86. North Brookfield's French Canadian population experienced a substantial loss bewteen 1895 and 1905, possibly due to a religious controversy in that town between 1898 and 1901, but it has been included here because of the interest in that controversy. Among towns having a 20 percent *Canadien* population in 1895, two were excluded from this list of communities. One of these was West Boylston, the other was Brookfield, which had 711 French Canadians in 1895 but only 413 ten years later due to the formation of a new town, East Brookfield. In both cases the percentage of French Canadians in these towns was drastically reduced.

37. For evidence corroborating the observations made in this discussion of the characteristics of the three community types, see tables in the appendix.

38. See appendix table 5. Note the rapid growth rate among primary centers, especially between 1885 and 1895. The percentage of French Canadians who are immigrants may be used as a measure of the length of time the group has been in a given locality and reflects the rate of growth of the *Canadien* colony.

39. See appendix tables 2 and 7. Among the eighteen cities, French Canadians ranked first among ethnic groups in only six in 1905; the Irish ranked first in twelve.

40. Vicero, "Immigration of French Canadians," pp. 95, 173.

41. Some examples of small, single-industry towns are Dudley, Hardwick, Sturbridge, and Auburn. See Jonathan Prude, *The Coming of Industrial Order; Town and Factory Life in Rural Massachusetts, 1810–1860* (Cambridge: Cambridge University Press, 1983).

42. The following are examples of case studies about French Canadians in various communities in New England: Therese Bilodeau, "The French in Holyoke (1850–1900)," *Historical Journal of Western Massachusetts* 3 (Spring 1974): 1–12; David J. Blow, "The Establishment and Erosion of French-Canadian Culture in Winooski, Vermont, 1867–1900," *Vermont History* 43 (Winter 1972): 59–74; Joseph Carvalho III and Robert Everett, "Statistical Analysis of Springfiled's French Canadians (1870)," *Historical Journal of Western Massachusetts* 3 (Spring 1974): 59–63; Frances H. Early, "Mobility Potential and the Quality of Life in Working-Class Lowell, Massachusetts; The French Canadians ca. 1870," *Labour/Le Travailleur* 2 (Fall 1977): 214–228; Tamara K. Hareven, "Family Time and Industrial Time: Family and Work in a Planned Corporation Town, 1900–1924;" *Journal of Urban History* 1 (May 1975): 365–89; Tamara K. Hareven, "The Laborers of Manchester, New Hampshire, 1912–1922: The Role of Family and Ethnicity in Adjustment to Industrial Life," *Labor History* 16 (Spring 1975): 249–65; and Tamara K. Hareven, *Family Time and Industrial Time: The Relationship Between the Family and Work in a New England Industrial Community* (Cambridge: Cambridge University Press, 1982).

43. Philip T. Silvia Jr., "The Position of 'New' Immigrants in the Fall River Textile Industry," *International Migration Review* 10 (1976): 221–32; "The 'Flint Affair': French Canadian Struggle for Survivance," *Catholic Historical Review* 65 (July 1979): 414–35; D.M.A. Magnan, *Notre-Dame de Lourdes de Fall River* (Quebec: Le Soleil, 1925); Sister

Florence M. Chevalier, S.S.A., "The Role of French National Societies in the Sociocultural Evolution of the Franco-American of New England from 1860 to the Present: An Analytical Macro-Sociological Case Study in Ethnic Integration Based on Current Social Systems Models," (Ph.D. diss., Catholic University of America, 1972), pp. 97–108.

44. See the discussion of French Canadian politics in Fall River in chapter 5.

45. T. A. Chandonnet, *Notre-Dame-des-Canadiens*, trans. Kenneth J. Moynihan (Worcester: n.p., 1977).

46. See chapter 5.

47. See chapter 6.

48. E. Hamon, *Les Canadiens-français de la Nouvell-Angleterre* (Quebec: Hardy, 1891), pp. 58–61; Chevalier, "The Role of French National Societies," pp. 42–43; Felix Gatineaux, *Histoire des franco-américains de Southbridge, Massachusetts* (Framingham, Mass.: Lakeview Press, 1919); Vicero, "Immigration of French Canadians," pp. 108–109; Wade, *The French Canadians*, pp. 359, 390–91. For examples of different types of French Canadian settlements in the Midwest see D. Aidan McQuillan, "Territory and Ethnic Identity," in *European Settlement and Development in North America*, ed. James R. Gibson (Toronto: University of Toronto Press, 1978), pp. 136–69, and Virgil Benoit, "Gentilly: A French Canadian Community in the Minnesota Red River Valley," *Minnesota History* 44 (Winter 1975): 279–89.

49. Concerning the slow rate of assimilation among French Canadians in New England see Herve B. Lemaire, "Franco-American Efforts on Behalf of the French Language in New England," in *Language Loyalty in the United States*, ed. Joshua Fishman (London: Mouton, 1966), pp. 253–79. For a different perspective that points toward relatively rapid assimilation, see Blow, "The Establishment an Erosion of French Canadian Culture," pp. 59–74.

50. Hamon in his *Les Canadiens-français* reported the following comment, which helps to explain why French Canadians willingly left the declining agricultural society of Quebec for New England:

> "On vit bien ici, vous dit-on, on est bien logé, bien chauffe, bien vetu, on a de la viande fraiche tous les jours et plus d'argent à la fin du mois qu'on n'en avait en Canada à la fin d'une année entière." (p. 16.)

In effect, French Canadians could look to a higher standard of living in New England. It is important to emphasize that such judgements largely depend on one's point of departure. Faced with a declining economic position, French Canadians might find conditions in American industrial cities attractive; but this attraction reflected more the desperate state of affairs in Canada than rosy conditions of life in America. Frances Early, "Mobility Potential," is no doubt correct in her assessment that life was "grim" for the *Canadien* immigrant. It is safe to assume that immigrants probably have an optimistic view of their situation in America as compared with the American view of the same situation.

51. Vicero, "Immigration of French Canadians," pp. 323, 332. Almost no French Canadian male immigrants reported that their wives were living abroad in the Dillingham report. This was typical of many early immigrants and probably reflects their longer residence in the United States. But the percentage of new immigrants reporting a wife abroad was not uniformly high, suggesting that there existed significant intergroup differences. Among Polish and Portuguese immigrants the percentages were 23.0 and 15.9 percent, while for Greeks it was an unusually high 74.7 percent. The average for all immigrants was 22.7 percent. See Jenks and Lauck, *The Immigration Problem*, pp. 514–15. For more detailed statistical data see U.S. Senate, Immigration Commission, *Immigrants in Industries*, vol. 20, pp. 961–78.

52. See Hareven, "Family Time and Industrial Time," and "Laborers of Manchester," for a description of the close relationship between the family and the textile industry. It is difficult to know whether the relationship she describes is typical of other textile centers or the unique product of the paternalism that characterized the Amoskeag corporation of Manchester. See also Vicero, "Immigration of French Canadians," p. 319; Lawrence French, "The Franco-American Working Class Family," in *Ethnic Families in America*, ed. Charles H. Mindel and Robert W. Habenstein (New York: Elsevier, 1976), pp. 323–46;

Ralph Piddington, "A Study of French Canadian Kinship," in The Canadian Family, ed. K. Ishwaran (Toronto: Holt, Rinehart and Winston of Canada, 1971); Philipe Garigue, "French Canadian Kinship and Urban Life," American Anthropologist 58 (December 1956): 1090–1101. William L. Warner and Leo Srole, The Social Systems of American Ethnic Groups (New Haven: Yale University Press, 1945), pp. 100–101, 106, point out the implications of family versus individual migration.

53. Hamon in his Les Canadiens-français, pp. 125–27, emphasized the proximity of Quebec as an important force helping the Canadiens to maintain their culture in New England. This theme has been echoed ever since. See George F. Theriault, "The Franco-Americans of New England," in Canadian Dualism, ed. Mason Wade, pp. 393–414; Lemaire, "Franco-American Efforts;" Richard S. Sorrell, "The survivance of French Canadians in New England (1865–1930): History, Geography, and Demography as Destiny," Ethnic and Racial Studies 4 (January 1981): 91–189.

54. Canadians generally had a very high rate of visits abroad as compared with immigrants from elsewhere. The following figures show the percent of foreign-born employees reporting one or more visits abroad for a few selected groups: Canadians, non-French, 58.2; Canadians, French 51.8; English, 27.3; Italians, South, 16.2; and Greek 8.6. The Canadians had the highest percentage of all immigrant groups, Jenks and Lauck, Immigration Problem, p. 493. For more complete data see U.S. Senate, Immigration Commission, Immigrants in Industry, vol. 20, pp. 979–1067.

55. The term "commuting immigrants" is taken from E. R. Barkan, "Proximity and Commuting Immigration: An Hypothesis Explored via the Bipolar Ethnic Communities of French Canadians and Mexican-Americans," in American Ethnic Revival, ed. Jack Kinton (Aurora, Il.: Social Science and Sociological Resources, 1977), pp. 163–83.

56. Wade, French Canadians, pp. 260–61, 432–35; Sorrell, "The survivance," pp. 97, 103.

57. For a general analysis of the role of the immigrant church in the process of assimilation see J. P. Dolan, The Immigrant Church: New York's Irish and German Catholics, 1815–1865 (Baltimore: Johns Hopkins, 1975); R. M. Linkh, American Catholicism and European Immigrants, 1900–1924 (New York: Center for Migration Studies, 1975); Victor Greene, For God and Country: The Rise of Polish and Lithuanian Ethnic Consciousness in America (Madison: State Historical Society of Wisconsin, 1975); S. Tomasi, Piety and Power: The Role of Italian Parishes in the New York Metropolitan Area (New York: Center for Migration Studies, 1975); and Raymond A. Mohl and Neil Betten, "The Immigrant Church in Gary, Indiana: Religious Adjustment and Cultural Defense," Ethnicity 6 (March 1981): 1–17.

58. Hamon, Les Canadiens-français, pp. 58–68; Mason Wade, "The French Parish and Survivance in Nineteenth-Century New England," Catholic Historical Review 36 (1950): 163–89; Abbe A. Verrette, "La Paroisse Franco-Américaine," Canadian Catholic Historical Report (1947–48): 125–39; Chevalier, "The Role of French National Societies," pp. 42–44, 54–57; Sorrell, "The survivance," pp. 96–97; Theriault, "The Franco-Americans," pp. 400–403.

59. Many of the references cited in the previous note are also relevant here. In addition, see Warner and Srole, The Social Systems, p. 241.

60. Ibid. See also Chevalier, "The Role of French National Societies," and Edward B. Ham, "French National Societies in New England," New England Quarterly 12 (1939): 315–32.

61. Warner and Srole, The Social Systems, pp. 275, 280–81.

62. Chandonnet, Notre-Dame-des-Canadiens, pp. 1–2; Hamon, Les Canadiens-français, pp. 233–46, 367–402, passim; see also William MacDonald, "The French Canadian in New England," Quarterly Journal of Economics 12 (1896): 249; Mason Wade, "The French Canadian Parish," pp. 175–76; and Felix Gatineaux, Historique des conventions des canadiens-français aux Etats-Unis, 1865–1901 (Woonsocket, R.I.: L'Union Saint-Jean-Baptiste d'Amérique, 1927), p. 42.

63. Based on information in Hamon, Les Canadiens-français, passim, and Guide des addresses des Canadiens-français de la Nouvelle-Angleterre (Fall River, Mass.: Fall River Publishing Co., 1899), pp. 223–26.

64. The term "institutional completeness" is attributed to Raymond Breton, "Institu-

tional Completeness of Ethnic Communities and the Personal Relations of Immigrants," *American Journal of Sociology* 70 (1964): 193–205.

65. See Hamon, *Les Canadiens-français; Guide des addresses de Canadiens-français de la Nouvelle-Angleterre* (Fall River, Massachusetts, 1899); Paul P. Chasse, "Church," Franco-American Ethnic Heritage Study Program, 1975, pp. 6–8.

66. Chevalier, "The Role of French National Societies," p. 28; Sorrell, "The Survivance," pp. 96–97; Wade, "The French Parish," p.69.

67. Hamon, *Les Canadiens-français*, pp. 120–21.

68. "Religion and language are the two natural guardians of a people's nationality," Hamon, *Les Canadiens-français*, p. 116. See also pp. 74–75; "He who loses his language, loses his faith."

69. Chevalier, "The Role of French National Societies," pp. 26–27; Linkh, *American Catholicism;* Robert D. Cross, *The Emergence of Liberal Catholicism in America* (Cambridge: Harvard University Press, 1958), pp. 88–94; Robert H. Lord, John E. Sexton, and Edward T. Harrington, *History of the Archdiocese of Boston* (Boston: Sheed and Ward, 1945), vol. 3, pp. 200–201.

70. Chevalier, "The Role of French National Societies," pp. 30–34, 76; Robert Rumilly, *Histoire des franco-américains* (Montreal: L'Union Saint-Jean-Baptiste-d'Amérique, 1958), p. 105–14, 130, 222, 238–39, 253–69. The most sensational conflicts were the Flint affair, the Corporation Sole controversy and the Sentinelle affair. For more details on each of these conflicts see Silvia, "The 'Flint Affair,'"; Kenneth Woodbury Jr., "An Incident Between the French Canadians and the Irish in the Diocese of Maine in 1906," *New England Quarterly* 40 (1967): 260–69; Richard S. Sorrell, "Sentinelle Affair (1924–1929)—Religion and Militant *Survivance* in Woonsocket, Rhode Island," *Rhode Island History* 36 (August 1977): 67–79.

71. See the brief parish histories given in Lord et al., *History of the Archdiocese of Boston*, vol. 3, pp. 197–215. The tolerance and sympathy that Archibishop Williams of Boston exhibited toward the French Canadians were not always matched by other bishops, as evidenced by Bishop Hendricken's inept handling of the Flint affair. The articles by Silvia, Woodbury, and Sorrell illustrate the importance of personalties and the role of fanaticism in precipitating crises.

72. See Rumily, *Histoire*, pp. 171–80. A detailed history of this controversy may be gleaned from reports in the *Worcester Daily Spy*, 5 August 1900; 1, 15, 18, 24–30 September 1900; 1, 5, 8, 11–14, 19–23, 31 October 1900; 2–4, 8, 11–14, 24 November 1900; 15 December 1900, and in nearly daily reports in *L'Opinion Publique*, September–November, 1900.

73. *Worcester Daily Spy*, 22 October 1900.

74. Ibid.

75. Ibid.

76. Ibid. For a discussion of the effect of this controversy in Worcester politics, see chapter 5.

77. *L'Opinion Publique*, 11 September, 29 October 1900.

78. See n. 72.

79. *Spencer Leader*, 3 November 1900. The French Canadians had very close ties with those of North Brookfield, who belonged to the Spencer French Canadian mutual aid society. It was surprising to find so little concern over the controversy in Spencer. The *Worcester Daily Spy* carried rumors that Dr. Marc Fontaine was personally involved in the incident. Only 33 persons from Spencer attended the meeting in that town. In part the poor showing may be attributed to the Rev. A. A. Lamy, pastor of the French Canadian parish in Spencer, who the previous Sunday in his sermon "touched very pointedly and forcibly upon the proposed meeting and his characterization of the man who is supposed to be behind the movement, Marc Fontaine, was not at all complimentary to that gentleman's honesty of purpose or church-going habits," (*Spencer Leader*, 3 November 1900.) There were political overtones to the controversy in Spencer as well. The French Canadians of Spencer were trying to bolster support for the candidacy of Democrat Eugene D. Marchessault for state representative that fall. Marchessault had been defeated the previous year because Fontaine had led a defection of about 50 French votes to the Republican candidate, (*Spencer Leader*, 11 November 1899.) The last thing the Franco-Irish

Democratic coalition in Spencer needed was the arousal of mutual antagonisms. Fontaine, who had been prominent in French Canadian politics locally, was spurned in the spring of 1900 by the French caucus, which was controlled by Democratic *Canadiens*, (*Spencer Leader*, 24 March 1900.) It is hardly surprising that the *Canadiens* in Spencer who were most deeply involved in the North Brookfield agitation were Republicans—Marc Fontaine, E. Comeau, Israel Wedge, Napoleon Cabana, Pierre Graveline. In a different vein, it should be noted that Bishop Beaven of Springfield, one of the principals in the controversy, had been pastor of the Catholic church in Spencer in the 1880s when Fontaine had helped to found a separate French Canadian parish in the town. What personal animosity existed between the two men is not known but it is likely that the events in North Brookfield were influenced by a clash of personalities as much as by a clash of cultures. Finally, Bishop Beaven pontificated at the funeral mass of John Kane in Spencer in mid-October because he was "a particular friend of the family, which is one of the most prominent Catholic families in town," (*Spencer Leader*, 13 October 1900.) The Rev. Lamy assisted him. What effect Beaven's presence in Spencer, in the past or in October as the controversy was heating up, had on the reaction of the town's French Canadians or on Lamy's sermon remains obscure. Nevertheless, the story related here leads one to caution in the jumping to conclusions about how such Franco-Irish animosities might have affected French Canadian politics. Comparing the response to the North Brookfield incident in Worcester and in Spencer, one can perceive, however dimly, the tangle of personality, politics, and religion.

80. Albert L. Bartlett, "The Transformation of New England," *Forum* 7 (1889): 643.

Chapter 3. Naturalization, Officeholding, and Voting

1. Massachusetts Bureau of Statistics of Labor, *Census of Massachusetts: 1895*, vol. 1, p. 319.

2. *Spencer Sun*, 4 April 1884.

3. Massachusetts Bureau of Statistics of Labor, *Report* 12 (1881), pp. 469–70.

4. The phrase is Carroll Wright's. See his summary of the report, "The Canadian French in New England," Massachusetts Bureau of Statistics of Labor, *Report* 13 (1882), p. 89.

5. Barbara Solomon, *Ancestors and Immigrants: A Changing New England Tradition* (Cambridge: Harvard University Press, 1956), pp. 66–67, 73, 77–78, 160–66, for a summary of the development of American views of the French Canadians. For examples of the contemporary literature concerning the *Canadiens*, see: Egbert C. Smyth, "The French Canadians in New England," American Antiquarian Society, *Proceedings* 7 (October 1891): 316–36; W. Blackburne Harte, "The Drift Toward Annexation," *Forum* 7 (June 1889): 361–72; "French Canada and the Dominion," *Forum* 10 (November 1890): 323–34; Edward Farrer, "The Inhabitant of Lower Canada," *Atlantic Monthly* 48 (December 1881): 771–80; "The Folk Lore of Lower Canada," *Atlantic Monthly* 49 (April 1882): 542–50; "New England Influences in French Canada," *Forum* 23 (May 1897): 308–19; Prosper Bender, "A New France in New England," *Magazine of American History* 20 (November 1888): 387–94; "The French Canadian Peasantry," *Magazine of American History* 24 (July 1890): 135–36; "The French Canadian in New England," *New England Magazine* 6 (July 1892): 569–77; A. R. Carmen, "Perplexities that Canada Would Bring," *Forum* 9 (July 1890): 562–68; Honore Beaugrand, "The Attitude of the French Canadians," *Forum* 7 (July 1889): 521–310.

6. For examples of this type of thinking, see especially Smyth, "French Canadians," pp. 329–30, and Henry Loomis Nelson, "French Canadians in New England," *Harper's New Monthly Magazine* 87 (July 1893): 180–87.

7. Albert L. Bartlett, "The Transformation of New England," *Forum* 7 (August 1889): 640.

8. Massachusetts Bureau of Statistics of Labor, *Report* 13 (1882), pp. 12, 89–92.

9. Concerning Wright's changing attitudes toward the French Canadians, see Alex-

andre Belisle, *Histoire de la presse franco-américaine* (Worcester: L'Opinion Publique, 1911), chap. 34, especially pp. 329–30

10. Smyth, "French Canadians," p. 336.

11. Bartlett, "Transformation," p. 644.

12. John Higham, *Strangers in the Land: Patterns of American Nativism, 1865–1925* (New Brunswick, N.J.: Rutgers University Press, 1955), and *Send These to Me* (New York: Atheneum, 1975), especially chap. 2, pp. 29–66; Howard C. Hill, "The Americanization Movement," *American Journal of Sociology* 24 (May 1919): 609–35, reprinted in *Race and Ethnicity in Modern America*, ed. Richard J. Meister (Lexington, Mass.: D. C. Heath, 1974), pp. 27–38.

13. Massachusetts Bureau of Statistics of Labor, *Report* 13 (1882), pp. 11–12.

14. Ibid., pp. 4–92, passim, especially pp. 18–19.

15. Ibid., p. 91.

16. Ibid., pp. 95–191, passim.

17. Henry Pratt Fairchild, who was critical of the Americanization movement of the early twentieth century, provided an insightful account of its premises. As he wrote in *The Melting Pot Mistake:*

[I]t should be perfectly clear that the true test of nationality is not what you know but how you feel. . . . Americanization is not an educational process, though the Americanization movement was, and is, essentially an educational program. True Americanization is a spiritual and emotional transformation. (pp. 50–51)

Fairchild pointed out that the early movement misunderstood the "psychological conditions of Americanization" by assuming that

. . . assimilation is a voluntary process, that it can be accomplished by an act of the will. . . . . The act of assimilation was conceived of much like the act of conversion in an old-fashioned revival. It was assumed that if sufficient pressure could be brought to bear upon the immigrant, and he could be worked up into a certain emotional state, he could deliberately 'take a stand' and thereupon go forth forever after an American. (p. 52)

(Pagination follows the excerpt of Fairchild's work in Meister, ed., *Race and Ethnicity.*) For an older but still useful work on the Americanization movement, see Edward G. Hartmann, *The Movement to Americanize the Immigrant* (New York: Columbia University Press, 1948). Hartmann's extensive bibliography on this subject is especially helpful.

18. Ferdinand Gagnon, in *L'Etendard National*, 25 July 1872, in Felix Gatineaux, *Historique des conventions des canadiens-français aux Etats-Unis, 1865–1901* (Woonsocket, R.I.: L'Union Saint-Jean-Baptiste d'Amérique, 1927), p. 32; "Naturalization," (1871), reprinted in Josaphat Benoit, ed., *Ferdinand Gagnon* (Manchester, N.H.: L'Avenir National, 1940), pp. 88–107.

19. Gatineaux, *Historique*, p. 32, trans., "Become American legally, but remain always *Canadiens* at heart."

20. Ferdinand Gagnon, "Discours Patriotique," 15 June 1876, in Benoit, *Ferdinand Gagnon*, pp. 135–41; "Restons Francais," 22 June 1882, pp. 172–85; trans., "Remain French; above all be *Canadiens.*"

21. Gatineaux, *Historique*, pp. 320–23; trans., "The variety of branches does not destroy the unity of a tree; ethnic diversity does not harm the unity of the nation" (p. 321). The cultural pluralism implicit in such ideas obviously put the French Canadians at odds with the advocates of total assimilation.

22. Gatineaux, *Historique*, p. 325, trans., "My faith to America; and my heart, to the beloved Province of Quebec."

23. Gatineaux, *Historique*, pp. 320, 322–23, 404, 410, and 413; Benoit, *Ferdinand Gagnon*, p. 180.

24. Gatineaux, *Historique*, pp. 161, 319, 405–07, 411–13, 415–16.

25. Ibid., p. 406

26. Ibid., trans., "*Canadiens* at heart and in thought;" "to perpetuate the traditions and virtues of the French race under the American flag."

27. Massachusetts Bureau of Statistics of Labor *Report* 19 (1888), p. 188. The rates among Irish, German, and English immigrants, for example, were 60, 56,and 51 percent respectively.

28. Ibid., 13 (1882), pp. 21, 23, 46, 83–84. The state constitution required that immigrants be able to read the constitution in English and have five years continuous residence in the United States to qualify for citizenship. The Bureau of Labor Statistics pointed out that the language requirement effectively excluded many French Canadians from citizenship; see *Report*, 19 (1888), pp. 218–219.

29. Ibid., *Report*, 13 (1882), pp. 57, 80–81.

30. Ibid., *Report*, 13 (1882), p. 91.

31. Ibid., *Report*, 19 (1888), pp. 188, 216. Illiteracy in this case was defined as "unable to read or write in the English language."

32. Ibid., *Report*, 19 (1888).

33. U.S. Bureau of the Census, *Thirteenth Census of the United States: 1910*, I, pp. 1068, 1084–85; *Fourteenth Census of the United States: 1920*, II, pp. 806, 826–31, 834–35. See tables 3.2 and 3.3 of Petrin, "Political Pragmatism," for a tabular summary of the naturalization rates for twenty-three groups, 1910–1920.

34. Recent studies on naturalization have shown that attitudes toward one's homeland and toward the United States, and the conditions that affected one's emigration and adjustment to the United States, have greater impact on naturalization than such socioeconomic variables as education, occupation, and income. See Elliot Robert Barkan and Nikolai Khokhlov, "Socioeconomic Data as Indices of Naturalization Patterns in the United States: A Theory Revisited," *Ethnicity* 7 (1980): 159–90. For an older view that emphasizes such factors as education, occupation, and income, see W. S. Bernard, "The Cultural Determinants of Naturalization," *American Sociological Review* 1 (1936): 943–53.

35. The Pearsonian correlation coefficient, a measure of the association between the naturalization rate and length of residence of twenty-three immigrant groups in 1910, was .81. Length of residence was measured by the percent of each foreign-stock group which was second generation in 1910. The assumption underlying this measure is that the second generation would be proportionately larger if the group had been in the United States for a longer period of time. See Truesdell, *The Canadian Born in the United States* (New Haven: Yale University Press, 1943), pp. 58, 114–15; Niles Carpenter, *Immigrants and their Children* (Washington, D.C.: Government Printing Office, 1927), pp. 259–60; Stanley Lieberson, *Ethnic Patterns in American Cities* (Glencoe, Il.: Free Press, 1963), pp. 141–46.

36. The nearness of Canada to the United States gave the Canadian immigrants a high mobility. One measure of this mobility was provided by the Dillingham reports on immigration, which show that 51.8 percent of the French Canadians and 58.2 percent of other Canadians had visited their homeland at least once since emigration. Among Russian Jews the percent visiting abroad was a very low 3.2 percent; for Greeks, 8.6 percent; for Northern Italians, 20.4 percent; and for Southern Italians, 16.2 percent. The rate of return for Canadians was about twice that for other immigrants, except Cubans. For a summary of the data contained in the Dillingham report, see Jeremiah W. Jenks and W. Lett Lauck, *The Immigration Problem*, 4th ed., (New York: Funk and Wagnalls, 1917), app. E, table 4, p. 492. See also Truesdell, *The Canadian Born*, pp. 109, 114–15.

37. U.S. Senate, Immigration Commission, *Immigrants in Industries*, vol. 10, p. 215; see also table 3.4 of Petrin, "Political Pragmatism."

38. For a comparison of naturalization rates by region, see U.S. Bureau of the Census, *Thirteenth Census of the United States: 1910*, vol. 1, pp. 1082–83. See also table 3.7, pp. 187–88, in Petrin, "Political Pragmatism."

39. U.S. Bureau of the Census, *Twelfth Census of the United States: 1900*, vol. 1, pt. 1, pp. 938–39, 942–43, 946–47, 950–51, 954–57; see also table 3.9 of Petrin, "Political Pragmatism."

40. John R. Commons, *Races and Immigrants in America* (New York: Macmillian, 1907), pp. 192–93, points out that Connecticut, Massachusetts, Maine, and New Hampshire were among the eight states that disenfranchised those who could not read or write the English language or read the United States Constitution.

41. Niles Carpenter, *Immigrants*, pp. 326–27, 410–21.

42. The Pearsonian correlation coefficient measuring the association between the percent naturalized and percent of *Canadien* families living on farms is .63; the coefficient for the association between percent naturalized and percent owning homes is .81.

43. For an analysis of the interrelationships between assimilation and residential segregation see O. D. Duncan and Stanley Lieberson, "Ethnic Segregation and Assimilation," *American Journal of Sociology* 64 (1959): 364–74; J. Fitzpatrick, "The Importance of the Community in the Process of Immigrant Assimilation," *International Migration Review* 1 (1967): 5–16; Stanley Lieberson, "The Impact of Residential Segregation on Assimilation," *Social Forces* 40 (1961): 52–57.

44. Massachusetts Bureau of Statistics of Labor, *Report* 13 (1882), pp. 18–19, 88. French Canadian leaders estimated that 1,765 naturalized *Canadien* males lived in eighteen centers of settlement in Massachusetts in 1880.

45. Massachusetts Bureau of Statistics of Labor, *Report* 19 (1888), p. 188. By contrast, 17 percent of the state's adult males but 13 percent of its voters were Irish born.

46. U.S. Bureau of the Census, *Thirteenth Census of the United States: 1910*, vol. 1, pp. 1084–85.

47. David B. Walker, "Presidential Politics of Franco-Americans," *Canadian Journal of Economics and Political Science* 28 (August 1962): 355–356; see also his *Politics and Ethnocentrism: The Case of Franco-Americans* (Brunswick, Maine: Bowdoin College, Bureau for Research in Municipal Government, 1961).

48. Ibid.

49. When the French Canadian average is compared with state averages, adjusted by excluding the vote in highly Democratic Suffolk County, the Democratic tendency of French Canadian communities becomes clearer. Suffolk County, comprising Boston, Chelsea, Revere, and Winthrop, contained about 20 percent of the state's population. Boston, having 92 percent of the county's total inhabitants, was strongly Democratic. As a result, the state averages are biased upwards, higher than could be expected for the rest of the state where 98 percent of French Canadians lived. The Democratic party received an average of 50.5 percent of the total vote cast in Suffolk County in nine presidential elections, while the average for the rest of the state was only 36.4 percent. Suffolk County contributed between 25 and 31 percent of all Democratic votes cast in the state in these elections.

Unless otherwise noted, percent Democratic was calculated as a proportion of the total vote, not just the major party vote. A similar pattern results when the Democratic vote is calculated as a percentage of the total vote; see table 1.2 of my dissertation, Petrin, "Political Pragmatism."

50. For twenty-eight gubernatorial elections the corresponding average Pearsonian coefficients were .46 for French Canadians and .62 for the Irish.

Statistical voting analyses must be interpreted with caution. Variables such as Democratic share of the vote, or percent French Canadian or Irish of the population describe communities. Drawing inferences about individual voter patterns from such data involves the so-called ecological fallacy. Thus, the fact that there is a correlation between percent French Canadian and percent Democratic vote for these seventy communities does not prove that French Canadians voted Democratic but points a direction for further research. I have tried to frame the analysis in ecological terms, arguing that the percent Democrat varied in proportion to the percent French Canadian for these localities, which suggests that French Canadians or their neighbors may have been responsible for the Democratic vote. I tested the correlation between percent Democrat and the proportion of other ethnic groups, e.g. native stock, Germans, English, Scot, English Canadian, Polish, Italian, and Irish. Of these groups only the Irish were positively correlated with percent Democrat. I also tested the correlation between percent Democrat with variables such as size of population and degree of industrialization (measured in terms of percent of the workforce in manufacturing and per capita investment in manufacturing) and found positive correlations. These last variables were, however, highly correlated with percent French Canadian and percent Irish. Because other forms of research I had done on politics indicated that both groups tended to approach politics in ethnic terms, rather than as city-dwellers or laborers, I decided in the end to restrict the analysis to ethnic groups and to focus attention on the sign of each coefficient and on the changes over time in its magnitude or direction. The emphasis is placed on the overall pattern that emerges for the seventy communities, which together account for more than 80 percent of the French Canadian stock in Massachusetts in 1895.

The well-established, close relationship between the Irish and the Democratic party was affirmed by the analysis, and it seems reasonable that the same method could be used to ascertain what, if any, association existed between percent French Canadian and percent Democrat. It remained possible that the positive correlation between percent French Canadian and percent Democratic for these communities was spurious, resulting from the proportion Irish of the population, not the proportion French Canadian. Because the correlation between the two groups was less than .10 for these seventy communities, percent French Canadian and percent Irish could be used as independent variables in a partial correlation analysis, which shows that the correlation coefficients for each group increased when controlling for the other. It is reasonable, then, to assume that both groups contributed independently to the variation in the Democratic vote.

51. This is a valid assumption. Partial correlational analysis shows that the correlation between the Democratic vote and the French Canadians increases when controlling for the Irish. See Hubert M. Blalock, *Social Statistics* (New York: McGraw-Hill, 1960), pp. 337–43 for a discussion of partial correlation and causal interpretation.

52. West Boylston, where more than 1,200 French Canadians formed 40 percent of the population in 1895, was excluded from the group of central towns because its *Canadien* population had dropped to less than 100 ten years later.

53. These conclusions regarding the primary cities are based on the percent Democratic and percent French Canadian for the cities as a whole, and therefore have limited applicability. Ideally the unit of analysis would be the precincts or wards of these cities. The lack of adequate data on that level make systematic analysis difficult. Unfortunately, the state censuses did not provide social data on the ward level. The federal census of 1910 does so in a limited way by providing the number of persons born abroad, by country of origin, for each ward of the largest cities. Since more detailed data was available in some cases from other sources, a closer investigation of French Canadians in certain primary cities was possible and is presented in chapter 5.

54. The pattern for these cities becomes especially apparent when examining gubernatorial elections. The contrasting pattern of voting between cities and towns remains evident when the analysis is expanded to include additional cities and towns. See table 5.10, figs. 5.1 and 5.2, tables 6.6 and 6.7, and figs. 6.1 and 6.2 of Petrin, "Political Pragmatism."

55. If eighteen French Canadian candidates for the state senate are combined with the state representative candidates, the percentages change little, as shown in table 3.16. None of the candidates for the state senate won election. As shown in table 3.17, French Canadian candidates from the towns were by far more successful than those originating in the cities.

Chapter 4. French Canadians and Massachusetts Politics, 1885–1895

1. Alexandre Belisle, *Histoire de la presse franco-américaine* (Worcester: L'Opinion Publique, 1911), p. 391; Granville Torrey Prior, "The French-Canadians in New England," (Master's thesis, Brown University, 1932), p. 268; Huge Dubuque, *Guide Canadienne de Fall River* (Fall River: Edmond F. Lamoureux, 1888), p. 131; Felix Gatineaux, *Histoire des franco-américains de Southbridge, Massachusetts* (Framingham, Mass.: Lakeview Press, 1919), pp. 102–3; Spencer, *Town Records,* 1875–1879. The first French Canadian city councillor in New England was elected in Lowell in 1874. In Fall River at least two *Canadiens* were appointed to law enforcement positions before 1880, while in Southbridge and Spencer several won election to positions such as overseer of the poor and constable. For a discussion of officeholding in Holyoke, see Peter Haebler, "Habitants in

Holyoke: The Development of the French Canadian Community in a Massachusetts City, 1865–1910." (Ph.D. diss., University of New Hampshire, 1976), pp. 150–53.

2. Massachusetts Bureau of Statistics of Labor, *Report*, 13 (1882), pp. 19, 43, 88, 175–81. French Canadians comprised about 17 percent of the total population of those eleven places but represented only 2.5 percent of the voters in 1880. Of nearly twelve thousand voters in Lowell, for example, only 232 were *Canadiens* but there were seven French Canadians in public office, including one member of the city council. In Fall River, where, as in Lowell, the French Canadians formed about 20 percent of the population but only 2 percent of the voters, they ran a candidate for the city council in 1880 and elected him in 1882 (Prior, "French Canadians in New England," p. 271). French Canadians in Spencer, forming nearly 40 percent of the population and ten percent of the voters, first won a seat on the board of selectmen in 1880, when two *Canadiens* had positions in town government. (Spencer, *Town Records*, 1880). Although French Canadians represented less than 4 percent of Holyoke's voters in 1880, they were usually able to elect one and sometimes two of their own to the city council between 1877 and 1885, largely because of their concentration in Wards Two and Four (Haebler, "Habitants in Holyoke," pp. 150–54). The eleven communities referred to here are: Fall River, Holyoke, Hudson, Springfield, Millbury, Northhampton, North Brookfield, Southbridge, Spencer, Worcester, and Lowell.

3. Thirteen of the nineteen naturalization/political clubs listed in *Guide des adresses des Canadiens-française de la Nouvelle Angleterre* (Fall River: Fall River Publishing Co., 1899), were founded during the 1880s, indicating the surge of interest in politics during this decade. Most were established after 1885. Only four were founded in the 1890s; the founding date of the remaining two was not given. It should be noted that these were not the only such clubs in Massachusetts.

4. Some of these social events assumed large proportions. Worcester's Ward Three Naturalization Club's third annual picnic, held at Quinsigamond Park, attracted about five thousand persons. About two-thirds attending came from Worcester. French Canadians from nearby towns attended in substantial numbers as well (West Boylston, 400; Millbury, 300; Spencer, 200). (*Worcester Daily Spy*, 6 September 1892). The practice of offering premiums for filing naturalization papers (fifty cents for final papers, twenty-five cents for first papers) by this club was considered illegal by some politicians (*Worcester Daily Spy*, 24 November 1900).

5. William L. Warner and Leo Srole, *The Social Systems of American Ethnic Groups* (New Haven: Yale University Press, 1945). Napoleon P. Huot, first president of the Ward Three Naturalization Club in Worcester (1885–86), received the Republican nomination for common councillor from that ward in 1887. Huot remained active in the Republican party, and became the first French Canadian alderman in the city, elected in 1896. Kenneth J. Moynihan, trans., *Le Worcester Canadien and Le Guide Français* (Worcester: Community Studies Program, Assumption College, 1979), p. 54; *Worcester Evening Gazette*, 14 December 1887; 5 November 1888; 10 September 1890; *Worcester Daily Spy*, 9 September, 25 November 1891. Such examples as Huot's could be multiplied to document the importance of naturalization clubs in generating ethnic politicians. See also Haebler, "Habitants in Holyoke," pp. 259–64.

6. Massachusetts Bureau of Statistics of Labor, *Report*, 13 (1882), pp. 18–19, 88, and *Report*, 19 (1888), p 188; E. Hamon, *Les Canadiens-français de la Nouvelle-Angleterre* (Quebec: Hardy, 1891); Egbert C. Smyth, "The French-Canadians in New England," American Antiquarian Society, *Proceedings* 7 (1891), p. 319, footnote 1.

7. Moynihan, *Le Worcester Canadien* (1899), p. 94.

8. Silvia, "The Spindle City," pp. 431–32. According to Richard Harmond, who does not mention Fall River specifically, Butler generally won the support of French Canadians, who, he says, were normally Republican. See his "The 'Beast' in Boston: Benjamin F. Butler as Governor of Massachusetts," *Journal of American History* 55 (1968–1969): 267, footnote 6.

9. Silvia, "The Spindle City," pp. 433–38, 445–47. Hugo Dubuque, active in the naturalization effort among *Canadiens* in that city, received the Republican nomination for school committee in 1883 and served two three-year terms. George Arcand, a Republican, won a seat on the city council in 1884. Although no French Canadians served

on the council between 1886 and 1888, Joseph Bonbonniere, also a Republican, had a seat on the common council in 1889 and 1890 (*City Directory*, 1880–1890). Dubuque was elected to the lower house of the general court in 1888 and 1889 with strong Republican support and won a third term on the school committee in 1889. He resigned from the school committee in 1890, however, following a personal crisis. (*Fall River Daily Herald*, 7 November 1888; *Fall River Daily Globe*, 4 December 1889; 3 December 1890. For details concerning the background of Dubuque's resignation see Silvia, "The Spindle City," p. 755, footnote 155.) In Holyoke, French Canadian leaders could be found in both parties but French voters appear to have voted Democratic between 1883 and 1885, according to Haebler, "Habitants in Holyoke," pp. 149–50.

10. *Spencer Sun*, 10 November, 30 March 1882; 23 March, 6 April, 2 November, 7 November 1883; 4 April 1884. Butler polled an especially strong vote in Spencer in 1884 when he ran for president, receiving 18 percent of the total vote, as compared to 9 percent in Worcester County as a whole. In nearby Southbridge, as in Spencer, the Democratic vote for governor rose as the number of French voters increased during this period, while the Republican vote remained stable. As also in Spencer, support for Butler coincided with a Franco-Democratic alliance on the local level. In 1884, for example, town democrats nominated four French Canadians for local office; the Republicans nominated none. Although no French Canadian Democratic candidates won in 1884, the following year a Democratic sweep brought four *Canadiens* into office. *Southbridge Journal*, 4 April 1884; 6 April 1885.

11. Allie E. Whitaker, *Southbridge Journal*, 1 November 1888, reprinted from the *Worcester Telegram*, 27 October 1888.

12. William MacDonald, "The French Canadians in New England," *Quarterly Journal of Economics* 12 (April 1898): 271–72

13. Ibid., p. 276.

14. Ibid., MacDonald explained further:

Neither the spirit nor the conditions of American life are favorable to the maintenance of distinct groups of population, bounded by lines of race, and kept together by the twin forces of a common language and religion; and so long as the French Canadians, either of their motion or under the direction of their leaders, occupy such a position, no amount of property-holding, no general exercise of the suffrage, and no patriotic declarations or services will suffice to remove the impression that they are still, in essential spirit, aliens and foreigners, living among us because to do so is pleasant and profitable, and not because they generally mean to become one with us.

15. Ibid., p. 277; see also pp. 276, 279.

16. Henry Loomis Nelson, "French Canadians in New England," *Harper's Weekly Magazine*, 87 (July 1893), pp. 180–87, reprinted in *Makers of America* (Encyclopedia Britannica Corporation, 1971), pp. 194–98.

17. Hamon, *Les Canadiens-français*, estimated the number of French Canadian voters in 1890 to be about 8,700. The six primary cities had 3,370 (39 percent); the following towns contained a total 2,118 (24 percent): Southbridge, Sutton, Spencer, Webster, Sturbridge, Millbury, Grafton, Oxford, Ware, Gardner, North Brookfield, Douglas, and Hardwick.

18. French Canadians became an important swing vote in local contests in Fall River, Holyoke, and Lowell. See Silvia, "Spindle City," p. 445; Haebler, "Habitants in Holyoke," pp. 315–17; and Mary H. Blewett, "The Mills and the Multitudes: A Political History," in Arthur L. Eno Jr., ed., *Cotton Was King* (Lowell: Lowell Historical Society, 1976), p. 175.

19. Nelson, "French Canadians in New England," pp. 195–96.

20. These victories did not severely impair the overall strength of the GOP. The governor's chair remained relatively weak in Massachusetts because the governor's council, usually in Republican hands, effectively limited the patronage power of the chief executive. The legislature and most local government, moreover, remained under Reb- pulican control through the years when Democrats held the governorship. Blodgett, *Gentle Reformers*, pp. 102–04. To take a longer perspective, only four democrats served as governor between 1884 and 1930, for a total of nine years. The GOP controlled the general court from the Civil War until 1948. See Peter K. Eisinger, "Ethnic Political Transition in

Boston, 1884–1933: Some Lessons for Contemporary Cities," *Political Science Quarterly* 93 (Summer 1978): 221. See also Duane Lockard, *New England State Politics* (Princeton: Princeton University Press, 1959), especially chapters 5 and 6, and Walter Dean Burnham, *Critical Elections and the Mainsprings of American Politics* (New York: Norton, 1970).

21. This discussion of Massachusetts Democrats relies heavily on Blodgett, *The Gentle Reformers*. See also Gerald MacFarland, *Mugwumps, Morals, and Politics, 1884–1920* (Amherst: University of Massachusetts Press, 1973), especially chapter 2.

22. Disgruntled with the reluctance of the GOP to enact state civil service reform, and feeling their ambitions constricted by their own party, the young reformers had organized themselves before 1884, creating a reform wing within the party. Butler's victory in 1882 had led the reformers to cooperate with the party regulars in 1883 to ensure Butler's defeat. Despite the passage of a civil service reform law in 1884, the reformers bolted that year and began working with the Democrats the next year. Blodgett, *Gentle Reformers*, chap. 1; MacFarland, *Mugwumps*, pp.17–19, 27.

23. Blodgett, *Gentle Reformers*, chap. 3; when one of the Republican bolters, John Andrews, received the Democratic nomination for governor (1886), for example, he failed to get the full support of the Irish democratic rank and file, pp. 64–66. See also MacFarland, *Mugwumps*, pp. 56–57.

24. Blodgett, *Gentle Reformers*, chap. 4.

25. Seven of the twelve Bay State congressmen elected in 1890 were Democrats: three Mugwumps and four life-long Democrats. The Democrats made substantial gains in the state legislature as well. These gains were part of a nationwide off-year Democratic sweep. See Albert Bushnell Hart, ed., *Commonwealth History of Massachusetts*, vol. 5, (New York: States History Co., 1930), pp. 169–70. Hugh O'Brien, the first Irish Democratic mayor of Boston (1884) was defeated in 1888. See also Eisinger, "Ethnic Political Transition," p. 221; Blodgett, *Gentle Reformers*, chap. 6, and MacFarland, *Mugwumps*, pp.65–67.

26. Massachusetts, *Public Document No. 43*, "Number of Registered Voters and Persons who Voted. . . ," 1887–1895. Between 1885 and 1888 the GOP had polled 50 percent of the total vote in national and state elections; less than 46 percent of the voters cast Democratic ballots. In 1888 high voter turnout characteristic of presidential years gave Oliver Ames, the Republican incumbent, a majority of twenty-eight thousand over Russell, who lost 53 percent to 45 percent. The following year, with eighty thousand fewer ballots cast, the Republican candidate once again defeated Russell, albeit by a smaller margin (48.4 to 45.8 percent) with the Prohibition Party taking the remainder. See table 4.2 of Petrin, "Political Pragmatism," for further detail.

27. Nelson, "French Canadians in New England," p. 197; see also Jacques Ducharme, *The Shadow of the Trees: The Story of French-Canadians in New England* (New York: Harper, 1943), pp. 167–68, and Silvia, "The Spindle City," p.752. For a summary of the Democratic platform, see the report on the state convention, held in Worcester, in the *Worcester Daily Spy*, 19 September 1890.

28. Blodgett, *Gentle Reformers*, pp. 120, 128–29, 130–32.

29. Belisle, *Histoire de la presse*, pp. 159, 168, 171.

30. Ibid., pp.279–80. Marier was a customs inspector in Boston from 1888 to 1891. In 1896, then living in Manchester, N.H., he supported Bryan.

31. Virulent anti-Catholicism in Massachusetts centered in Boston, where the Catholic Irish and British Canadians were embattled between 1887 and 1895; but French Canadians also came under fire. See, for example, *The American*, 28 December 1889, excerpted in Hamon, *Les Canadiens-français*, p. 133. See Frederick C. Luebke, *Immigrants and Politics: The Germans of Nebraska, 1880–1900* (Lincoln: University of Nebraska Press, 1969) and Richard J. Jensen, *The Winning of the Midwest* (Chicago: University of Chicago Press, 1971), for examples of how nativism affected ethnic groups elsewhere.

32. For more details on the school controversy see Robert H. Lord, *History of the Archdiocese of Boston* vol. 3, pp. 110–18, 126–33; and Lois B. Merk, "Boston's Historic Public School Crisis," *New England Quarterly* 31 (1958): 179–99.

33. Blodgett, *Gentle Reformers*, pp. 150–51, 53; Lord, *History*, vol. 3, pp. 125, 136.

Former Republican governor John D. Long was the lawyer who represented the anti-Catholic faction during this controversy in the legislature, a fact that did not go unnoticed by French Canadians. Charles A. Donnelly, assisted by Hugo Dubuque, who testified at one of the public hearings on this issue, represented the Catholic point of view (Belisle, *Histoire de la presse*, pp. 237–38).

34. *Worcester Daily Spy*, 31 October, 1 November 1890. Ambrose Choquet, of the French Republican Club in Worcester, listed as first among the campaign issues he explained to the club's membership the Republican party's desire to secure the ballot for all citizens—presumedly immigrants in Massachusetts as well as southern blacks. Although he probably was speaking to the already converted, the prominence he gave this issue may reflect his concern that Democratic promises might attract French Canadian voters in Worcester (*Worcester Daily Spy*, 24 October 1890).

35. *Worcester Daily Spy*, 23 October 1890.

36. Ibid., 1 November 1890.

37. *Worcester Evening Gazette*, 31 October 1890. John E. Russell of Leicester had been elected to Congress in Republican Worcester County in 1886 as a free trader, and was a leading advocate of tariff reform in the state before William E. Russell took up the cause. The popularity of his ideas among French Canadians probably helped wed them to the Democratic party in the towns of southern Worcester County. For a biographical sketch of Russell, see Blodgett, *Gentle Reformers*, pp. 76–77.

38. *Worcester Evening Gazette*, 14 October, 31 October 1890; Haggerty, the incumbent, won (5 November 1890).

39. *Spencer Leader*, 7 November 1889; election statistics were derived from Massachusetts, *Manual of the General Court, 1886–1895*. See table 4.3 of Petrin, "Political Pragmatism," for details.

40. *Worcester Evening Gazette*, 5 November 1889. Russell and Moreau received almost identical votes.

41. Ibid., in its editorial in the *Gazette* offered a view of the election similar to Walker's, emphasizing the central role of the tariff issue.

42. *Worcester Daily Spy*, 5 November 1890. Hamilton Coe, a member of the Worcester County Republican Committee, had stressed to the committee the need to turn out the vote in the rural areas of the county (30 October 1890). Statewide turnout (measured as the percentage of the registered voters who voted in the state election in 1890) was only 72.6 percent in the state's 326 towns, as compared with 83.2 percent in its twenty-five cities, a difference of 10.6 percentage points. The average difference in turnout between towns and cities in the twenty state elections from 1890 to 1909 was only 6.5 points, suggesting that poor turnout in the state's usually Republican rural areas was an important factor in Russell's victory in 1890, as Coe believed. Turnout in towns rose to 80.1 percent in 1891 and to 88.2 in 1892, very high as compared with the twenty-year average of 72.5 percent. The high turnout in the towns in 1891 and 1892 suggests that the Republican strategy of focusing on cultural issues to stimulate turnout probably contributed to Russell's diminishing pluralities in those years.

43. *Worcester Daily Spy*, 23 October 1891.

44. Ibid., 25 October 1891.

45. See Blodgett's discussion of the similarities between the social thought of Irish and Yankee Democrats during this era, *Gentle Reformers*, p. 155.

46. Statewide there was an increase of 4.4 percent in the number of registered voters, unusually high for an off-year election. Between 1890 and 1909, only in 1892, 1896, 1900, and 1904 was the percent increase in registered voters for state elections higher than 4.4. Most other years the increase was less than 2 percent, and in six years it actually declined. See table 4.2 of Petrin, "Political Pragmatism," for details.

47. Anti-liquor voters were particularly important to a GOP victory in a close election. The Prohibition Party vote, had it been added to the Republican totals in 1890 through 1892, would have given the GOP victory. Dissatisfaction among prohibitionists with the enforcement of state liquor laws by Republican administration in the 1880s revived the Prohibition Party after 1885. Governor Brackett's attempt to placate them by enforcing an absurd statute, which required serving liquor only with food and closing all

public bars, succeeded only in angering anti-liquor forces. As a result, they withheld support from the GOP from 1889 to 1891, allowing Russell to win. See Hart, *Commonwealth History*, vol. 4, pp. 608–10, and vol. 5, 169–70, and Blodgett, *Gentle Reformers*, p. 98.

48. *Worcester Daily Spy*, 8 September, 23 October, 27 October 1891; 21 August, 22 August, 24 August, 21 September, 28 September, 29 September, 30 September, 3 October 1892.

49. Ibid., 28 September 1981. See Massachusetts, Bureau of Statistics of Labor, *Report*, 21 (1891), pt. 3, pp. 177–258, for the program which worried the *Spy's* editor.

50. Ibid., 27 September 1892.

51. Ibid., 15 September, 30 September, 20 October, 23 October, 27 October, 28 October, 6 November 1892.

52. Ibid., 30 September, 19 October, 23 October 1892.

53. Ibid., 17 October, 24 October, 29 October 1890; 21 September, 10 October, 22 October 1892. Among the French Canadians who toured in Worcester County were the following: Republicans—Hugo Dubuque (Fall River), P.X. Angiers (Lewiston, Maine), Professor Debos (Boston), C. Herbert DeFosse (Worcester): Democrats—Dr. A.F. David (Willamantic, CT), Dr. C. Cote (Marlboro), Louis Rheims (Southbridge), Dr. L. DeGrandpre (Fall River), and E.H. Tarvidal (Worcester).

54. *Worcester Evening Gazette*, 9 November 1892; *Southbridge Journal*, 9 November 1893.

55 *Worcester Evening Gazette*, 30 October 1891; the Democratic County convention nominated Moreau for county treasurer but he declined (*Worcester Daily Spy*, 13 October 1891). A comparison of the vote for governor and state representative suggests that many *Canadiens* may have abstained from voting for the latter. (The French Canadian Republican candidate for representative was William Courtemanche. According to Hamon, *Les Canadiens-français*, Spencer had about 600 *Canadien* voters.)

	Rep.	Dem.	Other	Total
Governor	527	557	48	1132
State rep.	418	139	64	621

Unlike in Webster, the town Republicans in Spencer had brought French Canadians into their organization, as had the Democrats. This may help to explain why Russell did not do quite as well in Spencer as in Southbridge or Webster. (In 1892, four of sixteen Republican and nine of twenty-nine Democratic convention delegates from Spencer were French Canadians). *Worcester Daily Spy*, 4, 13 September 1892.

56. *Southbridge Journal*, 1885–1892; Southbridge *Town Records*, 1885–1895.

57. *Worcester Daily Spy*, 15, 20 October 1893.

58. The average yearly earnings of woolen textile workers fell from a high of $388 in 1892 to $343 in 1984, as low as they had been in 1887, see Massachusetts House Document No. 1750, *Report of the Commission on the Cost of Living*, (1910), p. 77. See also Arthur H. Cole, *The American Wool Manufacture* (Cambridge: Harvard University Press, 1926), vol. 2, pp. 128–29.

59. *Worcester Daily Spy*, 7, 18 October, 5, 12, 14 November 1894; 5–6 13, 20 October 1895. For a discussion of the APA in Massachusetts see Lord, *History of the Archdiocese*, vol. 3, chap. 7, and Blodgett, *Gentle Reformers*, p. 151. According to Blodgett, the term "entente cordiale" was used by G. H. Lyman, writing to Henry Cabot Lodge, 25 October 1895 (p. 314. footnote 12.) George Frisbie Hoar, unlike most other Republican leaders, finally denounced the APA in 1895. For his point of view on this controversy, see George F. Hoar, *Autobiography of Seventy Years* (New York: Scribner's Sons, 1903), vol. 2, pp. 278–93, and Richard E. Welch, Jr., *George Frisbie Hoar and the Half-Breed Republicans* (Cambridge: Harvard Univesity Press, 1971), pp. 187–93.

60. *Worcester Daily Spy*, 5 November 1893; 2–3 October 1895.

61. Ibid., 9, 27 October 1894; 2–3, 30 October 1895.

62. In 1896 George Fred Williams, running on four different tickets, managed to take only 27 percent of the total vote, a decrease of 10 percent from 1895.

63. *Worcester Daily Spy*, 6 November 1894.

64. According to the town's *Register of Voters,* 1892, there were about 320 *Canadien* voters in Spencer, judging by surname, and about 30 French Canadian names were added between 1893 and 1895. Note that the total drop in the combined Republican and Democratic vote in 1894 came to about 300 as well. Another bit of evidence pointing to the disaffection of French Republicans is that Dr. Marc Fontaine, a leading French Republican, addressed the French Canadian Democratic rally in 1894, not the Republican rally (*Worcester Daily Spy,* 1 November 1894). Fontaine, moreover, did not serve as a Republican convention delegate in 1894 as he usually did (*Worcester Daily Spy,* 4 September 1892; 24 September 1893; 21 September 1894; 25 September 1895). Bad relations between the *Canadiens* and the local GOP were reflected in town elections. Between 1884 and 1889 French Canadian Republicans elected to local office outnumbered *Canadien* Democrats twenty-two to ten; between 1890 and 1895 Democrats led Republicans twelve to four, and no *Canadien* Republicans were elected to office from 1893–1895 (*Spencer Sun,* 1884–90; *Spencer Leader,* 1891–95, see especially, 1 April 1894 and 16 March 1895.) To be sure, how French Canadians in Spencer actually voted is difficult to determine but the indirect evidence, while not conclusive, indicates that Barton's assessment may have been correct.

65. For a biographical sketch of Favreau, see *A Souvenir of Massachusetts Legislators,* (Brockton, Mass.: A. M. Bridgman, 1894), p. 158. In 1893, a number of French Canadians appeared with Republicans at campaign rallies and listened to *Canadien* speakers discuss the issues, indicating the possibility that at least some French in Marlboro were associated with the GOP. The following year Favreau and at least six other French Canadians were delegates to Democratic conventions (*Worcester Daily Spy,* 28 October 1893; 23 September 1894.)

66. Haebler, "Habitants in Holyoke," pp. 257–307, especially p. 282.

67. See Holyoke, *City Directory,* 1894–1896 and *Massachusetts Yearbook,* 1895–1896.

68. Blewett, "The Mills and the Multitudes," p. 175. French Canadians supported Courtney for mayor in 1894 and 1896. The Democratic party's nomination of Wilfrid Paradis for an unsuccessful bid for the lower house of the general court (1893) may have helped lay the foundation for Courtney's success (*Souvenir of Massachusetts Legislators,* 1894, p. 157).

69. For a discussion of the Flint affair, see Philip T. Silvia Jr., "The 'Flint Affair,'" pp. 414–35. Silvia's exhaustive dissertation, "Spindle City," is an indispensable source for understanding political life in Fall River; see chapter 14 especially for this period.

70. The successful democratic mayor during this period, Dr. John W. Coughlin, was the brother-in-law of Hugo Dubuque, the outstanding French Canadian Republican in Fall River. Democratic successes may be attributed at least in part on this connection as well as to heightened class and religious tensions arising from the Lizzie Borden case as Silvia points out, pp. 755–69. Since Franco-Democratic alliance appears to have occurred elsewhere as well, such forces as the tariff and liquor issues and anti-Catholic bigotry may have had at least an equally important role as local conditions that favored an Irish-French rapprochement. That such a rapprochement happened in Fall River, so soon after the Flint affair, suggests that incidents of religious hostility between the French and the Irish may not always have had so great or lasting an influence on French Canadian political preferences as such analysts as David Walker have believed.

71. *Fall River Daily Globe,* 4 December, 1889; 29 November, 3 December 1890; 9 December 1891; 7 December 1892. Although French Canadian candidates from Ward Six did not win, perhaps not receiving the full support of their group, election returns suggest they were able to draw at least some Republican *Canadiens* to Democratic columns.

72. In 1889 and 1890 Howard received over 65 percent in Ward Six, *Fall River Daily Globe,* 5 November 1889; 5 November 1890.

73. Estimates of how the French Canadians voted must rely on newspaper reports as well as election statistics as they formed a majority of the voters in no ward in 1890. In Ward Six, where they were strongest, about 46 percent of the assessed polled were *Canadiens* (Silvia, "Spindle City," and Massachusetts, *Public Document No. 43,* 1890), but I estimate that only about 25 percent of its voters were French Canadian.

Table 4.5 compares the vote in those wards (One, Five, Six, and Nine) with Democratic and Republican banner wards. Note that the Democratic gain in the French wards from 1888 to 1892. was larger than in the two banner wards. These four wards contained 75 percent of the city's French Canadian voters; Ward Six alone about one-third.

74. See tables 4.3, 4.4, and 4.5. In addition to nominating French Canadians for local offices, as they had before 1890, the GOP also nominated Hercule Beauparland for state representative in 1894 and 1895. Although he lost, this move probably helped to win back French Republican voters who had defected between 1889 and 1893. Cultural conflict colored the mayoral race in 1893, with the liquor issue, the APA, and recognition being the foremost issues among the *Canadiens*. Republican mayoral candidate Greene received a poor reception among French Canadians in Wards One, Two, Six, and Nine, while Coughlin was greeted with enthusiasm and endorsed by many leading French Republicans. Pro-Coughlin French Democrats hounded Greene, insisting that he publicly repudiate the APA, which he refused to do. Greene's response to the demand, as quoted in the *Globe*, a Democratic newspaper, was, "I cannot repudiate something I know nothing about." If the *Globe's* reporting was accurate, his answer would hardly have reassured *Canadien* voters that he was unaffiliated with that organization. The French Canadians reportedly gave Coughlin a majority of their votes; the vote in Ward Six, low as compared to that of 1891, probably reflected the British-American vote in that ward and the close ties between Ward Six French Canadian politicians and the local GOP (*Fall River Daily Globe*, 28 November, 1–2, 4, 6 December 1893). Cultural conflict had overtones of class differences as well, as the following exchange between a Republican candidate for alderman in Ward One and Dr. Couange, a pro-Coughlin French Canadian, indicates:

He [the Republican candidate] said that he could remember the time the French-Canadians first came here, and the fact that they were so generally employed in the factories was proving that the American people were with them. Who made your people in this city? Was it not the cotton industry?

Dr. DeCouange: No sir. It was the work of every man for himself. (*Fall River Daily Globe*, 28 November 1893)

75. The number of *Canadien* voters in Worcester rose from 375 in 1887, to 645 in 1891, and to 1,407 in 1895, *Le Worcester Canadien*, 1892, 1897, 1901.

76. Moynihan, *Le Worcester Canadien*, p. 4.

77. Worcester, *City Directory*, 1887–1892. Belisle's brother Eugene and his father were Ward Five Naturalization Club officers in 1887, and Alexander, Jr. himself became an officer in 1888, serving as president from 1890 to 1892.

78. Worcester, *City Directory*, 1887–1892. Lajoie was a Democrat candidate for the same position in 1893 as well. *Worcester Evening Gazette*, 10 December 1890; 16 December 1891; 12 December 1892; 13 December 1893.

79. Jandron later served on the common council in 1894–95, running as an independent Democrat but lost his bid for re-election in 1895. His bid for the Democratic nomination for common council in Ward Three in 1893 revealed the tension between the Irish and *Canadiens* in that ward. Jandron was accused of having brought "a brigade a Republicans . . . into a Democratic caucus to secure a nomination." Because the Democrats denied him their regular nomination, Jandron reportedly declared that he would never enter another Democratic caucus. Despite the obvious conflict between Jandron and Irish Democrats, he remained a party activist and financial supporter of the Democratic party until 1896 (*Worcester Evening Gazette*, 4, 13, December 1893; 6, 8, 12 December 1894; 11 December 1895). See the biographical sketch of Jandron in Moynihan, *Le Worcester Canadien*, p. 35.

80. The French Canadians were widely dispersed in Worcester, so that no ward contained more than 28 percent of the city's French Canadian voters in 1891 and they formed no more than 15 percent of the voters in any ward. Only in three precincts were there more than 80 French voters in 1891 (Six-2—95; Five-2—91; Three-2—80) and in these they represented between 10 and 15 percent of the voters. *Le Worcester Canadien*, 1892, 1896; Massachusetts Public Document No. 43 (1891, 1895). For details see tables 4.9 and 4.10 of Petrin, "Political Pragmatism."

81. *Worcester Daily Spy*, 1 November 1890; November 1893.

Chapter 5. The Fragility of Urban Franco-Republican Alliances, 1896–1915

1. In 1905 these cities contained 62 percent of the French Canadians in Massachusetts.

2. See also tables 5.3, 5.4, and 5.5 of Petrin, "Political Pragmatism." The correlation between the percentage French Canadian population and percentage of the quota achieved for city councils for seventeen cities, is .67 (Pearson's R). The correlation between the percentage of the quota filled for all other offices is .58.

3. Holyoke, Chicopee, and Marlboro had 102 of the total of 240 positions held by *Canadiens*. They had 37 of the 105 city council positions and 84 of the 135 other positions.

4. In 1910 only Haverhill (0), Lynn (0), and Springfield (2) had fewer than three French Canadian officials.

5. Massachusetts, *Public Document No. 43*, 1896–1915. For details, see table 5.8 of Petrin, "Political Pragmatism." Less than 10 percent of the Democratic candidates won, as compared to 35 percent of the Republicans.

6. See table 5.5 of Petrin, "Political Pragmatism."

7. Refer to table 5.7.

8. Haebler, "Habitants in Holyoke," pp. 272, 282. This discussion of *Canadien* political patterns in Holyoke relies substantially on Haebler's work but offers a somewhat different interpretation, based on the comparison of Holyoke to other cities.

9. Ibid., pp. 263, 270. In 1890, according to E. Hamon, *Les Canadiens-français de la Nouvelle-Angleterre* (Quebec: Hardy, 1891), there were about 450 *Canadien* voters in Holyoke, about 10 percent of the voters.

10. Ibid., pp. 271–73.

11. Ibid., "The Growth of French Canadian Political Power," Chap. 6, pp. 257–307, passim, especially pp. 273–78, 286–93.

12. Ibid., pp. 282–83.

13. *Massachusetts Yearbook*, 1895, pp. 480–81.

14. See Haebler's excellent discussion of the Keough scandal and its ramifications, pp. 280–85.

15. Ibid., p. 292; Holyoke, *City Directory*, 1897–1905; *Massachusetts Yearbook*, 1895–1901, 1903.

16. Haebler, "Habitants in Holyoke," pp. 290–92, 384. According to Haebler, Republicans were more generous in granting positions and recognition to the French Canadians in a number of ways, see pp. 289–97.

17. Massachusetts, *Public Document No. 43*, 1896–1915. For details on state representative elections see table 5.6 of Petrin, "Political Pragmatism."

18. Haebler, "Habitants in Holyoke," pp. 272, 286, 300.

19. See tables 5.10 and 5.11.

20. French Canadians formed 30 percent or more of the voters in six precincts in 1909: One-B, 30.6 percent; Two-A, 29.1 percent; Three-A, 31.5 percent; Six-A, 57.4 percent; Six-B, 43.4 percent; Nine-B, 31.8 percent.

21. In 1885 French Canadians comprised 2.8 and 6.4 percent of the legal voters in Fall River and Holyoke respectively. For 1890 and 1897, I have estimated that French Canadians formed about 8 and 12 percent of the voters in Fall River and 11 and 16 percent in Holyoke. Estimates of the percentages are based on the number of registered voters in the November elections, 1890, 1896.

22. See table 5.7.

23. French Canadians had been appointed to the board of register of voters and to the board of health. Additionally a *Canadien* served as city physician and another as inspector of animals. By 1895 French Canadians in Holyoke had established themselves on at least four of the city's governing boards, see *Massachusetts Yearbook* 1895, and Haebler, p. 290.

24. Silvia, "The Spindle City", pp. 808, 863; Massachusetts, *Public Document No. 43* (1909); between 1886 and 1905, 3,238 French Canadians registered to vote in Fall River.

Of this total, 799 (about 25 percent) registered between 1886 and 1894. Nearly three times as many registered between 1896 and 1905. These figures are based on Silvia's table 7, p. 861, which provides the number of registered voters by place of birth. I have assumed that those listed as born in Canada are actually French Canadians as few English Canadians migrated to Fall River. Silvia does not provide data for 1895.

25. See table 5.7.

26. Massachusetts, *Public Document No. 43*, 1894–1895; see table 5.13.

27. Data for tables 5.15 and 5.16 were derived from Massachusetts, *Public Document No. 43*, 1896–1915, Fall River, *City Directory*, 1890–1915, and the *Fall River Daily Globe*, 1890–1915. French Canadian candidates were identified by name, and in most cases, party identification was given in the newspaper reports on elections. In some cases, it is difficult to be certain that an individual was in fact French Canadian. For example, Alanson Abbe, who ran for alderman-at-large between 1902 and 1905, was included in this table as a French Canadian although his name is not obviously French. A Joseph A. L'Abbe is listed in the French Canadian directory in 1890, however, and Alanson J. Abbe, a physician, was listed in the city directory in 1900, residing at 375 Rock Street. The previous year *Le Guide des adresses des Canadiens-français de la Nouvelle-Angleterre* (Fall River: Fall River Publishing Co., 1899) listed one A. Y. Abbe, a physician, at 375 Rock Street among the *Canadiens* in Fall River. On this basis and on that of telephone calls to the L'Abbe family members listed in the Fall River telephone directory, 1982, I concluded that Abbe was indeed French Canadian. One cannot be certain, nevertheless, that Abbe identified himself with the French Canadian community. I could not find his name listed among the officers of any of about 60 French Canadian organizations that existed in Fall River between 1894 and 1915.

28. See table 5.13.

29. French Canadian Republicans were not nominated for state representative for the Eleventh District in 1898, 1899, 1900, 1909, and 1910. *Canadien* Democrats received nominations in five years (1898, 1899, 1908, 1911, and 1915) but all lost. Massachusetts, *Public Document No. 43*, 1896–1915.

30. See also figs. 5.3–5.5 of Petrin, "Political Pragmatism," which graphically illustrate voting patterns in Ward Six.

31. See Silvia, pp. 807–14. In 1897 Ward Six "paralyzed the Democrats" by turning in a 438 majority, at least 150 more than Democratic campaign managers had expected (*Fall River Daily Globe*, 8 December 1897). Republican candidate Jackson and French Canadian alderman candidate Edmund Cote received nearly identical total in Precinct Six-A. In 1898 the Republican vote dropped to 5,680, from 6,200 the previous year while the Democratic vote remained essentially unchanged. As a result, Jackson won by a mere 66 votes. The 400 vote majority for Jackson in Ward Six, where the Republican vote declined only 4 percent as opposed to 8 percent citywide, proved crucial to his victory. (*Fall River Daily Globe*, 7 December 1898)

32. Silvia, pp. 812–14. Cote was first elected alderman for Ward Six in 1897, and was re-elected in 1898 and 1899. His nomination for that position was an important ingredient in the Franco-Republican alliance until at least 1900, for Republican candidates were assured of victory in this ward where the Democratic organization was very weak. Hugo Dubuque had served as state representative and was a member of the school committee before 1890. His Republican nomination for state representative in 1896 and 1897 and for state senate in 1898 also helped the GOP to recapture the French Canadian vote in the mid-1890s.

33. According to the *Globe*, "the majority of 512 in Ward Six was secured after one of the most elaborate systems of enrollment ever attempted in a campaign." (6 December 1899) Mayor Abbott later appointed Hugo Dubuque as city solicitor (1900), a post Dubuque retained until 1910, and Cote became president of the board of aldermen in 1900. The mayor kept his promise, retaining French Canadians in appointive offices; see table 5.14.

34. See Silvia, pp. 812–18.

35. See table 5.18. Abbott expected to get a majority of 450 to 600 votes in Ward Six, not an extraordinary expectation in light of the ward's behavior since 1896. A majority of less than 300 was tantamount to defeat. In Ward Six Holland ran well on ballots cast for

Paul Maynard, a former Democrat who replaced Cote as Republican alderman in that ward. The *Globe* commented on the results in the ward, saying:

> The French vote did more for the Democratic ticket than it has done for many years. . . . The Ward Six vote gave Republicans something to worry about. It annoyed them yesterday and afterward the condition of affairs in the ward became apparent the Republican leaders were almost ready to concede the mayor's defeat. (5 December 1900)

In Precinct Six-A Holland received 39 percent of the vote, not especially high but 15 percentage points higher than the mean for the previous six elections.

36. When Dubuque first ran for state representative in 1896 he won but received the lowest vote total of the three GOP candidates, having done poorly in Republican non-French Canadian precincts Seven-B, Eight-B, and Nine-A. He was reelected the next year, when he did better than the other Republican candidates and was cut only in precinct Nine-A. In 1898 Dubuque did poorly again in Seven-B, Eight-B, and Nine-A precincts, where Republicans apparently voted for his opponent. An examination of state representative contests from 1896 to 1908 shows that *Canadien* candidates almost always polled a lesser vote than other GOP candidates in these three precincts. Massachusetts, *Public Document No. 43, 1896–1910, Fall River Daily Globe*, 7 December 1898; 6 December 1899.

37. *Fall River Daily Globe*, 4 December 1901. Buron, the Republican convention nominee lost to a popular independent candidate, who polled the highest vote total of the four. Precincts Seven-B and Eight-B contained the largest number of registered women voters of all the city's precincts. Women could vote only in school committee elections. Many women in these two precincts voted in 1901 and probably were responsible for Buron's especially poor showing there. Massachusetts, *Public Document No. 43*, 1901.

38. *Fall River Daily Globe*, 4 December 1901.

39. French Canadian dissatisfaction in 1902 stemmed in part from a quarrel between Cote and Mayor Grime over *Canadien* appointments to city offices. As a result, Cote tried to wrest the Republican mayoral nomination from Grime. He failed, and then supported Grime in the December election. See Silvia, pp. 818–20. Despite Cote's support, and that of Dubuque's as well, Grime did poorly among French Canadian voters in Wards One, Two, and Six and would have lost the election had Irish Democrats not split their vote because of a factional dispute. As the *Globe* observed:

> The Republican party and the French American voters split in a manner to indicate that the leaders of that section of the party have lost their grip. The French voters refused to be led about by the men who handled them in former years. (10 December 1902)

See also figs. 5.4–5.7 of Petrin, "Political Pragmatism," which graph voting patterns in precincts Six-A, Six-B, One-B, and Three-A.

40. For the background on charter reform see Silvia, pp. 803–06. As Silvia points out, the drive for charter reform was primarily an effort to reduce public corruption. Its potentially damaging, though indirect, effect on French Canadian political influence should not be overlooked however. Because they dominated Ward Six, *Canadiens* could be certain of four of the thirty-six seats on the city council (11 percent). From 1899 to 1902 they had won also a seat on the common council in Ward Two giving them 14 percent of council seats. Under the new charter the Franco-Americans could be sure of only two seats (ward aldermen elected in Ward Six). They would have to rely on Republican or Democratic voters citywide to elect a *Canadien* alderman-at-large.

41. The mean in eight Republican precincts in the charter vote was 73 percent; in five Democratic precincts the mean was 60 percent; in six French Canadian precincts it was only 56 percent. Precincts One-B, Six-A, Six-B were among the precincts most opposed to the charter.

42. *Fall River Daily Globe*, 10 December 1902. In three previous elections Gagnon had received strong Republican support. But when representation for the ward was cut from three to two representatives by the new charter, the GOP apparently decided to freeze Gagnon out.

43. *Fall River Daily Globe*, 16 December 1903.

44. Ibid., 7 November 1904. Bad feeling between Republicans and the *Canadiens* were exacerbated in 1903 in a controversy over the Luce law, which provided for joint party caucuses. Some French leaders favored the bill as a way of enhancing the influence of the French vote in the nomination process. Republican machine politicians opposed it for the same reason, according to one report (*Fall River Daily Globe*, 4 November 1903). Citywide, 66 percent of the voters opposed the Luce law; in Precinct Six-A only 56 percent of the voters opposed it.

45. Ibid., 7 November 1904.

46. Ibid., 16 November, 14 December 1904; Grime (5,007) lost to Irish Democrat John T. Coughlin (5,764). Coughlin actually received about 120 votes less than the Democratic candidate in 1902. He won because the Democratic vote remained relatively stable while the Republican vote suffered a 13 percent decline citywide, due to factional dispute within the party.

47. See table 5.18. A comparison of the mayoral vote in 1900, 1902, and 1904 in Ward Six suggests that Coughlin did not win any more French Canadians than Democratic candidates in 1900 or 1902. Rather than vote for Coughlin *Canadiens* punished Grime by withholding their vote in 1904 as did many other Republican voters. Turnout (the total mayoral vote divided by the number of registered voters) dropped to 70 percent in 1904 as contrasted with a mean of 83 percent for several elections from 1896 to 1902 and 90 percent for six elections from 1906 to 1916.

48. *Fall River Daily Globe*, 14 December 1904. The voting patterns in Precincts One-B and Two-A suggest that French Canadians abstained in the mayoral contest, as they did in Ward Six.

49. See table 5.18 above the fig. 5.8 of Petrin, "Political Pragmatism." The correlation coefficients in fig. 5.8 are not especially high but compared over time show that the association between the French Canadians and the Democratic vote in mayoral contests grew stronger after 1900 and weaker after 1910. Although such a measure does not provide proof that the French Canadians were voting Democratic, it does reinforce the interpretation I have offered here, since it coincides with the voting patterns, with officeholding patterns, and supports newspaper accounts of *Canadien* voting during this period.

50. See table 5.17. The percentage increase in the Democratic vote was about the same in both Ward Six precincts, but in Precinct Six-A, where French Canadians formed about 55 percent of the voters in 1909, the mean Democratic vote trailed that in Precinct Six-B. Thus, the stronger the French presence the less strong was the Democratic vote; note that the mean (1904–10) for Six-A was only 46 percent as opposed to 53 percent in Six-B. This evidence alone does not support the conclusion that most *Canadiens* voted Democratic. Newspaper reports, combined with the voting pattern, indicate clearly, however, that the Democratic party made significant gains in Ward Six. The likelihood seems to be that the *Canadiens* were split during this period, whereas they had been solidly Republican from 1896 to 1899.

51. *Fall River Daily Globe*, 9 December 1908. Republican campaign managers had expected Ward Six to provide a 200 to 300 vote majority in their favor. A comparison of the total vote for each party, from 1902 to 1910, suggests that voters in Ward Six who abstained in 1904 voted Democratic in 1906 and 1908, and possibly in 1910 as well, contributing to the closeness of these contests.

51. Ibid., 7 December 1910.

53. Because French Canadians comprised only about 30 percent of the voters in these precincts, how they voted is difficult to discern. The argument that Democrats made inroads among the *Canadiens* is based on the increase in the percent Democratic vote between 1904 and 1910, over the period from 1896 to 1902, and on the growth in the absolute number of Democratic votes while that for Republicans declined.

54. See tables 5.13 and 5.15. Note also the increase in the number of Democratic candidates for state representative. In 1911 and 1915 French Canadian Democrats ran for representative in the Eleventh Bristol County District; both lost. Edmond Talbot ran in the Tenth District three times (1913, 1914, 1915) and won in 1914.

55. See tables 5.13 and 5.16.

56. See table 5.14.

57. See table 5.13. See *Fall River Daily Globe*, 11, 12, 13 December 1905, for an example of how Lavoie coordinated his campaign with Irish Democrats. He and Eugene Sullivan, candidate for alderman-at-large campaigned together and won an identical vote citywide. As might be expected, Lavoie did better in French precincts that Sullivan (47 percent to 40 percent) and Sullivan did better than Lavoie in Irish Democratic precincts (67 percent to 62 percent). Ward Six provided the vote crucial to Lavoie's victory.

58. Silvia, p. 824, footnote 135.

59. *Fall River Daily Globe*, 9 December 1908.

60. Silvia, pp. 821–31; *Fall River Daily Globe*, 6 December 1911.

61. *Fall River Daily Globe*, 4 December 1912. In 1911 there were only 2,875 registered women voters, 80 percent of whom voted. The next year the number of women registered to vote increased to 11,360, 92 percent of whom voted. Over the next three years, female participation remained high, though not as high as in 1912. By 1916 turnout among women fell to less than 20 percent. Massachusetts, *Public Document No. 43*, 1910–1916.

62. Silvia, p. 831; Fall River *City Directory*, 1910–1915.

63. See tables 5.17, 5.18 and 5.19. Kay helped to solidify the *Canadien* vote by appointing a French Canadian as his secretary and by appointing to the board of port development Edmund Cote, who supported Kay in 1914. Kay probably benefited when the Republicans nominated a French Canadian for the school committee in 1914 (*Fall River Daily Globe*, 4 December 1914, 6 December 1916).

64. The Irish dominated Wards Three, Four, and Five. Of the 72 common councillors elected from these wards between 1888 and 1896, only one was Republican (in 1888). Although the Republicans gained one or two of the three seats in Ward Five between 1897 and 1905, and again in 1912–13 by running French Canadian candidates, Wards Three and Four elected no Republicans to the common council from 1888–1915. Republican aldermen elected in these wards outnumbered Democrats seven to five (1890–93) but only Democrats were elected between 1904 and 1915. (During the intervening years the board of aldermen was elected at large.) The Republican dominated Wards One, Two, Six, Seven, and Eight, and after 1902, Wards Nine and Ten also. Only very rarely was a Democrat elected to the city council from these wards. For example, only two of 120 aldermen elected between 1904 and 1915 in these wards were Democrats.

65. Democratic mayors were elected in 1895, 1896, 1900, 1905, 1906, and 1911. None received more than 55 percent of the vote. The mean vote for Republican mayors from 1886 to 1914 was 57 percent; in seven elections they won 60 percent or more of the two-party vote.

66. *Le Worcester Canadien*, 1888–95; *Worcester Evening Gazette*, 1887–95.

67. *Worcester Evening Gazette*, 7 December 1896.

68. *Worcester Evening Gazette*, 7 December 1896.

69. Ibid., 9 December 1896.

70. N. P. Huot, 1897–99; W. Levi Bousquet, 1900–01; John F. Jandron, 1902, served as aldermen; John Rivard served as common councillor in 1899.

71. Worcester, *City Directory*, 1898.

72. *Worcester Daily Spy*, 24 August 1900.

73. A comparison of the vote given to French Canadian candidates for school committee and common council with that for Republican mayoral candidate Dodge shows them to be nearly identical.

74. *Worcester Evening Post*, 21, 26 November 1900.

75. *Worcester Daily Spy*, 3 December 1900. French Canadians formed rallying committees in each ward to generate support for Bousquet. All told 131 *Canadiens* joined these committees, an unusually large group. The day after these committees were formed the French Republicans decided to form a permanent organization "to further the best interests of the French-speaking people." Explained one leader, the "French people want representation in the city government, and this organization will help choose candidates." (The *Spy*, 4 December 1900)

76. *Worcester Daily Spy,* 3 December 1900.

77. Ibid., 12 December 1900.

78. *Worcester Daily Spy,* 17 December 1900. Favreau's comment was in response to a letter to the *Spy* objecting to *L'Opinion Publique's* claim that the French vote had been overwhelmingly Republican in the municipal election (16 December 1900). Favreau's claim may have been exaggerated by partisanship since he was a member of the Republican city committee and editor of the Republican newspaper. Additional evidence, however, tends to support his claim. Favreau buttressed his claim by pointing out that many more *Canadiens* had served as Republican convention delegates than as Democratic delegates. In contrast with previous years, moreover, no French Canadian speakers attended Democratic rallies as the November election closed (*Worcester Daily Spy,* 7 November 1900; *Worcester Evening Post,* 3, 5 November 1900). Moreover, Alexander Belisle, a four-time Democratic common councilor (1887–91) appeared at Republican rallies (*Worcester Daily Spy,* 7 November 1900). Andre J. Lajoie, who had been a member of the Democratic city committee (1894–96) was by 1900 an independent and urged his Democratic friends to support Bousquet's candidacy (*Worcester Daily Spy,* 3 December 1900).

79. The North Brookfield controversy may be traced in the columns of the *Worcester Daily Spy,* 5 August, 1, 18, 24–30 September, 5, 8, 11–14, 19–20, 23, 27, 31 October, 2, 4, 8, 11–14, 24 November, 12 December 1900, and in nearly daily reports in *L'Opinion Publique,* September–December.

80. *Worcester Daily Spy,* 22 October 1900. Fontaine went on to point out that the Irish hierarchy had been opposing the creation of French parishes for more than thirty years.

81. *Worcester Daily Spy,* 22 October 1900.

82. *Worcester Evening Post,* 26 November 1900. The *Post* bluntly characterized the party's choice of O'Connell as a blunder. See Albert B. Southwick, "The City's First Irish Mayor," *Worcester Sunday Telegram,* 16 December 1979, for an account of the 1900 campaign.

83. *Worcester Evening Post,* 10 December 1900.

84. Ibid., 12 December 1900.

85. Ibid., 15, 17, 18 December 1900; 14, 16 February 1901.

86. Ibid., 20 February 1901.

87. Ibid.

88. Armenians were angry with the Republican city committee for having one Manoog Sherinjan arrested for voting in both fall primaries (*Worcester Evening Post,* 11 February 1901). According to the *Post,* all seventy-five voters of the Swedish Quinsigamond Social Club had pledged to vote for O'Connell because, as one of them explained "we are always good wheel horses but none of the plums happened to come our way after election." (*Worcester Evening Post,* 16 February 1901) Swedes had other reasons for punishing the Republican party. The *Worcester Daily Spy* had reported that they wanted an alderman but were divided over whom they should back (9, 10 October 1900). Perhaps because they could not decide on a candidate, no Swede was nominated for alderman by the Republicans in the fall of 1900, although B. Emil Nystrom was a Republican common council candidate (*Worcester Evening Post,* 21 November 1900). The *Post* reported Swedish and French Canadians voting for O'Connell in Ward Five (19, 20 February 1901).

89. *Worcester Evening Post,* 20 February 1901.

90. *Worcester Evening Post,* 5 March 1901.

91. *Worcester Evening Gazette,* 16 September, 11 December 1901. Democratic voters cut O'Connell again in 1902 (*Worcester Evening Gazette,* 10 December 1902).

92. A comparison of the mean vote received by all non-French Canadian alderman Republican candidates in Republican wards One, Two, Six, Seven, and Eight to that received by French Canadian Republican candidates shows that the *Canadiens* received between 8 and 35 percent fewer votes.

93. Between 1896 and 1902, ten French Canadians were nominated by the GOP for common council or school committee seats. All were in Wards Three, Four, and Five and all lost.

94. See n. 70.

95. C. Herbert DeFosse had been appointed sealer of weights and measures by Mayor Dodge in 1898.

96. The mean vote in favor of the new charter in the five Republican wards was 57 percent. The three Democratic wards opposed it, with only 44 percent voting in favor. In strongly French precincts even fewer voted to accept the new charter: 57 percent voted against it in precincts Three-3; Three-4 and Five-1 (*Worcester Evening Gazette*, 10 December 1902).

97. *Worcester Evening Post*, 21 February 1902; Worcester, *City Directory*, 1901, 1902.

98. *Worcester Evening Gazette*, 10 December 1902.

99. See tables 5.20 and 5.21. From 1902 to 1906 Democrats nominated six French Canadians; Republicans nominated nine. All Republicans lost. Democrat Louis A. Belisle was alderman-at-large in 1903 and Louis P. deGrandpre served one three-year term on the school committee. These two men were the only *Canadiens* in city government between 1903 and 1906.

100. *Worcester Evening Gazette*, 10 December 1902.

101. Ibid.

102. See figs. 5.9–5.11 in Petrin, "Political Pragmatism," which graph voting patterns in precincts 3-3, 3-4, and 5-1, 1896–1915.

103. *Worcester Evening Gazette*, 23 November 1904.

104. See table 5.20. Between 1907 and 1909 Republican *Canadien* candidates outnumbered Democrats thirteen to two.

105. From 1893 to 1903 only 19 of 264 (7 percent) of Republican ward committeemen were *Canadiens*. Between 1904 and 1906 the French Canadian percentage rose to 12 percent; in 1907 and 1908 it rose to 19 percent, when thirty-three of the 180 committeemen were French Canadians. Worcester, *City Directory*, 1893–1908.

106. See figs. 5.9–5.11 in Petrin, "Political Pragmatism."

107. *Worcester Evening Gazette*, 11 December 1907, 9 December 1908, 3, 10, 15 December 1909.

108. Ibid., 8 December 1909.

109. *Worcester Evening Post*, 15, 17 December 1910.

110. *Worcester Evening Post*, 18–19, 22 November 1910.

111. Ibid., 23 November 1910.

112. Ibid., 5, 8 November, 12 December 1910.

113. Ibid., 30 November, 12 December 1910.

114. Ibid., 10 December 1910. See also 30 November and 5 December 1910.

115. Ibid., 12–14 December 1910; *Worcester Evening Gazette*, 14 December 1910.

116. *Worcester Evening Post*, 21 November, 4, 8 December 1911; *Worcester Evening Gazette*, 6, 13 December 1911.

117. *Worcester Evening Gazette*, 6, 7 December 1912.

118. Ibid., 9–11 December 1911.

Chapter 6. France-Democrats and Partisan Politics: A Two-Town Case Study, 1896–1915

1. By 1910 French Canadians filled 13 percent of town offices but only 7.5 percent of elective positions in the cities. Compare tables 5.1 and 6.1.

2. A comparison of the percent of the quota filled by French Canadians in the cities and towns shows little difference between the two. For seventeen cities, it was 27.5; for twenty-two towns it was 24.2. For more detail, see table 6.2 in this chapter and table 5.5 of Petrin, "Political Pragmatism."

3. In the cities Republican candidates outnumbered Democrats by two to one; refer to table 5.7.

4. Compare figs. 5.1 and 6.1 of Petrin, "Political Pragmatism."

5. Compare figs. 5.2 and 6.2 of Petrin, "Political Pragmatism."

6. See chap. 4, nn. 1 and 2.

7. *Spencer Sun*, 30 March 1882.

8. Ibid.

9. Ibid., 23 March 1883.

10. Town elections in Spencer were not run on party lines. The conclusion that the Democrats remained out of power is based on cross referencing persons identified in the newspaper as belonging to each faction with persons chosen as delegates to party conventions during this period and with town officers.

11. *Spencer Sun*, 4 April 1884. The editor went on to say:

Sensible voters will take no notice of this un-American system of politics but will vote for the best man, and the best measures despite the dictation of racial fanatics. Racial distinctions, which are universally odious when applied to the negro, ought to bring a blush of shame to the cheeks of those who apply them to white men. It is time to call a halt. This thing has gone far enough. We will not place the blame at anybody's door, but we hope this town meeting will bury racial distinctions for all time. This is America and as citizens we are all free and equal, and we must sink all racial feelings in the desire to benefit our common country.

See also *Spencer Sun*, 9 March 1883, for an expression of similar opinions.

12. *Spencer Sun*, 4, 11 April 1884.

13. *Spencer Leader*, 27 March 1890; see chap. 4, n. 67.

14. *Spencer Leader*, 25 March 1893.

15. *Spencer Leader*, 3 April 1897. See also *Spencer Leader*, 25 April, 2 May, 3 October 1896, for more detailed information on the formation of the French Naturalization Club.

16. *Spencer Leader*, 5 March 1898.

17. Ibid., 12 March 1898.

18. In 1885 there were about 140 French Canadian-born voters in Spencer (Massachusetts Bureau of Statistics of Labor, *Report*, 19 (1888). The town's *Register of Voters, 1884–1891* shows that there were about 100 American-born *Canadien* voters as well. Together these two groups formed about 18 percent of the town's 1,300 voters in 1885.

In 1892 the *Register of Voters* again compiled a list of current voters which included about 320 French names, about 20 percent of the total. Despite the addition of many French voters to the list between 1884 and 1892 the proportion of Spencer's voters who were *Canadien* did not rise because a larger number of voters were also dropped from the list for various reasons. Of a sample of thirty-one French Canadians on the list in 1884, thirteen had been removed by 1892. Only one had died; the remainder had been removed from the list for non-payment of taxes or because they had left town. The register gives the names of persons who were added to the list between 1893 and 1916. See also *Spencer Leader*, 3 March 1897; 1 April 1899; and 18 March 1910, for estimates of the number of *Canadien* voters in the town.

19. *Spencer Leader*, 3 March, 10 April 1897.

20. Ibid., 3 April 1897.

21. Ibid., 3 March, 10 April 1897.

22. Ibid., 5, 12, 26 March, 6 April 1898.

23. Ibid., 11 March 1905; 7 April 1911; 5 April 1912. Until 1897 Spencer voted wet only in 1883, 1891, and 1893. After 1897 it voted against license only in 1900 and 1911. Between 1882 and 1897 the mean vote in favor of license was 45 percent, between 1898 and 1912, 53 percent.

24. Ibid., 10 April 1897; 12 March, 6 April 1898.

25. From 1876 to 1885, 18 of 20 representatives were Republicans; from 1886 to 1897, 10 of 12; and from 1898 to 1912, only 4 of 18. See also fig. 6.3 of my dissertation, Petrin, "Political Pragmatism," which graphically illustrates the preference for French Canadian and Democratic contests by contrasting voting in gubernatorial and state representative contests between 1890 and 1915.

26. *Spencer Leader*, 1, 22 October, 2 November 1898. Marchessault was president of the French Naturalization Club and was expected to carry most of its 450 votes as well as the Democrats of the town. He won in part because about 235 Republicans, many of them probably *Canadiens*, voted for him. For biographical information on Marchesault, see *Spencer Leader*, 22 October 1898, and *Worcester Daily Spy*, 17 October 1900.

27. *Spencer Leader*, 30 September, 12 October, 11 November 1899; 9 November 1901; *Worcester Daily Spy*, 3 November 1900. In late September Dr. Marc Fontaine was reported to be planning a "vigorous canvas against the re-election" of Marchessault. Fontaine predicted that as many as 125 *Canadiens* would attend the Republican caucus but only 25 actually attended. He also predicted that the French Canadian Republicans would unite in favor of Luther Hill over Charles Allen for state representative but this claim was repudiated by other French Republicans who denied that Fontaine had much influence among French voters in Spencer. They were probably correct. Republican party leaders expected Fontaine to deliver about 150 French votes for their candidate in the November election and were disappointed with the mere 50 French votes they received. These votes were enough to give the election to the GOP nominee nonetheless. According to the *Leader*, "Had the French voters stood by Mr. Marchessault as they had the previous year, it is conceded that he would have easily carried Spencer and possibly the district." (11 November 1899). Fontaine's actions angered many French Canadians in Spencer who grumbled about the defection of their compatriots to Allen.

28. See table 6.10. As the following figures suggest, French Canadians in Spencer tended to favor *Canadiens* over non-French candidates of either party.

The vote for state representative, 1898–1912:

	Democrats			Republicans		
	No.	%	# of candidates	No.	%	# of candidates
All candidates	581	51.7	(15)	535	47.8	(15)
Non-*Canadiens*	534	48.0	(9)	511	45.2	(13)
Canadiens	651	57.4	(6)	690	65.1	(2)

29. *Spencer Leader*, 1, 8 April 1899.
30. Ibid., 18 March, 8 April 1899.
31. Ibid., 17, 24 March, 7 April 1900.
32. Ibid., 17, 24 March, 7 April 1900.
33. *Worcester Daily Spy*, 22 October 1897.
34. *Spencer Leader*, 20 March 1902.
35. Ibid., 29 March, 12 April 1902.
36. Ibid., 7, 21 March, 14 April 1903; 26 March, 19 April 1904; 18 March 1905; 24 February, 24 March 1906.
37. Ibid., 24 February 1906. Dr. Marc Fontaine's justification of the French Republican cause, though long, is worthwhile quoting at length:

For many years we had a citizen's and a non-license caucus. It is a well-known fact that the citizen's caucus was a democratic caucus and that the no-license caucus was conducted by temperance people. As a result the republicans were left out altogether. The no-license people would simply ask if the candidate presented by the French people was a temperance man. The republicans tired of this thing and decided to have a caucus of their own two years ago. The democrats stayed with their own, the citizen's caucus.

The French people several years ago held a caucus of their own. The Yankees told us if we would unite on a man and present him they would support him, but we always found that the nominees were democrats. We have learned from the past that we got nothing.

It has been said that we might elect two French candidates for selectman, but in the *Spencer Leader* of last week, one of our people says that even if we had 900 French voters we ought not to ask for more than one French representative and in private this man says that if we ask for too much Charles N. Prouty and Erastus Jones would soon change the complexion of this town, so that the French people would be in the minority.

Now let us look at this. In 1888 we had a great strike here and the French people were the worst strikers in the lot. Were the French expelled from the town? No. They were not employed for their sweet eyes but because they are the best workmen in the world. Though Carroll D. Wright called them the 'Chinamen of the East,' he admitted that same fact as to their ability as workmen.

We want a republican representative once in a while and that is why we have called this caucus.

38. *Spencer Leader*, 3, 17, 31 March, 7 April 1906.
39. Ibid., 24 March 1906.
40. Ibid., 29 September 1906; 30 September 1907; see also 15 March 1907; 10 April 1908; 12 March 1909.

41. Ibid., 18, 25 March 1910.

42. Felix Gatineaux, *Histoire des franco-américains de Southbridge, Massachusetts* (Framingham, Mass.: Lakeview Press, 1919), pp. 101, 242. According to Gatineaux, 265 *Canadien* voters were registered in the town by 1890. Before 1885 Clement Begin had been elected overseer of the poor (1879) but he resigned. As early as 1895 there were about 800 French Canadians in Southbridge (*Southbridge Journal*, 7 November 1895). See Gatineaux for more details on the French Canadians of the town; also see Massachusetts Bureau of Statistics of Labor, *Report* (1882, 1888), for the number of *Canadien* voters in 1875 and 1885.

43. Between 1884 and 1897 the GOP ran *Canadiens* for selectman only twice. The Democratic party nominated *Canadiens* for that position nine times during the same period and they won in 1888, 1892, and 1893. From 1897 to 1914 at least one, and sometimes two, French Canadian Democrats were nominated for selectman and twenty of the twenty-three nominees won. Of the six Republican nominees during that period, half won.

44. *Southbridge Journal*, 4 October 1900. According to Alexis Boyer, a leading Democrat, the *Canadiens* were six hundred strong and were entitled to a greater representation among party delegations to conventions. In his view, they constituted the voting strength of the party, and therefore "they would demand a larger share of representation." A *Canadien* was nominated for state representative at this caucus meeting for the first time since 1893. According to Gatineaux, *Histoire*, p. 101, there were 330 French Canadian voters in 1895 but the *Southbridge Journal*, (7 November 1895), estimated there were 400.

45. The same pattern prevailed before and afterwards; see table 6.14.

46. Refer to table 6.10. See fig. 6.4 of Petrin, "Political Pragmatism," which graphically illustrates the preference in Southbridge for French Canadian and Democratic candidates by contrasting voting in gubernatorial and state representative elections between 1890 and 1915.

Chapter 7. Conclusion

1. Joseph Huthmacher, *Massachusetts People and Politics, 1919–1933* (Cambridge: Harvard University Press, 1959), pp. 12–13. See also John Higham, *Strangers in the Land: Patterns of American Nativism, 1865–1925* (New Brunswick, N.J.: Rutgers University Press, 1955), and Barbara Solomon, *Ancestors and Immigrants: A Changing New England Tradition* (Cambridge: Harvard University Press, 1956).

2. Alec Barbrook, *God Save the Commonwealth: An Electoral History of Massachusetts* (Amherst: University of Massachusetts Press, 1973), pp. 3–33.

3. Margaret Thompson, ed., *Presidential Elections since 1789*, 3d ed., (Washington, D.C.: Congressional Quarterly, 1983), pp. 91–105, 156–70.

4. Commonwealth of Massachusetts, *Manual for the Use of the General Court*, 1880–1940.

5. Thompson, *Presidential Elections*, pp. 106–19, 171–84. During the period from 1868 to 1924 Republican presidential candidates averaged 59.7 percent of the popular vote, as compared with 36.1 percent for Democrats. Only in 1884 and 1912 did a Republican receive less than 50 percent of the popular vote. By contrast, Republican candidates have averaged only 43.6 percent of the popular vote since 1928, the Democratic average having been 53.6 percent.

6. Commonwealth of Massachusetts, *Public Document No. 43: Number of . . . Registered Voters and Persons Who Voted . . . Together with the Number of Votes Received by Each Candidate*, 1890–1980; Huthmacher, *Massachusetts*, pp. 262–65. See also Barbrook, *God Save the Commonwealth*, especially p. 169; Edgar Litt, *The Political Cultures of Massachusetts* (Cambridge: M.I.T. Press, 1965); and Duane Lockard, *New England State Politics* (Princeton: Princeton University Press, 1959).

7. Huthmacher, *Massachusetts*, pp. 117–90.

8. Ibid., p. viii.

9. Ibid., pp. 119–25, 260–62.

10. Ibid., pp. 119–20.

11. John Buenker's work, *Urban Liberalism and Progressive Reform* (New York: Charles Scribner's Sons, 1973), traced the origins of social and economic liberalism to urban, ethnic workingclass politicians during the Progressive Era. He focused especially on the Irish of Boston when dealing with Massachusetts, paying scant attention to other groups or to the development of ethnic politics. Similarly Richard Abrams' study, *Conservatism in a Progressive Era*, largely overlooked the ethnic dimension of politics in the Bay State.

12. See especially Walker, *Politics and Ethnocentrism* and "Presidential Politics of Franco-Americans," pp. 353–63; and Duane Lockard, *New England State Politics* (Princeton: Princeton University Press, 1959). The works cited in n. 27 of chap. 1 are also relevant.

13. Lockard, *New England State Politics*, p. 66.

14. Ibid., p. 312.

15. Ibid.

16. Ibid., pp. 312–13.

17. Walker, "Presidential Politics," p. 355.

18. Ibid., pp. 355–56.

19. Ibid., p. 356; Walker, *Politics and Ethnocentrism*, p. 24.

20. Walker, *Politics and Ethnocentrism*, pp. 27–28.

21. Lockard, *New England State Politics*, pp. 31, 66, 98, 198, 241.

22. See especially Haebler, "Habitants in Holyoke," chap. 6; and Huthmacher, *Massachusetts People and Politics*, p. 15. The Irish blocked the rise of other immigrant groups in politics as well. See Robert A. Dahl, *Who Governs: Democracy and Power in an American City* (New Haven: Yale University Press, 1961), pp. 42–47; Elmer E. Cornwell Jr., "Party Absorption of Ethnic Groups: The Case of Providence, Rhode Island," *Social Forces* 38 (March 1960): 205–10; and "Bosses, Machines, and Ethnic Groups," *Annals of the American Academy of Political and Social Sciences* 353 (May 1964): 24–30.

23. Walker, "Presidential Politics," pp. 355–56.

24. Arthur M. Schlesinger Jr., ed., *Almanac of American History* (New York: G. P. Putnam's Sons, 1983), p. 415; Albert Bushnell Hart, ed., *Commonwealth History of Massachusetts*, vol. 5 (New York: States History Company, 1930), pp. 186, 367–69; *L'Opinion Publique* 6, 11, 27 September 2, 23 October, 4 November 1913.

25. Hart, *Commonwealth History*, pp. 168–72; Blodgett, *Gentle Reformers*, pp. 78–80, 92–99, 128–39.

26. Abrams, *Conservatism*, pp. 47, 85–93, 103–9, 230–34, 251–57; Hart, *Commonwealth History*, p. 177.

27. Hart, *Commonwealth History*, pp. 177–79; see also L. Ethan Ellis, *Reciprocity, 1911: A Study in Canadian-American Relations* (New Haven: Yale University, 1939); Orville John McDiarmid, *Commercial Policy in the Canadian Economy* (Cambridge: Harvard University Press, 1946), pp. 203–38.

28. Hart, *Commonwealth History*, pp. 180–86; Barbrook, *God Save the Commonwealth*, p. 26; Buenker, *Urban Liberalism*, pp. 10, 67–70.

29. Buenker, *Urban Liberalism*; Lockard, *New England State Politics*, pp. 312–13. Lockard's observations parallel that of V. O. Key, Jr., "Secular Realignment and the Party System," *Journal of Politics* 20 (1959): 198–210, that the Democratic trend in northern New England industrial towns reflected, at least in part, the growth of the ethnic working class, particularly French Canadians and Irish workers, in that region. See also V. O. Key, Jr., *Politics, Parties, and Pressure Groups*, 5th ed. (New York: Crowell, 1964), p. 539.

30. Massachusetts, *Public Document No. 43*, 1890–1920. See Huthmacher's perceptive discussion of the dangers and benefits that attended recognition politics in Massachusetts. His view is that in the long run the Republican party was hurt by its discomfiture with recognition politics in Massachusetts, while the Democrats made gains among ethnic voters by accommodating group demands for recognition, *Massachusetts People and Politics*, pp. 120–25.

31. Buenker, *Urban Liberalism*, pp. 10, 17, 107; Lockard, *New England State Politics*, pp. 305–20; Massachusetts, *Public Document No. 43*, 1890–1940.

32. *Massachusetts Yearbook*, 1895–1903.

33. Massachusetts, *Public Document No. 43*, 1896–1906.

34. For a discussion of the ways in which political recognition affects group politics see Litt, *Ethnic Politics in America*, pp. 28–35; Lane, *Why People Get Involved in Politics* pp. 236–43, 252; Wolfinger, "The Development of Persistence of Ethnic Voting," pp. 896–908; and "Some Consequences of Ethnic Politics," in *The Electoral Process*, ed. M. Kent Jennings and L. Harmon Zeigler (Englewood Cliffs, N.J.: Prentice-Hall, 1966), pp. 42–54. As Lane points out, "the more self-conscious and status-conscious an ethnic group, the more the members of that group will be sensitive to the politics of 'recognition,' i.e., appointment to office and political candidacy of fellow ethnics." (p. 243)

35. Lockard, *New England State Politics*, pp. 66, 312–13.

36. See Formisano, "Comment on Robert Kelly's 'Ideology and Political Culture from Jefferson to Nixon,'" pp. 571–73; Kleppner, *The Third Electoral System*, pp. 144, 362.

37. The relationship between parties and their constituent groups assumed here is drawn from Samuel J. Eldersweld's excellent *Political Parties: A Behavioral Analysis* (Chicago: Rand McNally, 1964).

38. Many French Canadian elites and their supporters remained identified with the GOP, largely because they had been integrated into the Republican city machine that rewarded party loyalty with patronage positions. This was especially true in the predominately French Canadian Ward Six of Falls River, where French Canadian Republicans dominated ward politics, enabling them to secure, practically without significant opposition, solid representation for the group on the city council as well as in the general court. It is also possible that upwardly mobile middle-class elites may have been attracted to the Republican party because it often stood for business-like government or that the GOP convinced them that it was the party of integrity and stability; see Haebler, "Habitants in Holyoke," pp. 285–86, 301. A split between middle-class and working-class French Canadians was evident in Lowell, where the former supported Republican efforts for charter reform that were successful but ironically enabled Irish Democrats to gain control of city government with the support of working-class *Canadiens*. See Blewett, "The Mills and the Multitude," p. 175.

39. Although there existed significant differences between these Massachusetts towns and those in the Midwest studies by Timothy L. Smith, his insights regarding differences in the ethnic experience between small towns and larger cities are relevant. See his "Religious Denominations as Ethnic Communities: A Regional Case Study," *Church History* 35 (1966): 207–26, and "New Approaches to the History of Immigration in Twentieth-Century America," *American Historical Review* 71 (July 1966): 1265–79.

40. For a more detailed discussion of these views see chapter 3. The speech by Camille Trahan of Worcester quoted at length in chapter 5 is an excellent example of the *Canadiens'* pluralistic conception of American politics.

41. Albert L. Bartlett, "The Transformation of New England," *Forum* 7 (August 1889): 640.

42. See Jensen, *Winning of the Midwest*, pp. 304–8; Walter D. Burnham, "The Changing Shape of the American Political Universe," *American Political Science Review* 59 (March 1965): 7–28; and Burnham's *Critical Elections and the Mainsprings of American Politics* (New York: Norton, 1970).

Bibliography

Public Documents

UNITED STATES

Bureau of the Census. *Tenth Census of the United States: 1880.*
——. *Eleventh Census of the United States: 1890.*
——. *Twelfth Census of the United States: 1900.*
——. *Abstract of the Thirteenth Census of the United States: 1910.*
——. *Thirteenth Census of the United States: 1910.*
——. *Fourteenth Census of the United States: 1920.*
——. *Special Reports, Occupations at the Twelfth Census, 1900.*
U.S. Congress. Senate. Immigration Commission. *Reports.* 41 vols. 61st Congress, 2d, 3d Sess. 1911.

COMMONWEALTH OF MASSACHUSETTS

Bureau of Statistics of Labor. *Annual Reports,* 1885–1920.
——. *Census of the Commonwealth of Massachusetts: 1885.*
——. *Census of the Commonwealth of Massachusetts: 1895.*
——. *Census of the Commonwealth of Massachusetts: 1905.*
——. *Census of the Commonwealth of Massachusetts: 1915.*
General Court. *Manual for the Use of the General Court.* 1880–1920.
——. *Report of the Commission on the Cost of Living.* House Doc. 1750, 1910.
——. *Report of the Commission on Immigration. The Problem of Immigration in Massachusetts.* House Doc. 2300, 1914.
Secretary of State. *Public Document 43,* "Number of Registered Voters and Persons who Voted . . . Together with the Number of Votes Received by each Candidate," 1890–1924.

MUNICIPAL

Chicopee. *City Directory.*
Fall River. *City Directory.*
Fall River. *City Documents.*
Fitchburg. *City Directory.*
Haverhill. *City Directory.*
Holyoke. *City Directory.*
Lawrence. *City Directory.*
Lowell. *City Directory.*
Lynn. *City Directory.*
Marlborough. *City Directory.*

Massachusetts Yearbook.
New Bedford. *City Directory.*
North Adams. *City Directory.*
Northhampton. *City Directory.*
Pittsfield. *City Directory.*
Salem. *City Directory.*
Southbridge. *Town Directory.*
Southbridge. *Town Records.*
Spencer. *Town Directory.*
Spencer. *Town Records.*
Spencer. *Register of Voters, 1884–1891.*
Spencer. *Register of Voters, 1892–1917.*
Springfield. *City Directory.*
Taunton. *City Directory.*
Worcester. *City Directory.*
Worcester. *City Documents.*

Newspapers

Fall River Daily Globe
Fall River Daily Herald
L'Independent (Fall River)
L'Opinion Publique (Worcester)
Southbridge Journal
Spencer Leader
Spencer Sun
Worcester Daily Spy
Worcester Evening Gazette
Worcester Evening Post
Worcester Telegram

Books

Abbott, Edith. *Historical Aspects of the Immigration Problem: Select Documents.* Chicago: University of Chicago Press, 1926.

Adell, Aaron I. *American Catholicism and Social Action: A Search for Social Justice, 1865–1950.* Garden City, N.Y.: Hanover House, 1960.

Abrams, Richard M. *Conservatism in a Progressive Era; Massachusetts Politics, 1900–1912.* Cambridge: Harvard University Press, 1964.

Abramson, Harold J. *Ethnic Diversity in Catholic America.* New York: Wiley, 1973.

Allswang, John W. *A House for All Peoples: Ethnic Politics in Chicago, 1890–1936.* Lexington: University of Kentucky Press, 1971.

Anctil, Pierre. *A Franco-American Bibliography; New England.* Bedford, N.H.: National Materials Development Center, 1979.

Anderson, Elin. *We Americans: A Study of Cleavage in an American City.* Cambridge: Harvard University Press, 1937.

Artman, Charles E. *Industrial Structure of New England.* Washington, D.C.: Government Printing Office, 1930.

Bailey, Harry A. Jr. and Ellis Katz. *Ethnic Group Politics.* Columbus, Ohio: Charles E. Merrill Publishing Co., 1969.

Banfield, Edward C. and James Q. Wilson. *City Politics.* New York: Vintage, 1963.

Barbrook, Alec. *God Save the Commonwealth: An Electoral History of Massachusetts.* Amherst: University of Massachusetts Press, 1973.

Bedford, Henry F. *Socialism and the Workers in Massachusetts, 1886–1912.* Amherst: University of Massachusetts Press, 1966.

Bélisle, Alexandre. *Histoire de la presse franco-américaine et des canadiens-français aux Etats-Unis.* Worcester, Mass.: L'Opinion Publique, 1911.

――――. *Livre d'Or des Franco-Américains de Worcester.* Worcester, Mass.: La Compagnie de Publication Bélisle, 1920.

Benoit, Josaphat. *L'Ame franco-américaine.* Montreal: Jouve, 1935.

Benoit, Josaphat, ed. *Fernand Gagnon, biographie, éloge, funèbre, pages choisies.* Manchester, N.H.: L'Avenir National, 1940.

Benson, Lee, et al. *American Political Behavior: Historical Essays and Readings.* New York: Harper & Row, 1974.

Benson, Lee. *The Concept of Jacksonian Democracy: New York as a Test Case.* Princeton: Princeton University Press, 1961.

Berelson, Bernard R., Paul F. Lazarsfeld, and William N. McPhee. *Voting: A Study of Opinion Formation in a Presidential Campaign.* Chicago: University of Chicago Press, 1954.

Berthoff, Rowland T. *British Immigrants in Industrial America, 1790–1950.* Cambridge: Harvard University Press, 1953.

Binstock, Robert H. *A Report on Politics in Worcester, Massachusetts.* Cambridge: Joint Center for Urban Studies of the Massachusetts Institute of Technology and Harvard University, 1960.

Blalock, Hubert M. *Social Statistics.* New York: McGraw-Hill, 1960.

Blodgett, Geoffrey. *The Gentle Reformers: Massachusetts Democrats in the Cleveland Era.* Cambridge: Harvard University Press, 1966.

Bodnar, John. *The Transplanted: A History of Immigrants in Urban America.* Bloomington: Indiana University Press, 1987.

Boston University. *Bibliography on State and Local Government in New England.* Boston: Boston University, Bureau of Public Administration, 1952.

Bourbonnière, Avila, ed. *Les Canadiens-français de Lowell.* Lowell, Mass.: L'Union franco-américaine, 1896.

Bracq, Jean C. *The Evolution of French Canada.* New York: Macmillan, 1924.

Brault, Gerard J. *The French-Canadian Heritage in New England.* Hanover, N.H.: University Press of New England and McGill-Queen's University Press, 1986.

――――, ed. *Les Conferences de l'institut Franco-Américain de Bowdoin College.* Brunswick, Maine: Bowdoin College, 1961.

Brayton, Alice, comp. *Life on the Stream.* 2 vols. Newport, R.I.: Wilkinson Press, 1962.

Brewer, Daniel C. *The Conquest of New England by the Immigrant.* New York: G. P. Putnam's Sons, 1926.

Buenker, John D. *Urban Liberalism and Progressive Reform.* New York: Charles Scribner's Sons, 1973.

Burnham, Walter D. *Critical Elections and the Mainsprings of American Politics.* New York: Norton, 1970.

Campbell, Angus, et al. *The American Voter.* New York: Wiley, 1960.

Cantor, Milton, ed. *American Workingclass Culture: Explorations in American Labor and Social History.* Westport, Conn.: Greenwood, 1979.

Carpenter, Niles. *Immigrants and their Children, 1920.* Washington, D.C.: Government Printing Office, 1927.

Chambers, William N. and Walter D. Burnham. *The American Party Systems; Stages of Political Development.* New York: Oxford, 1967.

Chandonnet, Thomas A. *Notre-Dame-des-Canadiens et les Canadiens des Etats-Unis.* Trans. by Kenneth J. Moynihan. Worcester, Mass.: n.p., 1977. Originally published in Montreal: George E. D. Desbarats, 1872.

Clark, Victor S. *History of Manufactures in the United States.* 3 vols. New York: McGraw-Hill, 1929.

Cohen, Morris H. *Worcester's Ethnic Groups: A Bicentennial View.* Worcester, Mass.: Worcester Bicentennial Commission, 1976.

Cole, Arthur H. *The American Wool Manufacture.* 2 vols. Cambridge: Harvard University Press, 1926.

Cole, Donald B. *Immigrant City: Lawrence, Massachusetts, 1845–1921.* Chapel Hill: University of North Carolina Press, 1963.

Commanger, Henry Steele, ed. *Immigration and American History.* Minneapolis: University of Minnesota Press, 1961.

Commons, John R. *Races and Immigrants in America.* Chautauqua, N.Y.: Chautauqua Press, 1907.

Crane, Ellery Bicknell. *Worcester County, Massachusetts.* 4 vols. New York: Lewis Publishing Co., 1907.

Creighton, D. G. et al. *Minorities, Schools, and Politics.* Toronto: University of Toronto Press, 1969.

Cross, Robert D. *The Emergence of Liberal Catholicism in America.* Cambridge: Harvard University Press, 1958.

Dahl, Robert A. *Who Governs: Democracy and Power in an American City.* New Haven: Yale University Press, 1961.

Devine, Donald J. *The Political Culture of the United States; The Influence of Member Values on Regime Maintenance.* Boston: Little, Brown, 1972.

Dinnerstein, Leonard and David M. Reimers. *Ethnic Americans; A History of Immigration and Assimilation.* New York: Dodd, Mead, 1975.

Dinnerstein, Leonard and Frederic C. Jaher. *Uncertain Americans.* New York: Oxford, 1977.

Dolan, J. P. *The Immigrant Church: New York's Irish and German Catholics, 1815–1865.* Baltimore: Johns Hopkins University Press, 1975.

Dollar, Charles M. and Richard J. Jensen. *Historian's Guide to Statistics.* New York: Holt, Rinehart, & Winston, 1971.

Drummond, William Henry. *The Habitant and Other French-Canadian Poems.* New York and London: G. P. Putnam's Sons, 1897.

———. *Poetical Works.* New York and London: G. P. Putnam's Sons, 1912.

Dubuque, Hugo A. *Les Canadiens-français de Fall River, Massachusetts.* Fall River, Mass.: H. Boisseau, 1883.

———. *Le Guide Canadian-français de Fall River et notes historiques sur les Canadiens de Fall River.* Fall River, Mass.: Edmond F. Lamoureux, 1888.

Ducharme, Jacques. *The Shadow of the Trees: The Story of French-Canadians in New England.* New York: Harper, 1943.

Eisenmenger, Robert W. *The Dynamics of Growth in New England's Economy, 1870–1964.* Middletown, Conn.: Wesleyan University Press, 1967.

Eldersweld, Samuel J. *Political Parties: A Behavioral Analysis.* Chicago: Rand McNally, 1964.

Ellis, John T. *American Catholicism.* 2d rev. ed. Chicago: University of Chicago Press, 1969.

Ellis, L. Ethan. *Reciprocity, 1911: A Study in Canadian-American Relations.* New Haven: Yale University Press, 1969.

Enloe, Cynthia H. *Ethnic Conflict and Political Development.* Boston: Little, Brown, 1973.

Eno, Arthur L., ed. *Cotton was King: A History of Lowell, Massachusetts.* Lowell, Mass.: Lowell Historical Society, 1976.

Erickson, Charlotte. *Invisible Immigrants: The Adaptation of English and Scottish Immigrants in Nineteenth-Century America.* Coral Gables, Fla.: University of Miami Press, 1972.

Fairchild, Henry P. *Immigrant Backgrounds.* New York: Wiley, 1927.

Faulkner, Harold U. *Politics, Reform, and Expansion, 1890–1900.* New York: Harper, 1959.

Felt, Joseph B. *Statistics of Towns in Massachusetts.* Boston: Little, Brown, 1843.

Fenner, Henry M. *History of Fall River, Mass.* Fall River, Mass.: Fall River Merchants Association, 1911.

Fenton, John. *The Catholic Vote.* New Orleans: Hauser, 1960.

———. *People and Parties in Politics.* Glenview, Ill.: Scott, Foresman, 1966.

Finlay, J. I. *Canada in the North Atlantic Triangle: Two Centuries of Social Change.* New York: Oxford, 1975.

Fishman, Joshua A. *Language Loyalty in the United States: The Maintenance and Perpetuation of Non-English Mother Tongues by American Ethnic and Religious Groups.* London: Mouton, 1966.

Flanigan, William H. and Zingale, Nancy H. *Political Behavior of the American Electorate.* 3d ed. Boston: Allyn & Bacon, 1975.

Floud, Roderick. *An Introduction to Quantitative Methods for Historians.* Princeton: Princeton University Press, 1973.

Formisano, Ronald P. *The Birth of Mass Political Parties: Michigan, 1827–1861.* Princeton: Princeton University Press, 1971.

Fowler, Orin. *History of Fall River.* Fall River, Mass.: Almy & Milne, Printers, 1862.

Freeman, Stanley L. and Raymond J. Pelletier. *Initiating Franco-American Studies: A Handbook for Teachers.* Orono, Maine: University of Maine, 1981.

Fuchs, Lawrence H., ed. *American Ethnic Politics.* New York: Harper Torchbooks, 1968.

———. *The Political Behavior of American Jews.* Glencoe, Ill.: Free Press, 1956.

Gans, Herbert. *The Urban Villagers.* Glencoe, Ill.: Free Press, 1962.

Garraty, John A. *The New Commonwealth, 1877–1896.* New York: Harper Torchbooks, 1968.

Gatineaux, Felix. *Histoire des franco-américains de Southbridge, Massachusetts.* Framingham, Mass.: Lakeview Press, 1919.

———. *Historique des conventions des canadiens-français aux Etats-Unis, 1865–1901.* Woonsocket, R.I.: L'Union Saint-Jean-Baptiste, d'Amérique, 1927.

Gavit, J. P. *American by Choice.* New York: Harper, 1922.

Gérin, Léon. *Le type économique et social des Canadiens.* 2d ed. Montreal: Bibliothèque Economique et Sociale, 1948.

Gibson, James R., ed. *European Settlement and Development in North America.* Toronto: University of Toronto Press, 1978.

Giguere, Madeleine, ed. *A Franco-American Overview,* vol 3. Cambridge: National Assessment and Dissemination Center, 1981.

Gillon, Edmund V. Jr. *A New England Town in Early Photographs.* New York: Dover Publications, 1976.

Glazer, Nathan and Moynihan, Daniel P. *Beyond the Melting Pot.* Cambridge: M.I.T. Press, 1963.

Glazer, Nathan and Moynihan, Daniel P., eds. *Ethnicity: Theory and Experience.* Cambridge: Harvard University Press, 1975.

Gordon, Milton M. *Assimilation in American Life.* New York: Oxford, 1964.

Greeley, Andrew M. and McCready, William C. *Ethnicity in the United States: A Preliminary Reconnaissance.* New York: Wiley, 1974.

Greene, Constance McLaughlin. *Holyoke, Massachusetts: A Case History of the Industrial Revolution in America.* New Haven: Yale University Press, 1939.

Guide des addresses des Canadiens-français de la Nouvelle-Angleterre. Fall River, Mass.: Fall River Publishing Co., 1899.

Guide français de Fall River, Massachusetts, 1909. Fall River, Mass.: L. J. Gagnon, 1909.

Guignard, Michael J. *La Foi—La Langue—La Culture: The Franco-Americans of Biddeford, Maine.* Privately published, 1982.

Greene, Victor. *For God and Country: The Rise of Polish and Lithuanian Ethnic Consciousness in America, 1860–1910.* Madison: State Historical Society of Wisconsin, 1975.

Hammarberg, Melvyn. *The Indiana Voter: The Historical Dynamics of Party Allegiance during the 1870s.* Chicago: University of Chicago Press, 1977.

Hamon, Edouard. *Les Canadiens-français de la Nouvelle-Angleterre.* Quebec: Hardy, 1891.

Handlin, Oscar. *Boston's Immigrants; A Study in Acculturation.* Rev. and enl. ed. New York: Atheneum, 1977.

———, ed. *Immigration as a Factor in American History.* Englewood Cliffs, N.J.: Prentice-Hall, 1951.

———. *The Uprooted.* Boston: Little, Brown, 1951.

Hansen, Marcus Lee and Brebner, John B. *The Mingling of the Canadian and American Peoples.* New Haven: Yale University Press, 1940.

Hareven, Tamara K. *Family Time and Industrial Time: The Relationship Between the Family and Work in a New England Industrial Community.* Cambridge: Cambridge University Press, 1982.

———, and Randolph Langenback. *Amoskeag: Life and Work in an American Factory City.* New York: Pantheon, 1978.

Harris, R. Cole and John Warkenten. *Canada Before Confederation.* New York: Oxford, 1974.

Hart, Albert Bushnell, ed. *Commonwealth History of Massachusetts.* 5 vols. New York: States History Co., 1930.

Hartmann, Edward G. *The Movement to Americanize the Immigrant.* New York: Columbia University Press, 1948.

Hendrickson, Dyke. *Quiet Presence: Histoire de Franco-Americains en New England.* Portland, Maine: Guy Gannett Publishing Co., 1980.

Hennessy, Michael E. *Twenty-five Years of Massachusetts Politics.* Boston: Practical Politics, 1917.

Herberg, Will. *Protestant-Catholic-Jew: An Essay in American Religious Sociology.* Rev. ed. Garden City, N.Y.: Anchor, 1960.

Higham, John ed. *Ethnic Leadership in America.* Baltimore: Johns Hopkins University Press, 1978.

———. *Send These To Me: Jews and other Immigrants in Urban America.* New York: Atheneum, 1975.

———. *Strangers in the Land: Patterns of American Nativism, 1865–1925.* New Brunswick, N.J.: Rutgers University Press, 1955.

Hiller, Ernest T., Faye E. Corner, and Wendell L. East. *Rural Community Types.* Urbana, Ill.: University of Illinois Press, 1930.

Hoar, George F. *Autobiography of Seventy Years.* 2 vols. New York: Charles Scribner's Sons, 1903.

Holt, Michael. *Forging a Majority: The Formation of the Republican Party in Pittsburg, 1848–1860.* New Haven: Yale University Press, 1969.

Hourwick, Isaac. *Immigration and Labor: The Economic Aspects of European Immigration to the United States.* New York: G. P. Putnam's Sons, 1912.

Hughes, Everett C. *French Canada in Transition.* Chicago: University of Chicago Press, 1943.

Hurd, D. Hamilton, ed. *History of Worcester County, Massachusetts.* 2 vols. Philadelphia: J. W. Lewis & Co., 1889.

Huthmacher, J. Joseph. *Massachusetts People and Politics, 1919–1933.* Cambridge: Harvard University Press, 1959.

Ishwaran, J., ed. *The Canadian Family.* Toronto: Holt, Rinehart & Winston of Canada, 1971.

Jenks, Jeremiah W. and W. Jett Lauck. *The Immigration Problem; A Study of American Immigration Conditions and Needs.* 4th ed. New York: Funk & Wagnalls, 1917.

Jensen, Richard J. *The Winning of the Midwest: Social and Political Conflict, 1888–1896.* Chicago: University of Chicago Press, 1971.

Jones, Maldwyn Allen. *American Immigration.* Chicago: University of Chicago Press, 1960.

Kantowicz, Edward R. *Polish-American Politics in Chicago.* Chicago: University of Chicago Press, 1975.

Key, V. O., Jr. *American State Politics: An Introduction.* New York: Knopf, 1956.

———. *Politics, Parties, and Pressure Groups.* 5th ed. New York: Crowell, 1964.

———. *A Primer of Statistics for Political Science.* New York: Crowell, 1966.

Kinton, Jack, ed. *American Ethnic Revival.* Aurora, Ill.: Social Science and Sociological Resources, 1977.

Kleppner, Paul. *The Cross of Culture: A Social Analysis of Midwestern Politics, 1850–1900.* New York: Macmillan, 1970.

Kleppner, Paul, et al. *The Evolution of American Electoral Systems.* Westport, Conn.: Greenwood, 1981.

Kleppner, Paul. *The Third Electoral System, 1853–1892: Parties, Voters, and Political Cultures.* Chapel Hill: University of North Carolina Press, 1979.

Lahne, Herbert J. *The Cotton Textile Worker.* New York: Farrar & Rinehart, 1944.

Lane, Robert. *Political Life; Why People Get Involved in Politics.* New York: Free Press, 1959.

Laughlin, Harry H. *Immigration and Conquest.* New York: Chamber of Commerce, 1939.

Lavoie, Yoland. *L'Emigration des Canadiens aux Etats-Unis avant 1930.* Montreal: Les Presses de l'Université de Montreal, 1972.

Layer, Robert G. *Earnings of Cotton Mill Operatives, 1825–1914.* Cambridge: Harvard University Press, 1955.

LeBlanc, Robert G. *Location of Manufacturing in New England in the Nineteenth Century.* Dartmouth Geography Publication No. 7. Hanover, N.H.: Dartmouth College Geography Department, 1969.

Lenski, Gerhard. *The Religious Factor: A Sociological Study of Religion's Impact on Politics, Economics, and Family Life.* Garden City: N.Y.: Doubleday, 1961.

Levin, Murray B. *The Compleat Politician.* New York: Bobbs-Merrill, 1962.

Levy, Mark R. and Michael S. Kramer. *The Ethnic Factor; How America's Minorities Decide Elections.* New York: Simon & Schuster, 1973.

Lieberson, Stanley. *Ethnic Patterns in American Cities.* Glencoe, Ill.: Free Press, 1963.

Linkh, R. M. *American Catholicism and European Immigrants, 1900–1924.* New York: Center for Migration Studies, 1975.

Litt, Edgar. *Ethnic Politics in America.* Glenview, Ill.: Scott, Foresman, 1970.

———. *The Political Cultures of Massachusetts*. Cambridge: M.I.T. Press, 1965.

Lockard, Duane. *New England State Politics*. Princeton: Princeton University Press, 1959.

Lord, Robert H., John E. Sexton, and Edward T. Harrington. *History of the Archdiocese of Boston*. 3 vols. Boston: Sheed & Ward, 1945.

Lowi, Theodore J. *The End of Liberalism: Ideology, Policy, and the Crisis of Public Authority*. New York: Norton, 1969.

Lubell, Samuel. *The Future of American Politics*. 3d ed. New York: Harper, 1965.

Luebke, Frederick C. *Immigrants and Politics: The Germans of Nebraska, 1880–1900*. Lincoln: University of Nebraska Press, 1969.

McFarland, Gerald. *Mugwumps, Morals and Politics, 1884–1920*. Amherst: University of Massachusetts Press, 1975.

McGouldrick, Paul F. *New England Textiles in the Nineteenth Century; Profits and Investment*. Cambridge: Harvard University Press, 1968.

McSeveney, Samuel T. *The Politics of Depression: Political Behavior in the Northeast, 1893–1896*. New York: Oxford, 1972.

Magnan, D. M. A. *Notre Dame de Lourdes de Fall River, Massachusetts*. Quebec: Le Soleil, 1925.

Mann, Arthur. *Yankee Reformers in the Urban Age*. Cambridge: Harvard University Press, 1954.

Meister, Richard J., ed. *Race and Ethnicity in Modern America*. Lexington, Mass.: D. C. Heath, 1974.

Milbrath, Lester. *Political Participation*. Chicago: Rand McNally, 1965.

Mindel, Charles H. and Robert W. Habenstein, eds. *Ethnic Families in America: Patterns and Variations*. New York: Elsevier, 1976.

Miner, Horace. *St. Denis: A French-Canadian Parish*. Chicago: University of Chicago Press, 1939.

Moynihan, Kenneth J., trans. *Le Worcester Canadien (1888–1907) and Le Guide Français (1916–1917)*. Worcester, Mass.: Community Studies Program, Assumption College, 1979.

Munro, William B. *A Bibliography of Municipal Government in the United States*. Cambridge: Harvard University Press, 1915.

Nelli, Humbert S. *Italians in Chicago, 1880–1930: A Study in Ethnic Mobility*. New York: Oxford, 1970.

Nelson, John. *Worcester County; A Narrative History*. 3 vols. New York: American Historical Society, 1934.

Niemi, Richard G. and Herbert F. Weisberg, eds. *Controversies in American Voting Behavior*. San Francisco: W. H. Freeman, 1976.

Novak, Michael. *The Rise of the Unmeltable Ethnics; Politics and Culture in the Seventies*. New York: Macmillan, 1972.

Nutt, Charles. *History of Worcester and its People*. 4 vols. New York: Lewis Historical Publishing Co., 1919.

Olson, James S. *The Ethnic Dimension in American History*. 2 vols. New York: St. Martin's Press, 1979.

Ouellet, Ferdinand. *Histoire économique et sociale de Québec, 1760–1850*. Montreal and Paris: Fides, 1966.

Park, Robert E. and Miller, Herbert A. *Old World Traits Transplanted*. New York: Harper, 1921.

Perrault, Robert B. *La Presse Franco-Américaine et le Politique: L'Oeuvre de Charles-Roger Daoust*. Bedford, N.H.: National Materials Development Center for French, 1978.

Prude, Jonathan. *The Coming of Industrial Order: Town and Factory Life in Rural Massachusetts, 1810–1860*. Cambridge: Cambridge University Press, 1983.

Quintal, Claire, ed. *L'Emigrant québécois vers le Etats-Unis: 1850–1920.* Worcester, Mass.: French Institute/Assumption College, 1982.

———, ed. *The Little Canadas of New England.* Worcester, Mass.: French Institute/Assumption College, 1983.

Quintal, Claire and Vachone, André, eds. *Situation de la Recherche sur les Franco-Américains.* Worcester, Mass.: French Institute/Assumption College, 1980.

Rai, Kul B. and John C. Blydenburgh. *Political Science Statistics.* Boston: Holbrook Press, 1973.

Redfield, Robert. *The Little Community.* Chicago: University of Chicago Press, 1955.

Rioux, Marcel and Yves Martin, eds. *French-Canadian Society.* vol. 1 Toronto: McClelland & Stewart, 1964.

Rischin, Moses, ed. *Immigration and the American Tradition.* Indianapolis, Ind.: Bobbs-Merrill, 1976.

Rosenblum, Gerald. *Immigrant Workers: Their Impact on American Labor Radicalism.* New York: Basic Books, 1973.

Roy, J. Arthur, ed. *Le Worcester Canadien, directoire des Canadiens-français de Worcester.* 20 vols. Worcester, Mass.: J. Arthur Roy & Fils, 1886–1907.

Rumilly, Robert. *Histoire des franco-américains.* Montreal: L'Union Saint-Jean-Baptiste d'Amérique, 1958.

Santerre, Richard. *Bibliographie des imprimés franco-américain parus à Lowell, Massachusetts de 1837 à 1968.* Manchester, N.H.: Ballard, 1969.

———. *The Franco-Americans of Lowell, Massachusetts.* Lowell, Mass.: Franco-American Day Committee, 1972.

Schlesinger, Arthur M., Jr., ed. *Almanac of American History.* New York: G. P. Putnam's Sons, 1983.

Seller, Maxime. *To Seek America: A History of Ethnic Life in the United States.* Englewood, N.J.: Jerome S. Ozer, 1977.

Shlakman, Vera. *Economic History of a Factory Town: Chicopee, Massachusetts.* Northampton, Mass.: Smith College Department of History, 1935.

Simano, Irene M. *The French-American of New England: A Union List of Materials in Selected Maine Libraries.* Orono, Maine: University of Maine, the New England-Atlantic Provinces-Quebec Center, 1971.

Smith, Thomas R. *Cotton Textile Industry of Fall River, Massachusetts: A Study of Industrial Localization.* New York: Crown Press, 1944.

Solomon, Barbara. *Ancestors and Immigrants: A Changing New England Tradition.* Cambridge: Harvard University Press, 1956.

Sorauf, Frank J. *Party Politics in America.* 2d ed. Boston: Little, Brown, 1972.

A Souvenir of Massachusetts Legislators. 10 vols. Brockton, Mass.: A. M. Bridgman, 1894–1904.

Taft, Donald R. *Two Portuguese Communities in New England.* New York: Longmans, Green, 1923.

TeSelle, Sallie, ed. *The Rediscovery of Ethnicity.* New York: Harper & Row, 1973.

Tetrault, Maximilienne. *Le Rôle de la presse dans l'évolution du peuple franco-américain de la Nouvelle-Angleterre.* Marseille: Imprimerie Ferran, 1935.

Thernstrom, Stephan, ed. *Harvard Encyclopedia of American Ethnic Groups.* Cambridge: Harvard University Press, 1980.

Thomas, Brinley. *Migration and Economic Growth.* Cambridge, England: Cambridge University Press, 1954.

Thompson, Margaret, ed. *Presidential Elections since 1789.* 3d ed. Washington, D.C.: Congressional Quarterly, 1983.

Tomasi, S. *Piety and Power: The Role of Italian Parishes in the New York Metropolitan Area.* New York: Center for Migration Studies, 1975.

Truesdell, Leon E. *The Canadian Born in the United States: An Analysis of the Canadian Element in the Population of the United States, 1850–1930*. New Haven: Yale University Press, 1943.

Underwood, Kenneth W. *Protestant and Catholic: Religious and Social Interaction in an Industrial Community*. Boston: Beacon Press, 1957.

Wade, Mason, ed. *Canadian Dualism; Studies of French-English Relations*. Toronto: University of Toronto Press, 1960.

———. *The French Canadians, 1760–1967*. Rev. ed. Toronto: MacMillan Company of Canada, 1968.

Walker, David B. *Politics and Ethnocentrism: The Case of the Franco-Americans*. Brunswick, Maine: Bowdoin College, Bureau for Research in Municipal Government, 1961.

Walkowitz, Daniel J. *Worker City, Company Town: Iron and Cotton Worker Protest In Troy and Cohoes, New York, 1855–1884*. Urbana: University of Illinois Press, 1978.

Warner, Sam Bass. *Streetcar Suburbs: The Process of Growth in Boston, 1870–1900*. Cambridge: Harvard University Press, 1962.

Warner, William L. and Srole, Leo. *The Social Systems of American Ethnic Groups*. New Haven: Yale University Press, 1945.

Welch, Richard E., Jr. *George Frisbie Hoar and the Half-Breed Republicans*. Cambridge: Harvard University Press, 1971.

Welkowitz, Joan, Robert B. Ewen, and Jacob Cohen. *Introductory Statistics for the Behavioral Sciences*. 2d ed. New York: Academic Press, 1976.

Williamson, Jeffrey. *Late Nineteenth Century American Economic Development: A General Equilibrium Model*. Cambridge, England: Cambridge University Press, 1974.

Wolkovich-Valkavicius, William. *Immigrants and Yankees in Nashoba Valley Massachusetts: Interethnic and Interreligious Conflict and Accommodation of Irish, French-Canadians, Poles, Lithuanians, and Italians*. West Groton, Mass.: by the author, 1981.

Articles

Abramson, Harold J. "Ethnic Diversity within Catholicism: A Comparative Analysis of Contemporary and Historical Religion." *Journal of Social History* 4 (Summer 1971): 259–388.

Alba, Richard D. "Social Assimilation among American Catholic National-Origin Groups." *American Sociological Review* 41 (1976): 1030–46.

Allen, James P. "Migration Fields of French Canadian Immigrants to Southern Maine." *Geographical Review* 62 (July 1972): 366–83.

Anderson, Grace M. "Voting Behavior and the Ethnic-Religious Variable: A Study of the Federal Election in Hamilton, Ontario." *Canadian Journal of Economics and Political Science* 32 (1966): 27.

Aniel, Dean. "Ethnicity: A Neglected Dimension of American History." *International Migration Review* 3 (Summer 1969): 58–64.

Arnell, William. "The French Population of New England." *Geography* 34 (1949): 97–101.

Barkan, Elliott Robert. "French Canadians." In *Harvard Encyclopedia of American Ethnic Groups*, pp. 388–401. Edited by Stephan Thernstrom. Cambridge: Harvard University Press, 1980.

———. "Proximity and Commuting Immigration: An Hypothesis Explored via the Bipolar Ethnic Communities of French Canadians and Mexican Americans." In *American Ethnic Revival*, pp. 163–83. Edited by Jack Kinton. Aurora, Il.: Social Science & Sociological Resources, 1977.

Barkan, Elliott Robert and Khokhlov, Nikolai. "Socioeconomic Data as Indices of Naturalization Patterns in the United States: A Theory Revisited." *Ethnicity* 7 (1980): 159–90.

Bartlett, Albert L. "The Transformation of New England." *Forum* 7 (August 1899): 634–44.

Beaugrand, Honoré. "The Attitude of the French Canadians." *Forum* 7 (July 1889): 521–30.

Belcourt, N. A. "The French Canadians outside of Quebec." *Annals of the American Academy of Political and Social Science* 112, no. 196 (May 1923): 13–24.

Bender, Prosper. "The French Canadian Peasantry." *Magazine of American History* 24 (1890): 126–36.

———. "The French Canadians in New England." *New England Magazine* 6 (July 1892): 569–77.

———. "A New France in New England." *Magazine of American History* 20 (November 1888): 387–94.

Benoit, Virgil. "Gentilly: A French Canadian Community in the Minnesota Red River Valley." *Minnesota History* 44 (Winter 1975): 279–89.

Bernard, W. S. "The Cultural Determinants of Naturalization." *American Sociological Review* 1 (1936): 943–53.

———. "Integration of Immigrants in the United States." *International Migration Review* 1 (1967): 23–32.

Bidwell, Percy W. "The Agricultural Revolution in New England." *American Historical Review* 26 (July 1921): 683–702.

———. "Population Growth in Southern New England." *Publications of the American Statistical Association* 15 (December 1917): 813–39.

Bieder, Robert E. "Kinship as a Factor in Migration." *Journal of Marriage and the Family* 35 (1973): 429–39.

Bilodeau, Therese. "The French in Holyoke (1850–1900)." *Historical Journal of Western Massachusetts* 3 (Spring 1974): 1–12.

Blewett, Mary H. "The Mills and the Multitude: A Political History." In *Cotton was King: A History of Lowell, Massachusetts*, pp. 161–89. Edited by Arthur L. Eno Jr. Lowell, Mass.: Lowell Historical Society, 1976.

Blocker, Jack S. Jr. "The Perils of Pluralism." *Canadian Review of American Studies* 4 (Fall 1973): 201–5.

Blow, David J. "The Establishment and Erosion of French-Canadian Culture in Winooski, Vermont, 1867–1900." *Vermont History* 43 (Winter 1975): 59–74.

Bocock, John P. "The Irish Conquest of our Cities." *Forum* 17 (April 1894): 186–95.

Brass, Paul R. "Ethnicity and Nationality Formation." *Ethnicity* 3 (1976): 225–41.

Brault, Gerard J. "Etat present des études sur les centres Franco-Américains de la Nouvelle-Angleterre." In *Situation de la Recherche sur les Franco-Américains*, pp. 9–25. Edited by Claire Quintal and André Vachon. Worcester, Mass.: French Institute/Assumption College, 1980.

Brault, Gerard J. "New England French Culture." *The French Review* 45 (March 1972): 831–37.

Breton, Raymond. "Institutional Completeness of Ethnic Communities and the Personal Relations of Immigrants." *American Journal of Sociology* 70 (1964): 193–205.

Brunet, Michel. "The British Conquest: Canadian Social Scientists and the Fate of the Canadiens." *Canadian Historical Review* 40 (June 1959): 93–107.

———. "L'Eglise catholique du bas-Canada et le partage du pouvoir à l'heure d'une nouvelle donne (1837–1854)." Catholic Historical Association, *Historical Papers* (1969): 37–51.

Burnham, Walter D. "The Changing Shape of the American Political Universe." *American Political Science Review* 59 (March 1965): 7–28.

Carman, A. R. "Perplexities that Canada Would Bring." *Forum* 9 (1890): 562–68.

Carvalho, Joseph III, and Robert Everett. "Statistical Analysis of Springfield's French-Canadians (1870)." *Historical Journal of Western Massachusetts* 3 (Spring 1974): 59–63.

Chasse, Paul P. "Church." Franco-American Ethnic Heritage Program. Title IX (ESEA) grant. Worcester, Mass.: Assumption College, 1976.

Clifford, N. K. "Religion and the Development of Canadian Society: An Historiographical Analysis." *Church History* 38 (1969): 506–23.

Cornwell, Elmer E. "Bosses, Machines, and Ethnic Groups." *Annals of the American Academy of Political and Social Science* 353 (May 1964): 24–30.

———. "Party Absorption of Ethnic Groups: The Case of Providence, Rhode Island." *Social Forces* 38 (March 1960): 205–10.

———. "Some Occupational Patterns in Party Committee Membership." *Rhode Island History* 20 (1961): 87–96.

Cumbler, John T. "The City and the Community: The Impact of Urban Forces on Working-Class Behavior." *Journal of Urban History* 3 (1977): 427–42.

Davidson, John. "The Growth of the French Canadian Race in America." *Annals of the American Academy of Political and Social Science.* 7 (1896): 213–35.

Dexter, Robert. "French-Canadian Patriotism." *American Journal of Sociology* 28 (1922–23): 694–710.

Dodd, Martin H. "Marlboro, Massachusetts and the Shoeworkers' Strike of 1898–1899." *Labor History* 20 (1979): 376–97.

Dolan, Jay P. "A Critical Period in American Catholicism." *Review of Politics* 35 (1973): 523–36.

Dumont, Fernand. "Idéologies au Canada français (1850–1900)" *Recherches sociographiques* 10 (1969): 145–56.

———. "La Representation idéologique des classes au Canada français." *Recherches sociographiques* 6 (1965): 9–22.

Duncan, O. D. and Lieberson, Stanley. "Ethnic Segregation and Assimilation." *American Journal of Sociology* 64 (1959): 364–74.

Early, Frances H. "Mobility Potential and the Quality of Life in Working-Class Lowell, Massachusetts: The French Canadians ca. 1870." *Labour/Le Travailleur* 2 (Fall 1977): 214–28.

———. "The Settling-In Process: The Beginnings of Little Canada in Lowell, Massachusetts, in the Late Nineteenth Century." In *The Little Canadas of New England*, pp. 23–43. Edited by Claire Quintal. Worcester, Mass.: French Institute/Assumption College, 1983.

Eisinger, Peter K. "Ethnic Political Transition in Boston, 1884–1933: Some Lessons for Contemporary Cities." *Political Science Quarterly* 93 (Summer 1978): 217–39.

Estus, Charles W. and Kenneth J. Moynihan. "Beyond Textiles: Industrial Diversity and the Franco-American Experience in Worcester, Massachusetts." In *The Little Canadas of New England*, pp. 104–15. Edited by Claire Quintal. Worcester, Mass.: French Institute/Assumption College, 1983.

Farrer, Edward. "The Folk of Lower Canada." *Atlantic Monthly* 49 (April 1882): 542–50.

———. "The Inhabitant of Lower Canada." *Atlantic Monthly* 48 (December 1881): 771–80.

———. "New England Influences in French Canada." *Forum* 23 (May 1897): 308–19.

Faucher, Albert. "L'émigration des canadiens-français aux Etats-Unis au XIXe siècle: Position du problème et perspectives." *Recherches sociographiques* 5 (1964): 277–317.

Fitzpatrick, J. "The Importance of the Community in the Process of Immigrant Assimilation." *International Migration Review* 1 (1967): 5–16.

Formisano, Ronald P. "Comment on Robert Kelley's 'Ideology and Political Culture from Jefferson to Nixon.'" *American Historical Review* 82 (1977): 567–77.

Frechette, Louis. "The United States for the French Canadians." *Forum* 16 (1893): 336–345.

French, Lawrence. "The Franco-American Working Class Family." In *Ethnic Families in America: Patterns and Variations*, pp. 323–46. Edited by Charles H. Mindel and Robert W. Habenstein. New York: Elsevier, 1976.

Garigue, Philippe. "French Canadian Kinship and Urban Life." *American Anthropologist* 58 (1956): 1090–1101.

Greeley, Andrew M. "Political Participation among American Ethnic Groups." *American Journal of Sociology* 80 (1974): 170–204.

Greene, Victor R. "For God and Country: The Origins of Slavic Catholic Self-Consciousness in America." *Church History* 35 (December 1966): 446–60.

Guignard, Michael J. "Geographic and Demographic Forces Facilitating Ethnic Survival in a New England Mill Town: The Franco-Americans of Biddeford, Maine." In *The Little Canadas of New England*, pp. 1–22. Edited by Claire Quintal. Worcester, Mass.: French Institute/Assumption College, 1983.

———. "Maine's Corporation Sole Controversy." *Maine Historical Society Newsletter* 12 (Winter 1973): 111–30.

Gutman, Herbert. "Work, Culture, and Society in Industrializing America, 1819–1918." *American Historical Review* 78 (1973): 531–88.

Haebler, Peter. "Holyoke's French Canadian Community in Turmoil: The Role of the Church in Assimilation." *Historical Journal of Western Massachusetts* 7 (1979): 5–21.

Ham, Edward B. "French National Societies in New England." *New England Quarterly* 12 (June 1939): 315–32.

———. "French Patterns in Quebec and New England." *New England Quarterly* 18 (December 1945): 435–447.

———. "Journalism and the French Survival in New England." *New England Quarterly* 11 (March 1939): 89–107.

Handlin, Oscar. "Historical Perspectives on the American Ethnic Group." *Daedalus* 90 (Spring 1961): 220–32.

Handlin, Oscar and Mary F. Handlin. "The New History and the Ethnic Factor in American Life." *Perspectives in American History* 4 (1970): 5–24.

Hansen, Marcus L. "The Second Colonization of New England." *New England Quarterly* 2 (October 1929): 539–60.

Hareven, Tamara K. "The Family as Process: The Historical Study of the Family Cycle." *Journal of Social History* 7 (1974): 322–29.

———. "Family Time and Industrial Time: Family and Work in a Planned Corporation Town, 1900–1924." *Journal of Urban History* 1 (1975): 365–89.

———. "The Laborers of Manchester, New Hampshire, 1912–1922: The Role of Family and Ethnicity in Adjustment to Industrial Life." *Labor History* (1975): 249–65.

Harmond, Richard. "The 'Beast' in Boston: Benjamin F. Butler as Governor of Massachusetts." *Journal of American History* 55 (June 1968–March 1969): 266–80.

Harte, W. Blackburn. "The Drift Toward Annexation." *Forum* 9 (June 1889): 361–72.

———. "French Canada and the Dominion." *Forum* 10 (November 1890): 323–34.

Hays, Samuel P. "The Changing Structure of the City in Industrial America." *Journal of Urban History* 1 (1974): 6–38.

———. "The Politics of Reform in Municipal Government in the Progressive Era." *Pacific Northwest Quarterly* 55 (October 1964): 157–69.

———. "The Social Analysis of American Political History, 1880–1920." *Political Science Quarterly* 80 (1965): 373–94.

Hill, Howard C. "The Americanization Movement." *American Journal of Sociology* 24 (May 1919): 609–35.

Hill, Peter J. "Relative Skill and Income Levels of Native and Foreign Born Workers in the United States." *Explorations in Economic History* 12 (1975): 47–60.

Jackson, G. E. "Emigration of Canadians to the United States." *Annals of the American Academy of Political and Social Science* 107 (May 1923): 25–34.

Johnson, Clark. "Burlington Since the 1930s: Change and Continuity in Vermont's Largest City." *Vermont History* 37 (1969): 52–62.

Jones, Robert L. "French Canadian Agriculture on the St. Lawrence Valley, 1815–1850." *Agricultural History* 16 (July 1942): 137–48.

Kalijarivi, Thorsten V. "French Canadians in the United States." *Annals of the American Academy of Political and Social Science* 223 (September 1942): 132–37.

Kelley, Robert. "Ideology and Political Culture from Jefferson to Nixon." *American Historical Review* 82 (1977): 531–62.

Key, V. O., Jr. "A Theory of Critical Elections." *Journal of Politics* 17 (February 1955): 198–210.

———. "Secular Realignment and the Party System." *Journal of Politics* 20 (1959): 198–210.

Keyes, Charles F. "Towards a New Formulation of the Concept of Ethnic Group." *Ethnicity* 3 (1976): 202–13.

Laflamme, J. L. K., David E. Lavigne, and J. Arthur Favreau. "French Catholics in the United States," in *The Catholic Encyclopedia*, vol. 6, pp. 271–77. New York: Robert Appleton Co., 1909.

Lemaire, Herve B. "Franco-American Efforts on Behalf of the French Language in New England." In *Language Loyalty in the United States*, pp. 253–79. Edited by Joshua Fishman. London: Mouton, 1966.

Leslie, Peter M. "The Role of Political Parties in Promoting the Interests of Ethnic Minorities." *Canadian Journal of Political Science* 2 (December 1969): 419–33.

Lieberson, Stanley. "The Impact of Residential Segregation on Assimilation." *Social Forces* 40 (1961): 52–57.

Lower, A. R. M. "New France in New England: A Study of French Canadian Immigration into New England from 1860 to 1920." *New England Quarterly* 2 (April 1929): 278–95.

McCormick, Richard L. "Ethnocultural Interpretations of Nineteenth-Century American Voting Behavior." *Political Science Quarterly* 89 (1974): 351–77.

MacDonald, William. "French Canadians in Maine." *Nation* 67 (15 October 1896): 285–86.

MacDonald, William. "French Canadians in New England." *Quarterly Journal of Economics* 12 (April 1898): 245–79.

McQuillan, D. Aidan. "Territory and Ethnic Identity: Some New Measures of an Old Theme in the Cultural Geography of the United States." In *European Settlement and Development in North America*, pp. 136–69. Edited by James R. Gibson. Toronto: University of Toronto Press, 1978.

McSeveney, Samuel T. "Ethnic Groups, Ethnic Conflicts, and Recent Quantitative Research in American Political History." *International Migration Review* 7 (1973): 14–33.

Marty, Martin E. "Ethnicity: The Skeleton of Religion in America." *Church History* 41 (1972): 5–21.

Merk, Lois B. "Boston's Historic Public School Crisis." *New England Quarterly* 31 (1958): 179–99.

Miller, Abraham H. "Ethnicity and Party Identification: Continuation of a Theoretical Dialogue." *Western Political Quarterly* 27 (1974): 479–90.

———. "Ethnicity and Political Behavior: A Review of Theories and an Attempt at Reformulation." *Western Political Quarterly* 24 (1971): 483–500.

Mohl, Raymond A., and Neil Betten. "The Immigrant Church in Gary, Indiana: Religious Adjustment and Cultural Defense." *Ethnicity* 8 (March 1981): 1–17.

Moreau, Peter L. "The Preservation of Ethnic Identity in the Franco-American Villages of

Lincoln, Rhode Island." In *The Little Canadas of New England*, pp. 84–103. Edited by Claire Quintal. Worcester, Mass.: French Institute/Assumption College, 1983.

Myers, Jerome K. "Assimilation in the Political Community." *Sociology and Social Research* 35 (1951): 175–82.

———. "Assimilation to the Ecological and Social Systems of a Community." *American Sociological Review* 15 (1950): 367–72.

Nelson, Henry Loomis. "French Canadians in New England." *Harper's New Monthly Magazine* 87 (July 1893): 180–87.

Paquet, Gilles. "L'Emigration des canadiens-français vers le Nouvelle-Angleterre, 1870–1910: prises de vue quantitatives." *Recherches sociographiques* 5 (1964): 319–70.

Parenti, Michael. "Ethnic Politics and the Persistence of Ethnic Identification." *American Political Science Review* 61 (September 1967): 717–26.

Petrin, Ronald A. "Culture, Community, and Politics: French Canadians in Massachusetts, 1885–1915." In *The Little Canadas of New England*, pp. 66–83. Edited by Claire Quintal. Worcester, Mass.: French Institute/Assumption College, 1983.

Picher, Robert L. "The Franco-Americans in Vermont." *Vermont History* 28 (1960): 59–62.

Piddington, Ralph. "The Kinship Network among French Canadians." In *Kinship and Geographical Mobility*. Edited by Ralph Piddington. Leiden, Netherlands: E. J. Brill, 1965.

Plax, Martin. "Towards a Redefinition of Ethnic Politics." *Ethnicity* 3 (1976): 19–33.

Podea, Iris S. "Quebec to Little Canada: The Coming of the French Canadians to New England in the Nineteenth Century." *New England Quarterly* 23 (September 1950): 365–380.

Rimbert, Silvie. "L'Immigration Franco-Canadienne au Massachusetts." *Revue Canadienne de Géographie* 8 (July–October 1954): 75–85.

Sait, E. M. "Theocratic Quebec." *Annals of the American Academy of Political and Social Science* 45 (January 1913): 69–82.

Savard, Pierre. "La vie du clergé Québecois au XIXᵉ siècle." *Recherches sociographiques* 8 (1967): 253–73.

Schneider, Mark. "Migration, Ethnicity, and Politics: A Comparative State Analysis." *Journal of Politics* 38 (1976): 938–62.

Séguin, Marcel. "Le Régime seigneurial au pays de Québec, 1760–1854." *Revue d'histoire de l'Amérique français* 1 (1948): 519–32.

Sepenuk, Norman. "A Profile of Franco-American Political Attitudes in New England." In *A Franco-American Overview*, vol. 3, pp. 213–33. Edited by Madeleine Giguere. Cambridge, Mass.: National Assessment and Dissemination Center, 1981.

Silvia, Philip T., Jr. "The 'Flint Affair': French Canadian Struggle for Survivance." *Catholic Historical Review* 65 (1979): 414–35.

———. "Neighbors from the North: French-Canadian Immigrants vs. Trade Unionism in Fall River, Massachusetts." In *The Little Canadas of New England*, pp. 44–65. Edited by Claire Quintal. Worcester, Mass.: French Institute/Assumption College, 1983.

———. "The Position of 'New' Immigrants in the Fall River Textile Industry." *International Migration Review* 10 (1976): 221–32.

———. "The Position of Workers in a Textile Community: Fall River in the Early 1800s." *Labor History* 6 (1975): 230–48.

Smith, Timothy L. "New Approaches to the History of Immigration in Twentieth Century America." *American Historical Review* 71 (July 1966): 1265–79.

———. "Religious Denominations as Ethnic Communities: A Regional Case Study." *Church History* 35 (1966): 207–26.

Smyth, Egbert C. "The French Canadians in New England." *American Antiquarian Society, Proceedings* 7 (October 1890): 316–36.

Sorrell, Richard S. "Franco-Americans in New England." *Journal of Ethnic Studies* 5 (1977): 90–94.

———. "Sentinelle Affair (1924–1929)—Religion and Militant Survivance in Woonsocket, Rhode Island." *Rhode Island History* 36 (August 1977): 67–79.

———. "Sports and Franco-Americans in Woonsocket, 1870–1930." *Rhode Island History* 31 (November 1972): 117–26.

———. "The survivance of French Canadians in New England (1865–1930): History, Geography, and Demography as Destiny." *Ethnic and Racial Studies* 4 (1981): 91–109.

Stauffer, Anne Tholen, comp. "The French-Americans and the French-Canadians: A Select Bibliography of Materials in the Library of the Vermont Historical Society." *Vermont History* 44 (1976): 110–14.

Swierenga, Robert P. "Ethnicity in Historical Perspective." *Social Science* 52 (Winter 1977): 31–44.

———. "Ethnocultural Political Analysis: A New Approach to American Ethnic Studies." *Journal of American Studies* 5 (April 1971): 59–79.

Theriault, George F. "The Franco-Americans of New England." In *Canadian Dualism: Studies of French-English Relations*, pp. 393–414. Edited by Mason Wade. Toronto: University of Toronto Press, 1960.

Vecoli, Rudolph J. "Ethnicity: A Neglected Dimension of American History." In *The State of American History*, pp. 70–88. Edited by Herbert J. Bass. Chicago: Quadrangle Books, 1970.

Verrette, A. "La Paroisse Franco-Américaine." *Canadian Catholic Historical Association, Report* (1947–48): 125–39.

Vicero, Ralph D. "L'exode vers le Sud: Survol de la migration canadienne-française vers la Nouvelle-Angleterre au XIXe siècle." In *The Little Canadas of New England*, pp. 6–8. Edited by Claire Quintal and André Vachon. Worcester, Mass.: French Institute/Assumption College, 1980.

Wade, Mason. "The French Parish and Survivance in Nineteenth-Century New England." *Catholic Historical Review* 26 (July 1950): 163–89.

Walker, David B. "La Politique Présidentielle des Franco-Américains: quelques observations sommaires." In *Les Conferences de l'Institut Franco-Américain de Bowdoin College*, pp. 64–72. Edited by Gerard J. Brault. Brunswick, Maine: Bowdoin College, 1961.

———. "The Presidential Politics of Franco-Americans." *Canadian Journal of Economics and Political Science* 28 (August 1962): 353–63.

Wallot, Jean-Pierre. "Religion and French Canadian Mores in the Early Nineteenth Century." *Canadian Historical Review* 52 (March 1971): 51–91.

Wicket, S. Morley. "Canadians in the United States." *Annals of the American Academy of Political and Social Science* 45 (January 1913): 83–98.

———. "French Canadians in the United States." *Political Science Quarterly* 21 (June 1906): 190–205.

Wolfinger, Raymond E. "Some Consequences of Ethnic Politics." In *The Electoral Process*, pp. 49–61. Edited by M. Kent Jennings and L. Harmon Ziegler. Englewood Cliffs, N.J.: Prentice-Hall, 1964.

———. "The Development and Persistence of Ethnic Voting." *American Political Science Review* 59 (December 1965): 896–908.

Woodbury, Kenneth, Jr. "An Incident between the French Canadians and the Irish in the Diocese of Maine in 1906." *New England Quarterly* 40 (1967): 260–69.

Woolfson, Peter. "The Heritage and Culture of the French-Vermonter: Research Needs in the Social Sciences." *Vermont History* 44 (1976): 103–9.

Wright, James E. "Ethnocultural Model of Voting: A Behavioral and Historical Critique." *American Behavioral Scientist* 16 (May–June 1973): 35–56.

Theses

Chevalier, Sister Florence Marie, S.S.A. "The Role of French National Societies in the Sociocultural Evolution of the Franco-Americans of New England from 1860 to the Present: An Analytical Macro-Sociological Case Study in Ethnic Integration Based on Current Social System Models," Ph.D. diss., The Catholic University of America, 1972.

Creveling, H. F. "The Patterns of Cultural Groups in Worcester." Ph.D. diss., Clark University, 1951.

Cumbler, John. "Continuity and Disruption: Working-Class Community in Lynn and Fall River, Massachusetts, 1880–1950." Ph.D. diss., University of Michigan, 1974.

Dexter, Robert C. "The Habitant Transplanted: A Study of the French Canadian in New England." Ph.D. diss., Clark University, 1923.

Doiron, Gerald J. "The French Canadian Migration into New England," Master's thesis, University of Rhode Island, 1959.

Guignard, Michael J. "Ethnic Survival in a New England Mill Town: The Franco-Americans of Biddeford, Maine." Ph.D. diss., Syracuse University, 1976.

Haebler, Peter. "Habitants in Holyoke: The Development of the French-Canadian Community in a Massachusetts City, 1865–1910." Ph.D. diss., University of New Hampshire, 1976.

Harmond, Richard P. "Tradition and Change in the Gilded Age: Political History of Massachusetts, 1878–1893." Ph.D. diss., Columbia University, 1968.

Hogan, William V. "Demographic Aspects of a Maturing Economy: New England, 1850–1900." Ph.D. diss., Cornell University, 1976.

Kistler, Ruth B. "Religion, Education, and Language as Factors in French Canadian Cultural Survival." Ph.D. diss., New York University, 1947.

Lortie, Leo A. "Dynamics of the French Canadian Family," Master's thesis, Clark University, 1967.

Petrin, Ronald A. "Ethnicity and Political Pragmatism: The French Canadians in Massachusetts, 1885–1915." Ph.D. diss., Clark University, 1983.

Prior, Granville T. "The French Canadians in New England." 2 vols. Master's thesis, Brown University, 1932.

Silvia, Philip T., Jr. "The Spindle City: Labor, Politics, and Religion in Fall River, Massachusetts, 1870–1905." Ph.D. diss., Fordham University, 1973.

Sorrell, Richard S. "The Sentinelle Affair (1924–1929) and Militant Survivance: The Franco-American Experience of Woonsocket, Rhode Island." Ph.D. diss., State University of New York, Buffalo, 1975.

Vicero, Ralph D. "Immigration of French Canadians to New England, 1840–1900: A Geographic Analysis." Ph.D. diss., University of Wisconsin, 1968.

Index

RANDALL LIBRARY-UNCW

3 0490 0496569 C